You Can Pass the CPA Exam

Second Edition

GET MOTIVATED

Debra R. Hopkins

WILEY

JOHN WILEY & SONS

Library of Congress Cataloging-in-Publication Data

Hopkins, Debra R.
    You can pass the CPA exam: get motivated: knowledge and confidence-building techniques/Debra R. Hopkins.—2nd ed.
        p.cm.
    Includes index.
    ISBN 0-471-45389-7 (paper/cd-rom)
    1. Accounting—Examinations. I. Title: CPA exam. II. Title.
    HF5661 .H58 2005
    657'.076–dc22   2004019370

Printed in the United States of America

10 9 8 7 6 5 4 3 2 1

This book is dedicated to the thousands of CPA candidates who have motivated me to believe in my abilities. Special recognition goes to my favorite CPAs, Mortimer Buckley, Beata Debek, Edward Gin, Mark Kramer, Leslie Kivi, Shyree Sanan, and Jennie Wong. They make me believe!

CONTENTS

Chapter	Title	Page No.
1	Believe That You Can Pass!	1
2	Content and Overall Exam Format	9
3	Scheduling and Applying for the Exam	32
4	A Time and Place for Everything	43
5	Assessing Your Strengths and Weaknesses	57
6	The Multiple-Choice Component	65
7	The Communications Component—Formerly Called Essays	75
8	The Simulation Component: No Fear, It's Here	82
9	The Research Component: How Many Hits?	87
10	CPA Exam Grading	94
11	Developing Your Personal Study Plan	99
12	Study Strategies to Improve Your Memory	111
13	Coping with Family, Friends, and Coworkers	127
14	Revising Your Personal Study Plan	136
15	How Will I Ever Pass? Practice Makes Perfect!	143
16	The Art of Auditing and Attestation	152
17	Financial Accounting and Reporting: Tough It Out	160
18	Regulation: The Rule-Oriented Section	166
19	Business Environment and Concepts: It's New, It's Different	174
20	Surviving the Prometric Experience	181
21	Nerves of Steel	187
22	Time Management	195
23	It's Show Time	205
24	The Waiting Game	212
25	Regrouping after an Unsuccessful Attempt	216
26	Congratulations—You Are a CPA!	226

PREFACE

Over the past twenty years, I have witnessed thousands of CPA candidates pass the Uniform Certified Public Accountant's (CPA) examination. Although there are many manuals and courses that outline the CPA exam's technical material, there is not much available to help CPA candidates manage the entire preparation process. This is especially true now that the CPA exam is offered in a computerized format.

With so little information available about the new computer-based test (CBT), it is no wonder that hundreds of candidates find themselves overwhelmed by the entire process. Now that the exam is offered one section at a time over various time periods, more information is needed. It is vital that CPA exam candidates understand the entire examination process, from the simple question of: "Which section should I sit for first?" to the issue of how best to prepare for the new simulation question format. Beginning with applying to sit for the CPA examination, to the technical knowledge, and ending with the exam-taking process itself, candidates need guidance. The purpose of this book is to provide such overall assistance. With a pass rate of 40-45% per section, I know how important it is for candidates to meet the demands of such a rigorous examination. Passing the computer-based CPA exam will continue to be a formidable undertaking. Use the strategy and study tips outlined in this book to maximize your study efforts and minimize your exam-taking time. Knowledge is power. Become fully informed about the entire examination process so that you can fulfill your dream of becoming a CPA by acting in a commanding manner. Whether you enroll in a formal CPA course or choose to self-study, this book will help you deal with the emotional side of your preparation process. You have made a considerable investment in your career so far. Why waste time and money in the last leg of the journey? Passing the CPA exam is the crowning glory of the accounting degree. Save yourself time, anxiety, stress, and energy by doing the right things to increase your chances of passing.

Each year I have the pleasure of assisting over 1,000 CPA candidates. I have put all my experience as a faculty member and director of one of the highest-achieving review courses in the nation into this book. I want the information and guidance made available to as many people as it can reach. I believe that candidates from all over the world have made a considerable investment of time and money in preparing for the exam, and they deserve the best guidance when it comes to the preparation process. Enjoy the book, the CD recording, and even taking each exam section. It's much easier when you know what to expect and how to handle the difficult areas.

I am grateful to those who have inspired me to continue to help people from all over the world pass the CPA examination. Gratitude is expressed to Mary Hamell, my office assistant, for her strong belief in my abilities. I thank Leslie Kivi, a fellow CPA Review faculty member, for her capable editorial assistance. I thank Judy Howarth and John Deremigis of John Wiley & Sons for their expert guidance. Special thanks go to the thousands of CPA candidates who encourage me to share my exam-taking techniques. Finally, a heartfelt thank-you to Megan, Lorraine, Tony, and Roger. Without their loving support, I would accomplish nothing.

Good luck to you in achieving the worthwhile goal of becoming a CPA!

Debra R. Hopkins, CPA, CIA

ABOUT THE AUTHOR

Debra R. Hopkins directs the nationally acclaimed Northern Illinois University (NIU) CPA Review course in the Chicago, Illinois area. For over twenty years she has taught financial accounting and auditing topics and for the last three years she has taught governmental and nonprofit accounting topics.

As director, she assists over 1,000 CPA candidates each year. She has skillfully combined her education, experience, and enthusiasm into a format that is easy to follow and understand. In the classroom she works directly with busy candidates who work full-time or are completing demanding accounting programs. She knows firsthand how frustrating the exam-taking experience can be for a person who is unaware of how the CPA exam functions. She has seen and heard directly from the candidates.

1 BELIEVE THAT YOU CAN PASS!

Passing the Uniform Certified Public Accountant (CPA) examination is not easy. Ever since 1917, the CPA exam has been challenging candidates. With a first-time passing rate of 12 to 18% on the pencil-based exam and a less than 50% per exam section passing rate on the computer-based test (CBT), it is assumed that most people will fail one or more sections on their first attempt. That's right, the odds are against you. Yet the only way to become a CPA is to keep on trying. Completing the exam is one of the greatest accomplishments an accountant can achieve. Completing a degreed accounting program is an accomplishment to be proud of, but passing all four sections of the CPA exam is the crowning glory. The old story goes, anyone can earn an accounting degree, but only the best accountants can pass the CPA exam. Without the three initials CPA, you are just another accountant. How could three initials mean so much?

Being a CPA sends certain signals. People know that you have achieved a very difficult goal—you have passed the Uniform Certified Public Accountant exam, one of the most difficult certification examinations in the nation. In the business world, the CPA designation instills confidence and trust. Compared to an accounting graduate who has not yet attained certification, CPAs command higher salaries, are in greater demand in the workforce, and are given greater respect by the general public. The recent accounting problems experienced by a few large corporations have made the CPA certificate more valuable, rather than less valuable. With the Securities and Exchange Commission and various oversight boards watching the profession, the CPA designation sends the signal of professional achievement. You have attained a minimum level of competence required to perform your work.

Who wouldn't want more money, more job choices, and more respect? The desire to become a CPA should be yours. You must believe that you have the skills and knowledge necessary to pass this exam. If you can look at yourself in the mirror and say, "I can pass the CPA exam," you are ready to proceed. Believing that you can pass the exam is the first step. Now, what's next?

STEPS TO CPA EXAM SUCCESS

In today's highly technological and informational age, it is amazing how many people take the CPA exam without knowing much about the process. Perhaps this is the reason why over half of the people taking the exam fail on their first attempt. To complete the CPA exam successfully, you must understand much more than the technical material. The three to four hours that it will take you to read this book will save you countless hours of study time, not to mention the stress and anxiety that goes along with a high-stakes exam. *Get Motivated* is designed not only to keep you pumped throughout the study process, but also to help you

- Increase your memory power
- Design a personalized study plan that is customized to fit your busy lifestyle
- Eliminate the fear of failure by understanding the exam process
- Decrease test anxiety by increasing your overall knowledge of the exam process
- Improve your study habits for the CPA exam, other professional certifications, and other study programs, such as graduate and certification programs
- Maximize the efficiency and effectiveness with which you study

Taking the CPA exam is a costly venture. When you add up the cost of a review course, textbooks, software, the exam application and related fees, the time off work, and the cost of travel to and from review courses and the exam, the total investment can easily exceed $3,000. Yet many exam candidates have the attitude that they will just "go try the exam to see what I can learn." If you were running a business, would you waste time and money just to understand the process? I doubt it. You would hire a consultant who not only understands the process but who can quickly teach you how to make the most out of the experience. This book provides you with just such tips and strategies. For over twenty years I have assisted thousands of people from all over the world pass the CPA exam. I have witnessed firsthand what it takes to pass. I know why people fail. I know how the successful people proceed. Why take chances? Learn how to attack the CPA exam and beat the odds of failure. Learn from other people's mistakes. Learn from other people's successes. Why reinvent the wheel? Utilize a best practices management plan that has been developed, tested, and found to be successful. Use the tips in this book as if a CPA exam consultant personally developed them for you.

You are ready to proceed. You have the desire to pass the CPA exam. The next step is to understand why so many people fail; failure is what you want to avoid.

FAILURE

Failure is the act of nonperformance. Failure means you were not successful at this attempt. Failure is temporary. Failure does not last forever. If you did not pass the exam, you are not awful, stupid, or careless. You just did not perform in the manner that was required. There is no need to provide excuses as to why you did not or will not pass the CPA exam. Making excuses takes time, bores the person who is listening to you, and reminds you that you were not successful. Move on; failure is the wrong focus. Spend a brief amount of time analyzing why you or others before you have failed. Then use your knowledge to move on. Learn from other people's mistakes.

Why do so many candidates fail the exam? Less than half of the people taking each exam section pass. What makes this exam so difficult?

First, the exam probably is not similar to any other exam you have ever taken. The total exam time is fourteen hours; the longest section, Auditing and Attestation is four and one half hours. Most exams you took in college were much shorter in length, perhaps one to two hours. A four and one half-hour exam would be considered very long.

Next, the exam is given in a place and format that is unfamiliar to you. You are accustomed to taking your exams in a college classroom, not at a Prometric test center. Not only is the place unfamiliar to you, but the format of taking an exam on a computer is new to most CPA exam candidates. The exam is administered under the rules set by the American Institute of Certified Public Accountants (AICPA) and the Prometric test center using a well-defined navigational process. Most CPA candidates are not informed about the exact exam-taking rules or of how to navigate the computerized format.

Finally, the exam covers material you learned over four to five years during your college studies. Although you are permitted to schedule each exam section over several testing windows, you must successfully complete all four sections within an eighteen-month period. Learning about the exam process, the format, and then reviewing course content and material that you learned several months or years before is a daunting task. If you stack up your college textbooks and professional reference materials that support each of the four CPA exam sections, you will have a pile that is at least a foot high. Add the four piles together and you quickly see the tremendous amount of material that is tested. Dealing with such breadth of material is enough to destroy your confidence.

After the exam, you must wait for your scores. Unlike the timely feedback you received in college, receiving your CPA exam score may take as long as six to eight weeks. Your kind college professor will not be grading the exam. Accounting professionals and AICPA examinations staff, who do not personally know you, will be grading your responses using a predetermined grading guide. You will be expected to achieve at a certain level that has not been clearly demonstrated or defined for you. The passing level often is established well before the exam is given. When the scores are released, you will not see your answers. You will see only your overall score for each section and a brief summary of your performance called the "Uniform CPA Examination Performance Information" report. The uncertainty of the content, the exam format and environment, the grading process, and the sheer volume of material may make you want to give up. Don't give up!

If you give up, you will never become a CPA. Read this book and learn how to develop a customized study plan to maximize your study effectiveness. Learn how to remain motivated and confident during both the study process and the exam-taking process. On exam day, learn how to attack and control the exam. Learn step-by-step how to remember concepts, apply exam strategy, and achieve a passing score section by section. Don't think about what you can't or don't know how to do. Believe and it can happen. Believe that you have what it takes to become a CPA. If you don't believe in yourself, who else will? You must convince the exam graders that you possess the necessary knowledge to have earned the right to call yourself a CPA. If you keep saying "I can't pass the CPA exam," you are probably correct. A successful candidate does not accept an "I can't" attitude. If you so easily discount your ability to perform, imagine what the exam graders will do! From now on, even when you are feeling low or doubtful about your abilities, remind yourself that you *can* pass the CPA exam. You will believe in yourself. Believing is your first step to becoming a CPA.

The CPA exam is not a new experience. Ever since 1917, people just like you have been passing the exam. You aren't the only person in the world who will struggle from time to time in your exam preparation. You are not the only person in the world who will have distractions, crises, and problems during your study process. You are not the only person in the world who is anxious, fearful, or worried about the exam. Remember, you are not alone. If you dwell on your doubts, you will become distracted and lose focus. Take a lesson from the people who have failed. Failure on the CPA exam occurs for a variety of reasons including

- Fear of failure—not believing in yourself
- Lack of technical knowledge
- Lack of knowledge of the computer-based test format and navigational system
- Lack of knowledge about the exam environment at the Prometric test center
- Loss of focus on the task on hand

From this list, it's easy to see that people fail because of both a lack of knowledge about the exam and a lack of knowledge about themselves and their capabilities. Unfortunately, some people fail even after hours of studying. They study the wrong material. Using out-of-date study materials is one of the biggest mistakes a person can make. Material that is more than six months to one year old may be out of date. Currently the CPA exam is adjusted for professional changes every six months. If people spend hours studying old college textbooks, they probably are not only using out-of-date materials, but they also are studying material meant for a college course rather than material meant for a professional, computer-based exam. The CPA exam is written using a unique method. People can arrive at the testing center and find no correlation between the materials they studied and the material tested. Why study just to study? Your time is too valuable. Spend your time learning and using the concepts and the formats used on the real exam.

Well-studied people can fail because they allowed themselves to be overcome with test anxiety. Taking a computer-based exam in an unfamiliar test center, next to strangers, under strict time conditions, all while being videotaped on camera can be very stressful. What a shame to have spent weeks preparing for a section and then to be overcome with fear just because the setting and format were not what you had expected.

If you have attempted the CPA exam and did not pass, you are not a failure. You have just hit a temporary setback. You have the power to turn failure into success. Once you have passed the CPA exam, no one will ask you how many times you sat for each section before you passed. The question is always: "Are you a CPA?"

What can you learn from other people's mistakes? It takes more than just technical knowledge to pass. The successful candidate will

- Prepare an organized study plan
- Use the proper study materials
- Learn about the exam environment, the grading process, and the exam requirements
- Remain motivated throughout the study process
- Use knowledge about the exam process to control the exam
- Remain confident that you are better prepared than the average candidate
- Always believe that he or she can pass the CPA exam

Enough talk about failure. You must focus on obtaining positive results. Use your energies toward achieving a positive outcome. Believe that you are a successful person. Your focus is to pass the exam section by section. Your focus should never be failure, even if you learn that you have failed a section. Once you abandon the failure focus, you can begin to work on the steps to success. Success is easier to talk about than failure. However, success does not come easily or quickly. Wouldn't it be nice if someone could develop a CPA potion that you could purchase from a drive-up restaurant? You could drive through and order a burger with onions and one large CPA success drink. The inventor of the CPA success drink would be one very rich person. No, it is not that simple. There is no fast track to success. You must go one step at a time. Slowly, step-by-step, you learn the concepts. Slowly, step-by-step, you gain exam confidence by learning more about the exam process. Slowly, step-by-step, you understand the exam content, the grading process, the computer navigational format, and how to control the exam before it controls you. You are in command of the CPA exam.

HOW TO USE THIS BOOK AND THE CD

Each chapter is designed as a separate informational unit. After you read Chapter 2, Content and Overall Exam Format, feel free to skip around. If at the moment family, friends, and coworkers seem to be your biggest problem, read Chapter 13, Coping with Family, Friends, and Coworkers. Closer to exam day, read the chapter that pertains to the section that you are taking and review Chapter 22, Time Management. As you read this book, tab and label certain pages to refer to frequently.

This book serves as a useful reference source to supplement your actual review materials. Often review materials cover the technical issues only. Who's going to help you with the emotional side of passing the exam? What should you wear to the exam? How do you apply to sit for the exam? Which section should you take first? How do you navigate the computer-based test? How can you practice simulation format questions? How can you improve your long-term memory? This book will walk you through the complete CPA exam journey step-by-step. The following chapters will guide you from the moment you think you want to be a CPA to the moment when you receive your final results and a letter that says: "Congratulations—you are a CPA!"

At the end of each chapter, you will find a section entitled "*Personally Speaking*." Here I speak frankly to you about former candidates' fears, mistakes, and successes. Let these real-world situations teach you how to be a successful exam taker.

Use the CD recording to motivate yourself. When you are feeling totally overwhelmed, listen to my friendly voice reminding you that passing the CPA exam is an achievable goal. Enjoy your preparation process. If you begin your studies with a positive outlook, you might be surprised. You actually could *enjoy* studying.

As you read, listen, and study, always keep the end result in mind. Picture yourself walking across a stage receiving a certificate that names you as successfully completing the Uniform Certified Public Accountant exam. You are now a CPA! Don't lose hope. Visualize yourself as a CPA. Believe that you can pass!

PERSONALLY SPEAKING

At the beginning of every CPA Review course, the most common statement made by the candidates is: "I am not your typical CPA candidate. Do I have a chance to pass?" The answer is always the same: "Yes, you can pass if you are willing to correct your weaknesses, remain focused, and at all times continue to believe in your abilities." In other words, the key to passing is not to be categorized as the "typical CPA candidate." The key to passing is willingness to work toward your goal; there is no typical candidate. There is no magic age to sit for the exam. The youngest candidate I have ever worked with was a child genius who received his college degree early and sat for the exam at age eighteen. The oldest candidate was a seventy-year-old grandfather who sat for the exam with his twenty-six-year-old granddaughter. One was a recent college graduate; the other had completed his accounting coursework and degree several years before. They both worked very hard, and they both passed. When it comes to the CPA exam, being categorized as a "typical" candidate does not help you pass.

Part-time college students who earned their accounting hours over ten years have the same chance of passing the exam as recent college graduates as long as they all are willing to work for it. The person who received all A's in college courses is not guaranteed a better chance to pass than the person with a C average. You may be very bright, but perhaps you will not be able to cope with the stress and pressure of taking a technical computer-based exam administered with strict time constraints.

Let's face it, when we look around we can always find someone who seems to be brighter and who is younger, thinner, richer, and better-looking than we are. What do these things have to do with passing the CPA exam? Don't worry about other people and other situations. Use your time and energies to assess where you are and what you can improve. My age is out of my control, and I am not going to worry about it. I am going to enjoy today and use today to improve my life. I am concerned with what I can control and what I can improve. Focus on what you can do to improve your chances of passing the exam. All other concerns are not important now. Understand that you are the typical CPA candidate no matter how old you are, where you went to college, or what grade point average you earned. The typical CPA candidate is just like you—concerned about passing the exam. Believe me and believe in yourself. No matter who you are, you are the kind of person who, with hard work and dedication, can pass the CPA exam. To begin planning a successful CPA exam journey, complete the checklist in Exhibit 1.1 to determine your basic awareness level about the exam.

Exhibit 1.1: CPA Exam Awareness Level Questionnaire

Statement	*Yes*	*No*
1. With hard work and dedication, I believe I can pass the CPA exam.		
2. Candidates should apply to sit for the CPA exam three to four months in advance of the date in which they plan to take the first exam section.		
3. Candidates must prove certain educational requirements to qualify to sit for the exam.		
4. Candidates should select the exam section order and make a conscious decision about which section(s) to take in each testing window.		
5. Candidates should obtain and use study materials that have been printed within six months to one year from the date they plan to sit.		
6. Passing the CPA exam takes a great deal of time and effort, but if I plan ahead, budget my study time, and stick to a study plan, I will greatly increase my chances of passing.		
7. The CPA exam tests a candidate's writing skills as well as ability to research certain technical issues.		
8. Today's CPA exam tests more analytical, research, and critical thinking skills and less memorization.		
9. The CPA exam is a computer-based exam that can be taken one section at a time. However, all sections must be passed within eighteen months of the date in which a candidate sits for the first section that he or she successfully completes.		
10. By passing the CPA exam, I can increase my salary, earn the respect of others in the field, and increase my job mobility.		

The correct answer to all of the questions in the exhibit is "Yes." If you checked "No" to question 1, please stop here. You are not ready to attempt this difficult exam. You do not believe in yourself. If you checked "no" to questions 2 through 10, use this book to learn more about the exam and how you should prepare for it. Learn how to manage your time. Learn how to control your fears by controlling the exam. Someday you, too, will sign your name and add the three initials "CPA." Go for it—the results are well worth it.

CPA EXAM TIP:
Visualize yourself as a CPA—believe that you can achieve your goal!

2 CONTENT AND OVERALL EXAM FORMAT

The Uniform Certified Public Accountant (CPA) examination is just that—uniform. The term "uniform" means that all candidates taking a particular exam section will be required to answer questions that are developed by referencing a set of content specification outlines (CSOs) that are the same for each exam section and for each and every candidate. Although exam questions vary, the overall content and the exam format do not. The more CPA candidates understand about the content and the format of the exam, the better their exam experience will be. This chapter helps CPA candidates learn more about the exam structure, content, and format. This is important, since the exam is nondisclosed.

NONDISCLOSED EXAM QUESTIONS AND ANSWERS

Since 1996, the CPA exam has been nondisclosed, which means the candidates no longer have access to exam questions and answers after taking an exam section. Because the general public and CPA candidates are not allowed to see the actual exam, it is more difficult for candidates to learn about exam changes, areas tested, and the exam format. With the change to a computer-based exam format, it is very important that CPA candidates purchase a proven source, such as quality review manuals, software, and/or an up-to-date CPA review course to help them learn about the exam. The computer-based exam is very new, with the first candidates taking exam sections on April 5, 2004; the pencil-based exam had been in existence since 1917.

Review course directors, accounting professors, and other interested parties may purchase released questions from the AICPA. The AICPA tells candidates to work the CPA exam tutorial and the AICPA sample examinations available on the primary CPA Web site (www.cpa-exam.org) at least three times before they take an exam section. The tutorial and sample exams serve as excellent sources to witness firsthand how the exam looks and feels. Understand, however, that the sample exam is simply a sample of a few multiple-choice questions and one abbreviated simulation testlet. These questions are for sample, demonstration purposes only. The chances of one of these sample questions appearing on the actual exam are slim to none. The AICPA Board of Examiners is responsible for preparing the exam tutorial, the sample exams, and the database of questions and answers that are used to generate the actual exams.

To keep the nondisclosed exam secure, candidates are asked to sign a statement of examination confidentiality and break policy statement. This statement reads:

I hereby certify that I will respect the confidentiality of the Uniform CPA Examination. I attest that I will NOT:

- Divulge the nature or content of any Uniform CPA Examination question or answer under any circumstance
- Engage in any unauthorized communication during testing
- Refer to unauthorized materials or use unauthorized equipment during testing
- Remove or attempt to remove any Uniform CPA Examinations materials, notes, or any other items from the examination room

I understand that I am required to report to the AICPA any examination question disclosures or solicitations for disclosure of which I am aware.

I understand that breaks are only allowed between testlets. I understand that I will be asked to complete any open testlet/simulation before leaving the testing room for a break.

In addition, I understand that failure to comply with this attestation may result in invalidation of my grades, disqualification from future examinations, expulsion from the testing facility and possible civil or criminal penalties.[1]

The AICPA means business. **Do not** violate the nondisclosure exam policies by discussing the exam with anyone, even someone who took an exam section at the same time you did. If someone overhears your discussion you could be reported, and it is difficult to prove that no one could have overheard you. It is best to avoid the problem by not discussing the exam with anyone. This will benefit most candidates, as discussing the exam and finding out about possible errors could discourage them from continuing to study and sit for another exam section. After you have taken an exam section, don't look back. Move on and begin preparing for the next section. Begin your studies promptly. It can take several weeks to receive your score. There is no time to waste. Don't worry about an exam performance that you cannot change. Once an exam section is history, move ahead to the next section.

CPA Review providers are allowed to conduct postexam interviews about their products. However, the information must be requested in such general terms, such as: How was our coverage on internal controls? Candidates may respond in very general terms by indicating whether the coverage was poor, adequate, or overly detailed. This type of questioning provides guidance to interested parties without divulging the exact question content, format, or type. A wise CPA candidate will purchase current materials from a trusted source that is current and knowledgeable about the

---

[1] *"Uniform CPA Examination Candidate Bulletin," p. 16, AICPA Web site, www.cpa-exam.org.*

nondisclosure rules. Being current is critical, because the content and/or focus of the exam continue to change.

CPA EXAM STRUCTURE

The Uniform CPA exam consists of four distinct sections, each worth a total of 100 points. The exam is administered at one of 300 Prometric test centers located throughout the United States. All candidates must take the exam at a Prometric center, using a computer. Exhibit 2.1 lists the exam sections and length of each section.

Exhibit 2.1: Exam Sections and Time Breakdowns

Auditing & Attestation (AUDIT)	Financial Accounting and Reporting (FAR)	Regulation (REG)	Business Environment and Concepts (BEC)	Total Examination Time
4.5 hours	4.0 hours	3.0 hours	2.5 hours	14.0 hours

Candidates choose the order in which they sit for each exam section, as well as the Prometric test center location and the date. Notice that the total testing time is fourteen hours. It is impossible to sit for the entire exam in one day. In fact, most candidates sit for only one section per day, with several days, weeks, or months, in between sections. The scheduling is very flexible. This is why it is important for candidates to understand the required skills and the content of each exam section.

SKILLS FOR THE UNIFORM CPA EXAMINATION

In the *2000 Practice Analysis of Certified Public Accountants* the AICPA identified five key skills necessary to protect the public interest. This was the third study conducted by the AICPA to determine the entry-level skills required in the early years of public accounting. As a result of the most recent study, five testing skills were identified to serve as a basis to develop the new computer-based test (CBT). The skills are

1. Analysis
2. Judgment
3. Understanding
4. Communication
5. Research

The first three skills—analysis, judgment, and understanding—require candidates to comprehend professional standards, to interpret and apply those standards to practice situations, and to recognize business-related issues and their relevance to evaluating an entity's financial condition. Candidates should be able to organize, process, and interpret data to select the best option for the given situation. Most of the aforementioned information is meaningless to candidates who just want to find out what they need to know to pass the CPA exam. This is where a reliable set of review materials comes in. Before you purchase study materials, read the introductory section to determine if the authors have focused on the five essential skills identified by the AICPA. If the authors have, purchase the materials and confidently begin your study process. Most reputable course providers are well trained in question development and can easily help you meet the above criteria. When candidates take time to understand and learn the details of the overall exam content by exam section, their performance is improved.

EXAMINATION CONTENT

The AICPA publishes a detailed content listing of each exam section referred to as content specification outlines (CSOs). The outlines can be found at the main CPA examination Web site (www.cpa-exam.org). See Exhibits 2.2 through 2.5 for the CSOs as of the date of this publication. The AICPA advises candidates to check the Web site frequently, as in the early years of the computer-based exam, changes are to be expected. It is clear from reading the CSOs that they provide only the most general of content information. The exact detail or nature of the topics tested is not obvious. For example, while knowing that the topic of leases will be tested in the Financial Accounting and Reporting (FAR) section, this tells us little about the exam content. The area of leases contains several areas, such as operating leases, capital leases, and financing leases. Are all of these areas considered to be testable topics? We must assume that the answer is yes. Use the CSOs to get a general idea of the overall content tested. Candidates also find it useful to think about the exam in relation to their college coursework. Exhibit 2.6 shows what college courses link to each exam section. Although the list may vary by university, most college curriculums are standardized enough to make these broad generalizations.

Exhibit 2.2: Auditing & Attestation (AUDIT)

The Auditing & Attestation section covers knowledge of auditing procedures, auditing standards generally accepted in the United States of America (GAAS) and other standards related to attest engagements and the skills needed to apply that knowledge in auditing and other attestation engagements. This section tests such knowledge and skills in the context of the five broad engagement tasks in the outline that follows.

Auditing & Attestation Content Specification Outline

I. **Plan the engagement, evaluate the prospective client and engagement, decide whether to accept or continue the client and the engagement, and enter into an agreement with the client (22%–28% of the total exam)**

   A. Determine nature and scope of engagement

1. Auditing standards generally accepted in the United States of America (GAAS)
2. Standards for accounting and review services
3. Standards for attestation engagements
4. Compliance auditing applicable to governmental entities and other recipients of governmental financial assistance
5. Other assurance services
6. Appropriateness of engagement to meet client's needs

B. Assess engagement risk and the CPA firm's ability to perform the engagement

1. Engagement responsibilities
2. Staffing and supervision requirements
3. Quality control considerations
4. Management integrity
5. Researching information sources for planning and performing the engagement

C. Communicate with the predecessor accountant or auditor
D. Decide whether to accept or continue the client and engagement
E. Enter into an agreement with the client about the terms of the engagement
F. Obtain an understanding of the client's operations, business, and industry
G. Perform analytical procedures
H. Consider preliminary engagement materiality
I. Assess inherent risk and risk of misstatements from errors, fraud, and illegal acts by clients
J. Consider other planning matters

1. Using the work of other independent auditors
2. Using the work of a specialist
3. Internal audit function
4. Related parties and related-party transactions
5. Electronic evidence
6. Risks of auditing around the computer

K. Identify financial statement assertions and formulate audit objectives

1. Significant financial statement balances, classes of transactions, and disclosures
2. Accounting estimates

L. Determine and prepare the work program defining the nature, timing, and extent of the procedures to be applied

II. Consider internal control in both manual and computerized environments (12%–18%)

A. Obtain an understanding of business processes and information flows
B. Identify controls that might be effective in preventing or detecting misstatements
C. Document an understanding of internal control

    D. Consider limitations of internal control
    E. Consider the effects of service organizations on internal control
    F. Perform tests of controls
    G. Assess control risk

III. Obtain and document information to form a basis for conclusions (32%–38%)

    A. Perform planned procedures

        1. Applications of audit sampling
        2. Analytical procedures
        3. Confirmation of balances and/or transactions with third parties
        4. Physical examination of inventories and other assets
        5. Other tests of details
        6. Computer assisted audit techniques, including data interrogation, extraction and analysis
        7. Substantive tests before the balance sheet date
        8. Tests of unusual year-end transactions

    B. Evaluate contingencies
    C. Obtain and evaluate lawyers' letters
    D. Review subsequent events
    E. Obtain representations from management
    F. Identify reportable conditions and other control deficiencies
    G. Identify matters for communication with audit committees
    H. Perform procedures for accounting and review services engagements
    I. Perform procedures for attestation engagements

IV. Review the engagement to provide reasonable assurance that objectives are achieved and evaluate information obtained to reach and to document engagement conclusions (8%–12%)

    A. Perform analytical procedures
    B. Evaluate the sufficiency and competence of audit evidence and document engagement conclusions
    C. Evaluate whether financial statements are free of material misstatements
    D. Consider whether substantial doubt about an entity's ability to continue as a going concern exists
    E. Consider other information in documents containing audited financial statements
    F. Review the work performed to provide reasonable assurance that objectives are achieved

V. Prepare communications to satisfy engagement objectives (12%–18%)

    A. Reports

        1. Reports on audited financial statements
        2. Reports on reviewed and compiled financial statements
        3. Reports required by Government Auditing Standards
        4. Reports on compliance with laws and regulations

    5.   Reports on internal control
    6.   Reports on prospective financial information
    7.   Reports on agreed-upon procedures
    8.   Reports on the processing of transactions by service organizations
    9.   Reports on supplementary financial information
   10.   Special reports
   11.   Reports on other assurance services
   12.   Reissuance of reports

B.   Other required communications

    1.   Errors and fraud
    2.   Illegal acts
    3.   Communications with audit committees
    4.   Other reporting considerations covered by statements on auditing standards and statements on standards for attestation engagements

C.   Other matters

    1.   Subsequent discovery of facts existing at the date of the auditor's report
    2.   Consideration after the report date of omitted procedures

References—Auditing and Attestation

- AICPA Statements on Auditing Standards and Interpretations
- AICPA Statements on Standards for Accounting and Review Services and Interpretations
- AICPA Statements on Quality Control Standards
- AICPA Statements on Standards for Attestation Engagements
- US General Accounting Office Government Auditing Standards
- AICPA Audit and Accounting Guides
  - *Audit Sampling*
  - *Consideration of Internal Control in a Financial Statement Audit*
  - *Analytical Procedures*
  - *Auditing Revenues in Certain Industries*
- Current textbooks on auditing and other attestation services
- AICPA Auditing Practice Releases
- AICPA Audit and Accounting Manual
- AICPA Audit Risk Alerts and Compilation and Review Alerts
- Single Audit Act, as amended

Source: AICPA Web site, www.cpa-exam.org. Under "Learning Resources," click "Educator Resources," then click "Revised Uniform CPA Examination Content Specification Outlines (CSOs)."

Exhibit 2.3: Financial Accounting and Reporting (FAR)

The Financial Accounting & Reporting section tests knowledge of accounting principles generally accepted in the United States of America (GAAP) for business enterprises, not-for-profit organizations, and governmental entities, and the skills needed to apply that knowledge. Content covered in this section includes financial accounting concepts and standards, and their application. To demonstrate such knowledge and skills, candidates will be required to

- Obtain and document information for use in financial statement presentations
- Evaluate, analyze, and process entity information for reporting in financial statements
- Communicate entity information and conclusions
- Analyze information and identify data relevant to financial accounting and reporting
- Identify financial accounting and reporting methods and select those that are suitable
- Perform calculations
- Formulate conclusions
- Present results in writing in a financial statement format or other appropriate format

Financial Accounting and Reporting Content Specification Outline

I.   Concepts and standards for financial statements (17%–23%)

   A.   Financial accounting concepts

      1.   Process by which standards are set and roles of standard-setting bodies

      2.   Conceptual basis for accounting standards

   B.   Financial accounting standards for presentation and disclosure in general-purpose financial statements

      1.   Consolidated and combined financial statements

      2.   Balance sheet

      3.   Statement(s) of income, comprehensive income and changes in equity accounts

      4.   Statement of cash flows

      5.   Accounting policies and other notes to financial statements

   C.   Other presentations of financial data (financial statements prepared in conformity with comprehensive bases of accounting other than GAAP)

   D.   Financial statement analysis

II. Typical items: recognition, measurement, valuation, and presentation in financial statements in conformity with GAAP (27%–33%)

   A.   Cash, cash equivalents, and marketable securities

   B.   Receivables

   C.   Inventories

   D.   Property, plant, and equipment

   E.   Investments

   F.   Intangibles and other assets

   G.   Payables and accruals

   H.   Deferred revenues

   I.   Notes and bonds payable

   J.   Other liabilities

   K.   Equity accounts

   L.   Revenues, cost, and expense accounts

III. Specific types of transactions and events: recognition, measurement, valuation, and presentation in financial statements in conformity with GAAP (27%–33%)

    A. Accounting changes and corrections of errors
    B. Business combinations
    C. Contingent liabilities and commitments
    D. Discontinued operations
    E. Earnings per share
    F. Employee benefits, including stock options
    G. Extraordinary items
    H. Financial instruments, including derivatives
    I. Foreign currency transactions and translation
    J. Income taxes
    K. Interest costs
    L. Interim financial reporting
    M. Leases
    N. Nonmonetary transactions
    O. Related parties
    P. Research and development costs
    Q. Segment reporting
    R. Subsequent events

IV. Accounting and reporting for governmental entities (8%–12%)

    A. Governmental accounting concepts
        1. Measurement focus and basis of accounting
        2. Fund accounting concepts and application
        3. Budgetary process

    B. Format and content of governmental financial statements
        1. Government-wide financial statements
        2. Governmental funds financial statements
        3. Conversion from fund to government-wide financial statements
        4. Proprietary fund financial statements
        5. Fiduciary fund financial statements
        6. Notes to financial statements
        7. Required supplementary information, including management's discussion and analysis
        8. Comprehensive annual financial report (CAFR)

    C. Financial reporting entity including blended and discrete component units

    D. Typical items and specific types of transactions and events: recognition, measurement, valuation and presentation in governmental entity financial statements in conformity with GAAP
        1. Net assets
        2. Capital assets and infrastructure
       3. Transfers
        4. Other financing sources and uses

5. Fund balance
6. Nonexchange revenues
7. Expenditures
8. Special items
9. Encumbrances

E. Accounting and financial reporting for governmental not-for-profit organizations

V. Accounting and reporting for nongovernmental not-for-profit organizations (8%–12%)

A. Objectives, elements and formats of financial statements

1. Statement of financial position
2. Statement of activities
3. Statement of cash flows
4. Statement of functional expenses

B. Typical items and specific types of transactions and events: recognition, measurement, valuation and presentation in the financial statements of not-for-profit organizations in conformity with GAAP

1. Revenues and contributions
2. Restrictions on resources
3. Expenses, including depreciation and functional expenses
4. Investments

References—Financial Accounting and Reporting

- Financial Accounting Standards Board (FASB) Statements of Financial Accounting Standards and Interpretations, Accounting Principles Board Opinions, AICPA Accounting Research Bulletins, and FASB Technical Bulletins
- Codification of Statements on Auditing Standards
  - AU Section 411, *The Meaning of "Present Fairly in Conformity with Generally Accepted Accounting Principles"*
  - AU Section 560, *Subsequent Events*
  - AU Section 623, *Special Reports*
- FASB Statements of Financial Accounting Concepts
- AICPA Statements of Position
  - 93-7, *Reporting on Advertising Costs*
  - 94-6, *Disclosure of Certain Significant Risks and Uncertainties*
  - 96-1, *Environmental Remediation Liabilities*
  - 97-2, *Software Revenue Recognition*
  - 98-1, *Accounting for the Costs of Computer Software Developed or Obtained for Internal Use*
  - 98-2, *Accounting for the Costs of Activities of Not-for-Profit Organizations and State and Local Governmental Entities That Include Fund-Raising*
  - 98-5, *Reporting on the Costs of Start-Up Activities*

- AICPA Audit and Accounting Guides relating to governmental and not-for-profit organizations
- Governmental Accounting Standards Board (GASB) Statements, Interpretations, and Technical Bulletins
- Current textbooks on accounting for business enterprises, not-for-profit organizations, and governmental entities

Source: AICPA Web site, www.cpa-exam.org. Under "Learning Resources," click "Educator Resources," then click "Revised Uniform CPA Examination Content Specification Outlines (CSOs)."

Exhibit 2.4: Regulation (REG)

The Regulation section tests candidates' knowledge of federal taxation, ethics, professional and legal responsibilities, and business law and the skills needed to apply that knowledge.

Ethics, Professional and Legal Responsibilities, and Business Law

This portion covers knowledge of a CPA's professional and legal responsibilities and the legal implications of business transactions, particularly as they relate to accounting and auditing, and the skills needed to apply that knowledge. This section deals with federal and widely adopted uniform state laws. If there is no federal or uniform state law on a topic, the questions are intended to test knowledge of the law of the majority of jurisdictions. Professional ethics questions are based on the AICPA Code of Professional Conduct because it is national in its application.

Federal Taxation

This portion tests knowledge of principles and procedures for federal income, estate, and gift taxation and their application in practice. To demonstrate such knowledge, candidates will be required to

- Analyze information and identify data relevant for tax purposes
- Identify issues, elections, and alternative tax treatments
- Research issues and alternative tax treatments
- Formulate conclusions

Regulation Content Specification Outline

I.   Ethics and professional and legal responsibilities (15%–20%)

    A.   Code of Professional Conduct
    B.   Proficiency, independence, and due care
    C.   Ethics and responsibilities in tax practice
    D.   Licensing and disciplinary systems imposed by the profession and state regulatory bodies
    E.   Legal responsibilities and liabilities

        1.   Common law liability to clients and third parties
        2.   Federal statutory liability

    F.   Privileged communications and confidentiality

II. **Business law (20%–25%)**

    A. Agency

        1. Formation and termination
        2. Duties and authority of agents and principals
        3. Liabilities and authority of agents and principals

    B. Contracts

        1. Formation
        2. Performance
        3. Third-party assignments
        4. Discharge, breach, and remedies

    C. Debtor-creditor relationships

        1. Rights, duties, and liabilities of debtors, creditors, and guarantors
        2. Bankruptcy

    D. Government regulation of business

        1. Federal securities acts
        2. Other government regulation (antitrust, pension and retirement plans, union and employee relations, and legal liability for payroll and social security taxes)

    E. Uniform commercial code

        1. Negotiable instruments and letters of credit
        2. Sales
        3. Secured transactions
        4. Documents of title and title transfer

    F. Real property, including insurance

III. **Federal tax procedures and accounting issues (8%–12%)**

    A. Federal tax procedures
    B. Accounting periods
    C. Accounting methods including cash, accrual, percentage of completion, completed contract, and installment sales
    D. Inventory methods, including uniform capitalization rules

IV. **Federal taxation of property transactions (8%–12%)**

    A. Types of assets
    B. Basis of assets
    C. Depreciation and amortization
    D. Taxable and nontaxable sales and exchanges
    E. Income, deductions, capital gains and capital losses, including sales and exchanges of business property and depreciation recapture

V. **Federal taxation—individuals (12%–18%)**

    A. Gross income—inclusions and exclusions
    B. Reporting of items from pass-through entities, including passive activity losses
    C. Adjustments and deductions to arrive at taxable income

D. Filing status and exemptions
E. Tax computations, credits, and penalties
F. Alternative minimum tax
G. Retirement plans
H. Estate and gift taxation, including transfers subject to the gift tax, annual exclusion, and items includible and deductible from gross estate

VI. Federal taxation—entities (22%–28%)

A. Similarities and distinctions in tax reporting among such entities as sole proprietorships, general and limited partnerships, subchapter C corporations, subchapter S corporations, limited liability companies, and limited liability partnerships

B. Subchapter C corporations

1. Determination of taxable income and loss, and reconciliation of book income to taxable income
2. Tax computations, credits, and penalties, including alternative minimum tax
3. Net operating losses
4. Consolidated returns
5. Entity/owner transactions, including contributions and distributions

C. Subchapter S corporations

1. Eligibility and election
2. Determination of ordinary income, separately stated items, and reconciliation of book income to taxable income
3. Basis of shareholder's interest
4. Entity/owner transactions, including contributions and liquidating and nonliquidating distributions
5. Built-in gains tax

D. Partnerships

1. Determination of ordinary income, separately stated items, and reconciliation of book income to taxable income
2. Basis of partner's interest and basis of assets contributed to the partnership
3. Partnership and partner elections
4. Partner dealing with own partnership
5. Treatment of partnership liabilities
6. Distribution of partnership assets
7. Ownership changes and liquidation and termination of partnership

E. Trusts

1. Types of trusts
2. Income and deductions
3. Determination of beneficiary's share of taxable income

References—Regulation

Ethics, Professional and Legal Responsibilities, and Business Law

- AICPA Professional Standards: *Code of Professional Conduct and By-laws*
- AICPA Statements on Auditing Standards dealing explicitly with proficiency, confidentiality, independence, and due care
- AICPA Statements on Standards for Consulting Services
- AICPA Statements on Responsibilities in Personal Financial Planning Practice
- Pronouncements of the Independence Standards Board
- Current textbooks covering business law, auditing, and accounting

Federal Taxation

- Internal Revenue Code and Income Tax Regulations
- Internal Revenue Service Circular 230
- AICPA Statements on Standards for Tax Services
- US Master Tax Guide
- Current federal income tax textbooks

Source: AICPA Web site, www.cpa-exam.org. Under "Learning Resources," click "Educator Resources," then click "Revised Uniform CPA Examination Content Specification Outlines (CSOs)."

Exhibit 2.5: Business Environment and Concepts (BEC)

The Business Environment and Concepts section tests knowledge of general business environment and business concepts that candidates need to know in order to understand the underlying business reasons for and accounting implications of transactions, and the skills needed to apply that knowledge in performing financial statement audit and attestation engagements and other functions normally performed by CPAs that affect the public interest. Content covered in this section includes knowledge of business structure; economic concepts essential to obtaining an understanding of an entity's operations, business and industry; financial management; information technology; and planning and measurement.

Business Environment and Concepts Content Specification Outline

I.   Business structure (17%–23%)

A.   Advantages, implications, and constraints of legal structures for business

1.   Sole proprietorships and general and limited partnerships
2.   Limited liability companies (LLC), limited liability partnerships (LLP), and joint ventures
3.   Subchapter C and subchapter S corporations

B.   Formation, operation, and termination of businesses
C.   Financial structure, capitalization, profit and loss allocation, and distributions
D.   Rights, duties, legal obligations, and authority of owners and management (directors, officers, stockholders, partners, and other owners)

II.   Economic concepts essential to obtaining an understanding of an entity's business and industry (8%–12%)

    A.   Business cycles and reasons for business fluctuations

    B.   Economic measures and reasons for changes in the economy, such as inflation, deflation and interest rate changes

    C.   Market influences on business strategies, including selling, supply chain, and customer management strategies

    D.   Implications to business of dealings in foreign currencies, hedging and exchange rate fluctuations

III.   Financial management (17%–23%)

    A.   Financial modeling, including factors such as financial indexes, taxes and opportunity costs, and models such as economic value added, cash flow, net present value, discounted payback, and internal rate of return

        1.   Objectives
        2.   Techniques
        3.   Limitations

    B.   Strategies for short-term and long-term financing options, including cost of capital and derivatives

    C.   Financial statement and business implications of liquid asset management

        1.   Management of cash and cash equivalents, accounts receivable, accounts payable, and inventories
        2.   Characteristics and financial statement and business implications of loan rates (fixed vs. variable) and loan covenants

IV.   Information technology (IT) implications in the business environment (22%–28%)

    A.   Role of business information systems

        1.   Reporting concepts and systems
        2.   Transaction processing systems
        3.   Management reporting systems
        4.   Risks

    B.   Roles and responsibilities within the IT function

        1.   Roles and responsibilities of database/network/Web administrators, computer operators, librarians, systems programmers and applications programmers
        2.   Appropriate segregation of duties

    C.   IT fundamentals

        1.   Hardware and software, networks, and data structure, analysis, and application, including operating systems, security, file organization, types of data files, and database management systems
        2.   Systems operation, including transaction processing modes, such as batch, on-line, real-time, and distributed processing, and application processing phases, such as data capture; edit routines;

master file maintenance; reporting, accounting, control, and management; query, audit trail, and ad hoc reports; and transaction flow

D. Disaster recovery and business continuity, including data backup and data recovery procedures, alternate processing facilities (hot sites), and threats and risk management

E. Financial statement and business implications of electronic commerce, including electronic fund transfers, point of sale transactions, internet-based transactions and electronic data interchange

V. Planning and measurement (22%–28%)

A. Planning and budgeting

1. Planning techniques, including strategic and operational planning
2. Forecasting and projection techniques
3. Budgeting and budget variance analysis

B. Performance measures

1. Organizational performance measures, including financial and nonfinancial scorecards
2. Benchmarking, including quality control principles, best practices, and benchmarking techniques

C. Cost measurement

1. Cost measurement concepts (standard, joint product, and by-product costing)
2. Accumulating and assigning costs (job order, process, and activity-based costing)
3. Factors affecting production costs

References—Business Environment and Concepts

- Current textbooks on
  - Business law
  - Managerial accounting
  - Management
  - Finance
  - Economics
  - Accounting information systems
  - Management information systems
  - Budgeting and measurement
- AICPA Audit Risk Alerts
- Business periodicals provide background material that is helpful in gaining an understanding of business environment and concepts.

Source: AICPA Web site, www.cpa-exam.org. Under "Learning Resources," click "Educator Resources," then click "Revised Uniform CPA Examination Content Specification Outlines (CSOs)."

Exhibit 2.6: Comparison of College Courses to Exam Content

Exam Content by Section	College Courses and/or College Content
Auditing and Attestation	• Financial statement auditing performed by external auditors following generally accepted auditing standards (GAAS) • Statistical sampling • Auditing with technology (use of the computer to audit) • Attestation standards • Compilation and review standards • Use of the AICPA Professional Standards, a professional database of standards
Financial Accounting and Reporting	• Intermediate accounting or financial reporting (usually two semesters) • Advanced financial accounting covering the areas of partnership accounting, and combinations and consolidations • Derivatives and financial instruments • Governmental accounting • Not-for-profit accounting • Use of the Financial Accounting Research System (FARS), a professional database
Regulation	• Business law (usually two semesters) • Professional and legal responsibilities of auditors (sometimes covered in an auditing course) • Individual taxation • Corporate taxation • Partnership taxation • Taxation of estates, trusts, and exempt organizations • Tax return preparers' responsibilities • Use of a taxation database tool to search for various code sections
Business Environment and Concepts	• Microeconomics • Macroeconomics • Corporate finance • Business formation, operation, and dissolution of various business organizations • Information systems (can be an accounting emphasis) • Managerial/cost accounting

Once you become familiar with the content and types of information that is testable, it is necessary to understand the computer-based examination format.

OVERALL EXAMINATION FORMAT

Each of the four exam sections begins with three testlets of multiple-choice questions. What is a testlet? A testlet is defined as a small subset of items in a pool, preassembled to meet sets of content specifications.[2] In plain English, this means a set of questions that focus around the CSOs, similar to a quiz that you took in college. Look at a testlet as a group of questions. The topics, however, are not randomly selected. The AICPA examiners carefully write questions to match the items listed in the CSOs. For more detail on each exam section, refer to Chapters 16 through 19, which discuss the content, question format, and tips for all four exams. As of this book's publication date, the Auditing and Attestation (AUDIT), Financial Accounting and Reporting (FAR), and Regulation (REG) exam sections also include two additional testlets that are referred to as simulations.

What is a simulation and how does it work? The AICPA defines a simulation as "an assessment of knowledge and skills in context approximating that found on the job through the use of realistic scenarios and tasks, and access to normally available and familiar resources."[3] Consider a simulation to be similar to a short case study. The CPA exam simulations require candidates to utilize many of the tools and skills that today's entry-level accountants use in the real-world workplace. Typical question requirements include writing a memo to communicate an accounting issue, using a database research tool to locate a key passage, completing an income tax schedule, and answering questions that refer to a set of facts. Each simulation contains one question that requires candidates to write an essay-type response. This essay-type response is referred to as the communication component. Each exam section is worth a total of 100 points. Exhibit 2.7 presents the point and format breakdown as of this book's publication date.

Exhibit 2.7: Point and Test Format Allocation

Format	Auditing and Attestation (AUDIT)	Financial Accounting and Reporting (FAR)	Regulation (REG)	Business Environment and Concepts (BEC)
Multiple-choice	70%	70%	70%	100%
Communication (formerly called essays)	10%	10%	10%	None at this time— expected in 2005

---

[2] *Craig N. Mills, Maria T. Potenza, John J. Fremer, and William C. Ward,* **Computer-Based Testing** *(Mahwah, New Jersey and London: Lawrence Erlbaum Associates, 2002), p. 96*
[3] *"What Are Simulations?" www.cpa-exam.org/cpa/computer_faqs_2html.*

Format	Auditing and Attestation (AUDIT)	Financial Accounting and Reporting (FAR)	Regulation (REG)	Business Environment and Concepts (BEC)
Other Simulation Requirements	20%	20%	20%	None at this time— expected in 2005

Right now the BEC section is tested using only the multiple-choice question format. Plans are under way to add simulations to this section as early as 2005.

Do you want to see for yourself what the new exam looks like? Go to www.cpa-exam.org and take the AICPA sample exams. Don't be concerned about the content and getting the answers correct at this time. Just take a look to get the general idea of how the exam works. Then come back and continue reading to find out the specifics of this new, exciting, and ever-changing CPA exam.

After you see the sample exams, you will be eager to select a testing date and begin. Not so fast! You don't even know when the exam is administered.

EXAMINATION DATES

No more May and November blues. Although the pencil-based exam required all candidates to sit for the exam on the same two days in May and November each year, the CBT is flexible. To keep pace with today's rapidly changing profession, the CPA exam is offered at least five days a week during two out of every three months throughout the year. There are no more set dates. You pick the test date and you select the exam section. Under the pencil-based format, most candidates were required to sit for all four exam sections in two days. Now candidates select their testing times from the first two months of every quarter, referred to as testing windows. During the third month of each quarter, the testing window is closed. The AICPA uses the time to analyze results, determine the exam section grade(s), and communicate the score(s) to the various state boards of accountancy that then distribute the score(s) to the examinees. Exhibit 2.8 presents the testing windows as of this book's publication date.

Exhibit 2.8: Testing Windows

Open Testing Windows	January February	April May	July August	October November
No Testing	March	June	September	December

As with all the information about the new CBT, candidates should remain informed. The testing times could be expanded in the future. Before beginning your journey to pass the CPA exam, check (www.cpa-exam.org) to see what information might have changed.

Can candidates sit for more than one section within a testing window? Most definitely; candidates may sit for one to four sections within each testing window. Candidates are not, however, permitted to sit for an exam section more than once within each testing window. Only one attempt is allowed per section in each testing window.

Is there a deadline to complete all four sections? Yes, all four sections must be completed within eighteen months of the date you took the first exam section that you completed successfully. For example, if you sat for the AUDIT exam on April 6, 2004, you should have received your score by the middle of July. Perhaps the AICPA will speed up the scoring process. However, at this time the plan is to release scores within two weeks after the testing window closes. So, if you took the exam on July 1, 2004, the testing window closed on September 30, and you would find out your results sometime around October 15, 2004. By the exam score date, you would have already lost some study time because the eighteen months begins from **the date you sat for the first exam section that you passed**, not the date you receive your score.

What happens if a candidate fails to successfully complete all four sections within the eighteen months? The candidate will forfeit the "pass" on the first section passed, and the eighteen months begins rolling from the date the candidate passed the next section. This is why the eighteen-month rule is referred to as the rolling eighteen-month rule.

WHAT DOES IT TAKE TO PASS?

The magical score is a 75! A score of 75 does not indicate that a candidate answered 75 percent of the examination questions correctly. The printed score indicates the grade after an exam procedure using a psychometric process called equating is applied. Details of the scoring and grading process are covered in Chapter 10, CPA Exam Grading. As mentioned, all four sections must be successfully completed within a rolling eighteen-month period, which begins on the date that the first section(s) passed is taken. If a candidate does not pass all four sections within the rolling eighteen-month period, credit for any section passed outside the eighteen-month period will expire and that section must be retaken. There is a time limit to complete all four exam sections.

"Conditioning," a term used under the pencil-based exam, meant that a candidate had successfully completed some sections of the total exam and was given a time period to complete the remaining sections. The term "conditioning" is no longer used when discussing the CBT. Because candidates now take one exam section at a time, the term is no longer relevant. Candidates who had conditioned under the pencil-based exam and are transitioning over to the CBT to complete the remaining areas should consult their state boards of accountancy for transition rules.

Candidate anonymity is preserved throughout the grading process. Graders are not aware of how many times a candidate has attempted the section. Preferential treatment is not given to those candidates who are at risk of losing a pass on a section as they move outside an eighteen-month window. No personal information—name, gender, education, experience, age, or number of examination attempts—is available to graders.

SCORE RELEASE

Candidates do not receive grades at the test center. The CBT contains structured response questions that require transmission of answers to the AICPA for scoring. A minimum of two to four weeks is required to grade a section and to release scores. For 2004, the first year of the CBT, it is anticipated that scores will not be released to the various state boards of accountancy until the end of the testing window (the last month of every quarter). Candidates are likely to receive their results within two weeks of the end of the quarter.

Now that you have a general idea of the content and overall exam format, are you ready to schedule a date to take the CPA exam? That is the topic of Chapter 3.

PERSONALLY SPEAKING

Isn't flexibility great? Yes, sometimes it is great. However, there are downsides to being allowed to select the date, time, and the exam section that you plan to sit for. Are you confused and wondering which section to sit for first? Chapter 4, A Time and Place for Everything, will help you make your decision. For now, understand one fundamental idea of the computer-based exam: You the candidate are in control. This means you must not only select the optimal times for you, but you also must motivate yourself to remain focused and disciplined to complete the entire exam. Choices aren't going to make the exam super easy. The exam remains a force to be respected. Proper preparation remains paramount. In fact, because everyone else also will be taking extra time to prepare for a section, outperforming your fellow test takers just might be tougher. Accept the fact that you must look at the CPA exam preparation process like a job with a set deadline. Establish your deadline and stick to it. Eighteen months seems like a long time, but it really isn't—time will fly by. Don't make a career out of passing the CPA exam—just make a short-term time commitment. Once you have programmed yourself to complete the task, then you must think about content.

In the early discussions of the CBT, candidates would tell me that they thought passing the new exam would be easier. When asked why, they would reply: "Because I can use the computer to help me." I find this comment to be very naive. A computer is only as smart as the people who operate it. The computer will not provide the correct answers. The key to passing the exam remains with learning the content. Candidates must be informed and knowledgeable about all of the areas listed in the CSOs. The content outlines are presented for a reason. The CSOs are your blueprint for the exam. Take time to become acquainted with the content listings. Check your review materials to be sure that all areas are covered. As your studies progress, stop and review the CSOs. The week before you take each exam section, reread the CSOs to be sure you are prepared for each listed area. A successful candidate will have prepared for all areas.

Why is such a diverse base of knowledge required to pass the CPA exam? One look at the CSOs is enough to make you give up. Of course, giving up is not an option. This exam is greatly respected, and much of that respect comes from the rigor. Nothing that's easy commands much respect. Accomplish what others can't do and you are respected. No need to panic. Leave no stone unturned. Know something about every outline item.

Watch for content changes. The AICPA will change the content to respond to changes made in the profession. For example, the content outline is updated when a new auditing standard is issued. How soon should you expect a new pronouncement to be tested? The rule is roughly six months from the date the new pronouncement was issued. This constant updating is especially important in the areas of income taxation and auditing, which seem to be changing the most. The www.cpa-exam.org Web site will provide you with the updated content outlines. This Web site is your greatest friend as you take the exam. Before beginning your preparation for each and every exam section, consult the Web site and note the changes. Why lose points just for being out-of-date? Be prepared by practicing and remaining current. Also be sure your review materials are current. Don't buy materials ahead of time just to save money. If you plan to take a section one year from now, don't buy the materials today, as the necessary changes might not have been made to update the information.

Divulging exam information is cheating! You are not a cheater, and you certainly don't want to be caught cheating. If you are caught, you could risk losing all that you have worked so hard to accomplish. If someone attempts to solicit information from you, simply say, "Quiet please, you know we are not allowed to discuss the exam." Leave the exam with the proctors and forget about it. Let the graders do their job. Your job will be to move on and begin preparation for the next exam section.

When I took the CPA exam, candidates could talk about it freely. In fact, the AICPA mailed candidates the actual question booklet one week prior to the exam date. Immediately after completing my first exam section, another candidate asked me about how I answered a particular question.

After I explained my approach and answer, she went on to tell me that I was wrong. I will never forget how I felt. I began to doubt my abilities. I wanted to give up and go home. Fortunately, I found the courage to regroup by telling myself that perhaps both of us were correct—there could have been two approaches. Most accountants tend to be more critical of themselves and willing to believe that others must be correct and they must be incorrect. Well, I passed the exam, as did my fellow candidate. If someone is pushing you to talk about the exam, don't risk your passing score by becoming a snitch! Remain quiet. Keep all exam information to yourself. Retaining confidentiality is required by the rules. Confidentiality will also prevent you from being judged by a fellow candidate.

Continue to believe that you can pass. No matter how difficult the section, you can't change your score after you complete the exam. Worry does not earn points. Don't look back. Look forward to the next event. Take time to prepare so that after each exam section you can say: "I did my best! Let the graders do their work. I am moving on to begin preparing for the next exam section."

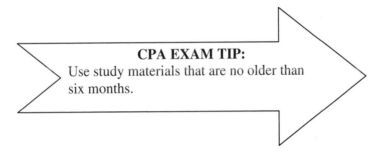

CPA EXAM TIP:
Use study materials that are no older than six months.

3 SCHEDULING AND APPLYING FOR THE EXAM

Before you sit for the first exam section, you must meet certain requirements. Although the exam itself is a national exam, written by the AICPA CPA Examinations staff in New Jersey, approval to sit for the exam is granted at the state level. Obtain approval from the state or territory in which you plan to practice or work as an accountant.

The exam is offered in fifty-four United States jurisdictions, which includes the fifty states, the District of Columbia, and three United States territories: Guam, Puerto Rico, and the Virgin Islands.

Each jurisdiction has specific requirements to sit for the exam and to become licensed as a certified public accountant. For a complete listing of the jurisdictions and the applicable contact information, consult the primary CPA exam Web site at www.cpa-exam.org or the National Association of State Boards of Accountancy (NASBA) at www.nasba.org.

The requirements always include proof of education. Most states/jurisdictions require candidates to earn 150 semester hours of college credit before approval to sit is granted. A few states require as few as 120 semester hours of college to qualify to sit for the CPA exam. Some states list specific accounting, auditing, and other business courses that candidates must complete before sitting for the exam. Other jurisdictions just count hours and not specific coursework. One state—Delaware—requires completion of a US income taxation course. An official sealed transcript from your college or university is the usual method used to prove the hours earned.

When should you begin the application process? As soon as possible, usually six months before the first day of the testing window in which you plan to sit. (Use the checklist in Exhibit 3.1 to monitor your application progress.)

Exhibit 3.1: Timetable checklist applying to sit for the CPA Exam

Task to complete	Due date	Date completed
Select the state/jurisdiction in which you plan to practice as a CPA. Consult the NASBA exam Web site, www.nasba.org, to obtain a list of state board Web sites and examination application information for the state in which you plan to practice.	6 – 7 months before your test date	

Task to complete	Due date	Date completed
Download the application for the state/jurisdiction of your choice. Prepare a file folder to keep all application materials accessible.	6 – 7 months before your test date	
Send international transcripts to the proper authorities for a foreign transcript evaluation.	7 – 8 months before your test date	
Obtain transcripts to prove your education. Determine if the Board of Examiners allows you to mail in official sealed transcripts directly. If the answer is yes, obtain official sealed transcripts. Do not open them. Save them to mail in with your completed exam application. If the answer is no, verify that your university has sent your transcript.	6 – 7 months before your test date	
Obtain the required identification photos.	6 – 7 months before your test date	
Complete the application. Ask a friend to check your application for completeness. Copy all supporting materials, even your check or credit card information.	6 – 7 months before your test date	
If necessary, complete any special needs or disability verification.	7 – 8 months before your test date	
Verify that the Board of Examiners has received all of the necessary application materials.	4 – 5 months before your test date	
Double-check your Prometric test center site and date.	4 – 5 months before your test date	
Verify that your two forms of identification match your name exactly as shown on the notice to schedule (NTS).	Check identification the day you receive your NTS.	

Suggested questions to ask the board when you request an application to sit are

- What are the hour requirements to sit for the exam—120 semester hours, or 150 semester hours or some combination in between? How are the hourly requirements measured—semester, trimester, or quarter hours?
- Must I possess a master's degree to sit? If so, what type of master's degree will fulfill the requirements?
- If a master's degree is not required, must I possess a bachelor's degree? If there is no requirement for an actual bachelor's degree, how many credit hours are considered to be equivalent to having earned a bachelor's degree?
- Are specific courses required to sit for the exam? If so, what are the courses? At what level are the courses to be taken (e.g., undergraduate or graduate level)?

- May I apply for approval to sit for the CPA exam before I complete the necessary coursework? If so, what special proof of class enrollment is required?
- If I earned my hours/degree outside of the United States, what are the procedures to obtain a special transcript evaluation of my international hours? How much time should be added to accommodate the international transcript evaluation? How much extra does the international transcript evaluation cost?
- Do grades of D or better count?
- Do pass/fail or satisfactory/unsatisfactory grades count toward the requirements?
- Must my college transcripts be "officially sealed," or will a copy of my transcripts suffice? May I enclose my transcripts along with the application, or must I ask that my university or college submit the transcripts directly to the state board?
- If I plan to apply to sit for the CPA exam in one state and later request that my CPA exam scores be transferred to another state, how is this accomplished? How much does it cost to transfer score results to another state?
- Must I submit a photo along with my application? If so, should the pictures be of any special specifications, such as color, official passport, or a certain size? May I simply take the picture and e-mail the picture to the board? Should the picture be just head and shoulders, or will a full-body picture be acceptable?

Many times you will be able to answer these questions by calling the appropriate board or by consulting their Web site. Begin early and leave nothing to chance.

COMPLETING THE EXAM APPLICATION

Most CPA exam applications can be downloaded from a Web site. For a complete listing of Web site addresses and state board phone numbers, refer to the NASBA Web site at www.nasba.org. NASBA is charged with the task of maintaining the official candidate database. This complete database lists all candidates who have been authorized to test. No candidate is permitted to apply to sit for the exam in more than one state or jurisdiction at a time. Candidates should select the state or jurisdiction in which they plan to practice as a CPA. When you receive your application, make a copy of it. Use the copy to prepare a rough draft.

Take the application process seriously. Read the instructions carefully. An incomplete or incorrect application can lead to a delay in acceptance. Wouldn't it be awful if you studied hard and were very prepared for an exam section in an upcoming testing window, only to discover a few weeks into the process that your state board has denied you admission for your selected testing window? If you are unclear as to the information required, clarify it with your board immediately.

Common exam application mistakes include

- Leaving requested information blank
- Illegible handwriting
- Questions answered incorrectly
- Questions skipped because they are on the back of the application form or on another sheet of paper
- Missing signatures
- Inappropriate fee enclosed or check made payable to the incorrect party
- Improper attachment of necessary photograph(s)
- Missing supporting information such as college transcripts
- Mailing the application to the wrong address
- Mailing the application too late to qualify to sit in the desired testing window

Ask a family member, colleague, or friend to review your application copy. Then carefully transfer the information to the original application. Use the appropriate writing instrument (usually a black or blue pen). Avoid using a mark that smears. Some states allow you to complete the application online. For downloaded applications, don't try to be fancy by typing the information unless it is clearly stated to do so. You can make numerous mistakes when typing an application. Watch the address section. Many application forms ask you to list a temporary and a permanent address. If you list your parents' home as your address and your parents plan to be in Europe on a twelve-week cruise of the Mediterranean, who will be home to give you the mail you might receive from the board? If you have made an error or omitted information, the board sometimes contacts you via regular mail. Be careful when giving e-mail addresses. Many work environments run virus protection software that prevents employees from receiving e-mails from a source such as the NASBA or your state board. If you plan to move, think about the time lag—will your local post office continue to forward mail long enough for you to receive your authorization to test? Be sure the mailing and e-mail addresses that you provide are addresses that you check frequently.

PHOTO IDENTIFICATION

Most jurisdictions require that one or more photos be attached to the actual application form. Read the instructions carefully and follow the exact procedures. For example, don't submit a color photo when a black-and-white photo is requested. If a color photo is acceptable, be sure that the color of your hair, eyes (for those who change the color of their eyes with contacts), and general look is what you will resemble when you arrive several weeks later at a Prometric test center to sit for an exam section. If you plan to wear glasses at the test center, wear glasses for the picture. If a passport photo is requested, having your picture taken in a photo booth will not suffice. If a regular photo will do, be sure you follow the directions and take the head and shoulders at a close range. Remember that the purpose of this photo is to verify your identity, as you will appear at the exam. If a discount is given for buying more than one photo, go ahead and buy two or more. You will use the photos when you reapply to take additional sections. Most states do not allow candidates to apply to sit for sections more than six months in advance. If you select two sections in the first six months, you will need that extra photo to apply for the remaining sections in the next six-month time frame.

Be sure to affix your photo in the correct area. Before you attach your photo, write your name on the back so if the photo falls off, the board will know to whom it belongs. Tape, staples, and paper clips often do not remain attached and could result in your photo or application form becoming torn. To affix the photo, use rubber cement.

TRANSCRIPTS

Exercise special care when providing the state board with transcripts. Some states require that your university mail the transcripts directly to the board. Other states will allow you to obtain official sealed transcripts and include the transcripts along with the application form. Note that transcripts are not considered to be "official" after they have been opened. To be safe, request two copies of your transcripts; open one set, inspect it to make sure the information is what you expected to receive, and then submit the second, unopened set along with your application.

Some colleges issue sealed transcripts that are considered to be official because a raised seal is pressed on the paper documents. Go ahead and submit the sealed transcripts; they are considered official proof of the coursework completed.

Some colleges have different forms of transcripts: official sealed transcripts and transcripts mailed to students. Speak with the records and registration department and ask if what you see on your latest transcript report is the same information that is included in the official sealed transcript. If your jurisdiction requires specific courses, you must be sure the transcript provides enough information so that an outsider looking at the transcript can tell the course subject and the number of credits granted. Beware; repeated courses will count only once, not twice. The good news, however, is that usually grades of A to D will count, and usually there is no time limit on how recently the courses must have been taken.

If you are unsure whether you will be authorized to take the test, call your board and ask if you can mail or fax a copy of your transcripts for review. Sometimes the board will perform a preliminary evaluation to let you know how close you are to meeting the requirements.

Don't ask a professor or friend to evaluate your transcripts. Even a CPA Review course manager or director is not qualified to conduct a transcript evaluation. Your state board is the only group that approves candidates to sit for the CPA exam.

INTERNATIONAL TRANSCRIPT EVALUATION

For degrees or college credit earned outside of the United States, many jurisdictions require that a foreign transcript service evaluate your transcripts. Always check with your jurisdiction before paying a fee to a foreign credential evaluation service. Most jurisdictions prefer to complete the task themselves and will not accept the work of another credential evaluation service. Allow for extra time when submitting foreign credentials. Having foreign transcripts evaluated often adds two to six weeks to the entire application process.

Some international schools do not issue a second set of transcripts. Graduates carry one original set with them. If this is your situation, be sure you send the original documents via a one-day service such as Fed Ex, UPS, or DHL. You wouldn't want to lose the only proof you have of your education.

Hours earned in international study abroad programs usually are not considered to be international credits and therefore do not require an international transcript evaluation. Verify this fact with your state board.

For those state boards who use outside evaluation services, conduct a follow-up with the evaluation service every two weeks. After the evaluation is complete, forward all of the information to your state board. Ask your board if it also needs the original documents. It is up to you to begin the process early enough to obtain all of the proper approvals in time to sit in your selected testing window.

EXAM APPLICATION DEADLINE

According to the various state boards, there is no longer an exam application deadline. However, to you, there is a deadline if you have prepared a plan and want to sit for a section or two within a certain testing window. Some boards may take as long as three months just to evaluate a domestic first-time exam taker's application. Add additional time for an international transcript evaluation, and you just might be precluded from sitting in your planned window. Avoid the stress—send the application in well before you plan to sit. If you are found to be deficient in hours earned, then you will have time to complete the necessary coursework.

Most state boards approve candidates for a certain time period, for example, six months. If a candidate plans to sit for three exam sections in the first six months and the remaining section six months later, he or she must complete a second application form. Although the process is not as rigorous as the first time, as transcripts are not required the second time around, the process still takes time. Budget the proper amount of time.

MAILING THE EXAM APPLICATION

Verify the mailing address. If you have any doubts about the correct address, phone the board and ask. If the board includes an envelope to return the application, use it. Clearly indicate a complete return address in case delivery problems occur. Again, avoid using markers that can smear if the envelope gets wet. Don't guess on the postage. Take the envelope to the post office and have it weighed.

Spend the extra money to send the transcripts and application certified mail. Use a mail process that allows you to track the receipt via the Internet. This is an effective and inexpensive method of assuring that your application arrives on time.

Don't throw away the instructions and the extra application forms. Prepare a file folder labeled "CPA Exam Application." Put your copy of the application in the file, along with extra forms and copies of transcripts. Make a copy of your check, and place it in the folder, too.

Keep the folder handy in case you receive a phone call or e-mail from the board. If you accidentally omitted a required form, you can consult your file, quickly complete the form, and promptly return it. Keep your mailing information in the same folder.

EXAM APPLICATION FOLLOW-UP

Don't leave the receipt of your application to chance. If you do not receive an acknowledgement from the board within two to three weeks after you mail your application, phone to inquire about your application status. Always be calm and courteous. Most board members are not CPAs. They often license many groups within the state, such as electricians, lawyers, barbers, and plumbers. Explain that you are just making sure that **you** followed the necessary procedures. You are not checking up on the board, you are checking on the status of your application.

When transcripts have been mailed directly by your college or university, be sure to verify with the board, not the university, that the transcripts have been received. The university or college may have sent the transcripts to the incorrect address or may not have sent them at all. You will be sure of meeting the requirements only if the board has received your documents on time.

SPECIAL CONSIDERATIONS FOR CANDIDATES WITH DISABILITIES

All fifty-four jurisdictions recognize their responsibilities under Title II of the Americans with Disabilities Act to provide reasonable, appropriate, and effective accommodations, including auxiliary aids, to qualified examination candidates with disabilities. A disability is defined as a physical or mental impairment that substantially limits one or more of the major life activities of an individual. Disabilities are usually of three types.

1. Physical
2. Mental
3. Learning

Mental impairment includes any mental or psychological disorder such as organic brain syndrome, emotional or mental illness, and specific learning disabilities. A learning disability is further defined as individual evidence of significant learning problems that substantially affect or limit one or more major life activities and that are not primarily due to cultural, conditional, or motivational factors. Typical impairments include

- Difficulty to attend and concentrate
- Reception, perception, and/or verbal comprehension difficulty
- Problems in the areas of memory, cognition, and/or expression

It is your responsibility to request special consideration for any disability. You are required to provide the necessary documentation, which often includes performance on reliable standardized tests and a doctor's or other qualified person's certification of the disability.

Don't be afraid. The laws are established to provide you with the same opportunities to succeed as others. Communicate with your state board well in advance of your planned testing date. Obtain all of the necessary forms and complete them carefully. When in doubt, call the board to clarify areas of uncertainty. The policies and procedures for reasonable accommodation of exam candidates with disabilities are there to help you.

AUTHORIZATION TO TEST

Finally, you receive notice that you meet the requirements to sit for the CPA exam. The verification letter will reference a form called an authorization to test (ATT). What is an ATT? The ATT is the notification from a state board to NASBA indicating that you are eligible to sit for the CPA exam. Candidates do **not** receive the ATT. Your name and pertinent information is forwarded to NASBA after a state or jurisdiction has approved your CPA exam application. As mentioned, NASBA is responsible for maintaining a national candidate database. NASBA will verify that you have registered to sit for the exam in only one jurisdiction and, usually within three business days, will send a payment coupon. What is a payment coupon? The payment coupon is a bill for computer time at the Prometric test center. You already have submitted a check along with your application. This is an application fee. Now, you must pay an exam sitting fee. Exhibit 3.2 shows the exam sitting fees as of this book's publication date. Understand that fees may increase. For example, as simulations are added to the Business Environment and Concepts (BEC) section of the exam, the fee is likely to rise.

Exhibit 3.2 Exam Sections and Prometric Fees Per Section

Auditing & Attestation (AUDIT)	*Financial Accounting & Reporting (FAR)*	*Regulation (REG)*	*Business Environment & Concepts (BEC)*	*Total Examination Fees*
$134.50	$126.00	$109.00	$100.50	$470.00

The fees are paid as requested on the payment request coupon. If a candidate is taking only FAR and REG, he or she would remit $235 to NASBA, **not** to Prometric. NASBA serves as the collection agency for the exam. A partial refund of fees is available by providing advance notice. The refund rules are spelled out in the "CPA Candidate Bulletin" on the www.cpa-exam.org Web site.

Once the fees are paid, a form called a "Notification to Schedule" (NTS) is generated and mailed or e-mailed to the candidate. The NTS is a very important document.

NOTIFICATION TO SCHEDULE

An examination identification number is shown on the NTS for each scheduled exam section. The identification number is needed to schedule an examination date and time and to request free software from the AICPA. Receipt of an NTS means the final approval has arrived. You are ready to schedule an exam time. You also can use the NTS to also obtain free software to practice search routines on the AICPA Professional Standards that are used by auditors and the Financial Accounting Research Systems (FARS) used by accountants to search for various accounting pronouncements. Chapter 9, "The Research Component: How Many Hits?" discusses using such databases in detail. Of interest here is how to use the NTS to schedule your exam date, time, section, and the test location.

SCHEDULING AN EXAM SECTION

To schedule a test appointment, you must have your NTS handy before contacting Prometric. Identify at least three alternative dates and two possible test center locations before contacting Prometric. If your first choice of test site, date, and time is not available, you will be ready with a second and third choice.

Prometric offers three methods for test scheduling.

1. Online scheduler at www.prometric.com/cpa
2. Calling 1-800-580-9648
3. On-site at a test center

To view test center choices, visit the Prometric Web site listed above. Note that candidates can schedule and take the exam in whatever state they choose regardless of where eligibility was obtained. That's right— candidates who apply to sit in the state of Illinois could travel to Colorado, for example, and sit at a Prometric test center site in Denver. Exam scores would be sent to the state board where the candidates applied to sit.

The online scheduler is very easy to use. After agreeing to a statement of examination policies, the candidate enters his or her NTS number, selects a test center, and then selects a date and time. Immediately after scheduling online, the candidate receives an online confirmation, with an e-mail confirmation following. The application process is complete! It's time to begin the examination preparation.

PERSONALLY SPEAKING

It always amazes me when people do not take the time to complete the CPA exam application carefully. If you are unable to properly complete the application, should you even attempt to become a CPA? The fact of the matter is that most people get very nervous about completing the application correctly and many times they make mistakes. TAKE YOUR TIME! Read everything carefully, and double check that you completed all the necessary pages and forms. One of my brightest CPA candidates was very disappointed because his testing date was delayed. He submitted his paperwork too late to test in his preferred testing window. He felt his knowledge was no longer as fresh as it had been just after completing the CPA review course.

Please keep the necessary funds in your checking account until you are sure that the board and NASBA has processed your check. Each year a few people in my classes assume improperly that their application check is cashed immediately on receipt. Ideally, every organization deposits checks daily for effective internal control, but things do not always work that way. After a check has bounced, a state board often requires that you drive to the location to pay cash or deliver a money order. Who needs this additional stress? Yes, sitting for the CPA exam is costly, so begin saving now. If it's your birthday or the holidays, ask family and friends to give you items such as note cards, CPA review software and manuals, or money to put to good use in your exam preparation.

Watch that photo ID! The picture I sent in with my CPA exam application showed me with a hair color that was very different from the color that I had when I arrived to sit for the exam. Besides the hair color change, I wore my contacts for the picture and my glasses to the actual exam. I was almost denied access to the site. The proctors thought I had paid someone to sit for the exam for me. Try to use a picture that looks as close as possible to how you will look when you arrive to sit for the section(s).

Women, be careful about those name changes. Your exam NTS must exactly match your other forms of identification. Don't use a married name until you have officially tied the knot. Your name does not change until you marry. If your name changes at a later date, contact the board, NASBA, and Prometric.

Watch that e-mail address. Your company may bounce the payment coupon because NASBA submits the e-mail under a name called "Gateway." Avoid using your employer's address—establish and use your own personal e-mail address such as a Yahoo or Hotmail address.

My final words of advice: Begin the process early. If you have your heart set on taking a section on a certain date at a preferred Prometric test center, you must plan ahead. Although Prometric advertises that it usually can meet your request if you apply to sit forty-five days ahead of time, your wishes do not always come true. Establish a backup plan, listing alternative dates, times, and test centers. Remain flexible.

CPA EXAM TIP:
Complete your CPA exam application at least six months in advance of the date you plan to sit.

4 A TIME AND PLACE FOR EVERYTHING

Passing the CPA examination is challenging. Every candidate hopes to take each section only once. What can you do to give yourself the best shot at passing each section on your first attempt? Sometimes it's the simple things we do in life that help us achieve our goals more effectively and efficiently. Are you hoping to find a time in your life when everything will be operating smoothly? Think again. There is never an ideal time to sit for the CPA exam. A better way to phrase the question is: Are you ready to make the commitment it takes to become a CPA? If your answer is YES! read on to find out when you should begin the study process, what materials and/or courses you should use to study, and where you should study. If you are unsure about making a commitment to the hard work it will take, at least read the next section about how soon after graduation you should take the CPA exam. Maybe you will see how important it is to start the process early.

HOW SOON AFTER YOU GRADUATE
SHOULD YOU TAKE THE EXAM?

My words of advice remain the same from year to year: take the CPA exam as soon after you complete the necessary college requirements to sit in the state or jurisdiction of your choice. One of the major benefits of the computer-based test (CBT) is that you are in control of when you sit for the exam. Likewise, you are also in control of how soon you begin the exam preparation process. See Chapter 3, Scheduling and Applying for the Exam, for details of the application process. This chapter's focus is on the timing of the event. Don't wait. If you have completed the necessary coursework, then prepare your study plan and apply to sit. It's a known fact that it is difficult to retain technical material. The old saying goes: "If you don't use it, you lose it." This couldn't be truer regarding accounting. The sooner you study and take the exam, the better your chances of passing it. Does this mean you should give up the idea of passing the exam if you graduated several years ago? No, definitely not. CPA candidates who have work experience and have reached a certain level of maturity have a good chance of passing. They may, however, need to budget additional time to study and practice the concepts learned.

If you already meet the requirements to sit for the CPA exam, then get going! There is no time to waste. Begin today. There are five factors to think about before choosing the date you will start the exam.

1. Have you fulfilled the necessary educational and degree requirements? See the Web site www.nasba.org for the requirements in your jurisdiction, review Chapter 3, and ask your state board of accountancy to examine your credentials to verify your eligibility.
2. Are you currently under pressure of losing your job or being overlooked for a promotion if you don't pass the CPA exam? This is not a scare tactic. Public accounting firms do not promote staff auditors to the managerial level until they have passed the exam. This is part of the quality control element of the accounting profession. CPAs are preferred for some corporate finance positions, as well.
3. Have you recently graduated from college or completed your accounting hours?
4. Do you see becoming a CPA as a priority in your life?
5. Do you believe that passing the CPA exam will give you greater job stability, job mobility, and a higher salary?

Obviously, you must be able to answer question 1 positively. You will not be permitted to sit for the exam until you meet the requirements in the jurisdiction where you plan to register as a licensed CPA.

An affirmative answer to question 2 indicates that you are under a considerable amount of pressure. Spend some time researching CPA exam preparatory courses. Establish a disciplined schedule to keep you focused and motivated. You are at risk of overreacting to the pressures and finding yourself giving up. Your boss is not being unreasonable, he or she is just following company rules. Don't look for someone to blame. Make up your mind to do it right this time.

Question 3 is not meant to discourage people who have completed their college work some time ago. However, we can't overlook the obvious fact: The CPA exam tests an accountant's entry-level skills and competencies. Accounting, auditing, and income tax rules change frequently. As a recent college graduate, you are accustomed to taking exams; the material is fresher in your mind, and your workload is not yet as demanding as it will be when you advance within the company. The best time to take the exam is as soon as you meet the requirements to sit, which is usually upon graduation.

What about those of you who completed your coursework several years ago? Don't give up! You, too, can pass. There is something to be said for work experience, especially in the area of tax and auditing. Work experience helps you to quickly analyze situations, write better, and read with greater understanding. At work you may utilize some of the software products that are used on the exam. Professionals use income tax software, the Financial Accounting Research System (FARS), and the AICPA professional standards daily.

Questions 4 and 5 are important to your decision. You must take becoming a CPA seriously. It just doesn't happen; it takes hard work. Are you concerned that you will never be able to make such a commitment? Don't be! You must not lose sight of the fact that people do pass this exam. Now that the exam is given in sections, the pressure is somewhat eased as you can take a short break in between preparing for each exam section. The point is to understand what those who passed did to become successful. Admitting to yourself that passing the CPA exam is going to require a great deal of work, which only you can do, is a key element. It's not easy, and that's why those three initials mean so much. If becoming a CPA were easy, many more people would be CPAs and the value of the title would be greatly diminished. Are you ready? Good. Now let's decide the order in which you should take the exam sections.

WHICH SECTION SHOULD YOU TAKE FIRST?

You might think it is wise to take the shortest section, Business Environment and Concepts (BEC), first. You could get your feet wet, so to speak, with a two and one-half hour section and then work your way up to the four and one-half hour Auditing and Attestation (AUDIT) section. If you are fearful of the overall testing process, taking the shortest section first might be beneficial. However, for most people, passing one of the two longer sections, such as AUDIT or Financial Accounting and Reporting (FAR), first is much more beneficial. Why does it matter? As soon as a candidate successfully completes a section, an eighteen-month time clock begins to tick. Once you pass a section of the examination, you are allowed a maximum of eighteen months from the date on which you sat for the first section to pass all remaining sections in order to retain credit on the passed section. If you do not pass all four sections within the eighteen-month time period, you will lose credit for the first section that you passed. A new eighteen-month period will commence on the date you pass the next section.

Why does this rule exist? The rule is in place to assure the general public that upon passing all four sections, a new CPA's total skill set is up-to-date and current. Do you want to be under time pressure to complete the longer sections or the shorter ones? Also, new accounting graduates are the most prepared for the audit, tax, and financial topics right out of school because they have recently completed the coursework. For these reasons, I suggest that you select either AUDIT or FAR to take first. Next register for Regulation (REG), and save BEC for last. However, if you don't have a choice because of other outside factors, such as the timing of an exam section review course, don't let the order bother you. It is more important to begin the process than to delay taking the exam just to follow a suggested plan. Passing the exam is your experience; plan it accordingly and be happy with your choices.

WHEN SHOULD YOU TAKE THE EXAM?

When you take each exam section is important. Don't set yourself up for failure by planning to sit for a section two days after a major event, such as a family wedding or completion of a large project at work. Your energy level will be low. Select a date when you will have time to study and review so your performance will be optimal. Poor exam timing selection might be part of the reason why people fail on their first attempt. They don't take the time to match taking the CPA exam to the events of their lives. Give yourself the best possible chance of passing. Plan for it.

Is it a good idea to sit for all four sections within one testing window? Remember, a testing window is the first two months of every calendar quarter. For example, if you graduate from college in the middle of May, should you hurry to complete all four sections by the end of May, doing this just to see what the exam looks like? I don't recommend doing this. You will gain little insight into the exam process just by taking a section. The questions are drawn from a large database. It is very unlikely that you will see any repeat questions during your second exam attempt. Previewing the exam just for informational content is costly in both money and confidence. Even though you may think that you just were previewing and didn't expect to pass, that little voice inside might say: "You aren't good enough to pass." You know you are smart enough to complete the task, but now your confidence has begun to erode. The most efficient and effective method is to prepare for each and every section. If this takes time, plan for it. Don't ignore it. Candidates must pay each time they take a section. There is no free exam or reduced fee for repeat takers. View each attempt as important.

Chapter 25, Regrouping after an Unsuccessful Attempt, will help you determine when to repeat an exam section. Think about why you failed; it doesn't hurt to face up to it now; perhaps you failed because you didn't plan well. If this has happened to you, don't focus on the failure. Look ahead and correct what you can. Admit that perhaps your results were partly affected by the timing of your exam attempt in relation to what was happening in your life at the time. The computer-based exam allows you flexibility. Make that flexibility work for you.

Think ahead. When you are entering the planned examination dates on your calendar, think about family birthdays and anniversaries, planned vacations, work deadlines, and any other events that you encounter during the year. Sure, it may sound like a good idea to take an exam section one week after the completion of tax season, but for most people, this is one of the absolute worst times to test. You are too exhausted to prepare properly. Most of us cannot jump from one big challenge to another without some down time to reenergize both our minds and bodies. If you know that the usual quarterly close takes three to five days of intense work, don't schedule to take a section around that time. Be proactive when determining the best possible situation. A little planning on your part can make your life so much easier in the long run.

A word of caution: Don't stretch your exam-taking experience out so long that you have not allowed time to retake a section or two. Remember, as soon as you successfully complete one section, the eighteen-month time clock begins ticking from the date that you sat for the first section. Build some extra time into your timetable.

Once you know when you plan to sit and which sections you will take first, it's time to think about what study aids might be helpful.

STUDY AIDS

CPA candidates often believe that their college textbooks and notes are the most helpful study aids. Think again. Usually college texts are some of the **least** effective tools. Why? By the time you complete a course, some of the material may already be out-of-date. Candidates are responsible for knowing accounting and auditing pronouncements six months after a pronouncement's effective date, unless early application is permitted. When early application is permitted, candidates are responsible for knowing the new pronouncement within six months of issuance date. In the tax area, candidates must know the tax laws in effect six months before the examination date. In the law area, candidates are responsible for knowing federal laws six months after their effective date and uniform acts affecting state laws, one year after they have been adopted by a simple majority of the jurisdictions. Over the past ten years there have been many changes to technical pronouncements. Every time the accounting profession changes an accounting rule, the auditing profession must respond with changes in audit techniques and procedures. The United States Congress also passes laws that affect the accounting and auditing profession. The passing of the Sarbanes-Oxley Act of 2002 was a momentous change.

On average, textbooks are revised every two to three years. Many of the testable topics on the CPA exam may not even be presented in recent college texts. In addition to being out-of-date, college texts usually contain more material than what is testable on the CPA exam. You don't have time to study extraneous facts. Your studies must be focused on the concepts that are tested on the CPA exam, not all of the concepts ever developed.

Another problem occurs with the presentation style. Material offered in a college class does not necessarily reflect the type of material that is tested on the exam. The CPA exam is more integrated than the typical college class. For example, each of the four exam sections could test overall knowledge of the business environment. Overall business knowledge affects how we audit, how we account for transactions, and the laws that are in place. In some college classes, professors discuss only their individual subjects. Your college texts can be useful reference sources, but understand that the CPA exam is unique, and your primary study materials should always be based on the CPA examination.

Where will you find CPA examination based materials? One source is the AICPA itself. At the time of this publication, it is unclear what tools and products the AICPA plans to provide. Since the AICPA writes the exam, it is always wise to check the www.cpa-exam.org Web site first. If you search the Internet, you will find a number of CPA exam review course providers.

SHOULD YOU ENROLL IN A CPA REVIEW COURSE?

Whether to enroll in a CPA review course is not a decision to make quickly. Review courses cost about $2,000. Price is only one of the many variables to consider. A quality CPA review course should offer you

- A focused study plan
- Exam-taking strategies
- Up-to-date materials
- Support material such as software and/or flash cards
- Confidence-building techniques
- Simulated practice exams
- Assistance in obtaining and completing the CPA exam application
- Follow-up counseling or regrouping for unsuccessful attempts

If the price is less than the going rate, the course may omit one or more of the listed features. That's OK if it is a feature that you feel you can live without.

Maybe you don't need a review course. If you learn better by working questions on your own, you might not want to take a course. Don't get too excited about saving money yet. If you choose to self-study, you still should purchase certain study materials and you must be highly disciplined. Do you have the ability to prepare a study plan and stick to it? If you think you do, go to the next section of this chapter, "CPA Review Manuals for Self-Study." Be honest; if you procrastinate, you would benefit greatly from the structure that a review course provides. Try a review for one section. If you think you benefited, then plan to take another course. If not, try the next section on your own.

Are you a visual learner? An online interactive review course might work for you. Like self-study, an online course puts the responsibility on the learner to stay on track. Online reviews are a good choice for busy people who travel frequently for their work, or for those who have small children and can't leave home to attend a class.

Before you enroll in an online course, or any review course for that matter, be sure to preview the format. Stay away from a course that does not allow you to attend or preview at least one session. You should evaluate the course style. Does the presentation style help you to learn? Avoid pushy sales representatives who call you at home and work and promise you the world. The decision is yours to make. In most instances, you do not need to make the decision quickly. Take the time you need to evaluate your choices.

Consider using more than one approach. Attending a live course and supplementing the classroom experience with flash cards and software is a wonderful choice. Live instruction can be the quickest method to help you review material that you have learned already and to help you understand new material. Live CPA review courses are usually more up to date than online "canned" programs. Live courses and online courses usually offer e-mail support.

Evaluate the timeliness and the quality of such support. Are real professionals, who are experts in a particular area, responding, or will you receive a generic response? You want and most often pay for detailed, customized answers tailored to your weaknesses. Be sure you understand the type of live instruction that the course is promising. Some courses advertise live classroom sessions when what the review course providers really are doing is playing an audio recording in a classroom setting. The person playing the recording may or may not be knowledgeable about the CPA exam and the subject matter presented. Live lectures keep the candidate in a structured environment that is motivational because the presenter is a real person who cares about audience members. Be sure to read the instructors' qualifications before you enroll. Are they part-time instructors who work at full-time accounting jobs during the day? This could indicate that they really are not fully informed about the CPA exam. Their everyday work experiences are not necessarily helpful in understanding today's CPA exam. Beware of the professor or working professional who relies only on personal experience. They most likely took the pencil-based exam, not the new computer-based test, one which is very different. Look to people who understand the new exam model, not the old one. Find an instructor who is up-to-date and who understands and studies today's CBT.

Are you a traveling auditor or accountant? If you are, don't automatically rule out a live course. Classes meet on weekends. Audio recordings may be made available to those who travel. Software is a great tool for candidates who are mobile. They can use their downtime on planes and in airports to work CPA exam questions.

Audio recordings are great for those who learn better by listening. If you are in the comfort of your own home, you can repeat lectures out loud. This will help you remember the ideas presented for a longer period of time. Video- or audio-taped lectures and online CPA reviews played in the home offer little or no structure. Procrastinators, beware. It is better for you to enroll in a live classroom setting where you feel you must attend. Today's CBT gives you more freedom to choose sessions that fit your schedule. Gone are the days where you would be required to attend classes for four months to learn all four sections' worth of material. Now you can enroll in one class for a short period, take that particular exam section, and take some time off from studying before you move on to the next section.

Should you select a review course based on passing percentages? This is almost impossible to do. The National Association of State Boards of Accountancy (NASBA) publishes externally generated CPA exam-passing percentages yearly in August. The booklet, entitled "Candidate Performance on the Uniform CPA Examination" (about $130), can be ordered by accessing the NASBA Web site at www.nasba.org. Passing percentages are presented not by CPA review courses but by universities and colleges. Proprietary CPA review courses quote their own internally generated passing rates. Providers may show only the passing rates of those who attended more than 95% of the lectures or those who worked each set of questions more than once and scored a certain percentage. Beware of a review course that promises a pass rate of 75 to 90%. It might be referring to a select group of people who passed. You want pass statistics for the average person.

Your best information about review courses comes from those who have passed. Ask your friends and coworkers about the study aids that they felt were most helpful. Recommendations from satisfied customers are powerful statements. Keep in mind that the methods used to pass the exam two or more years ago may now be out-of-date. Survey those who have passed within the last eighteen months.

CPA review courses are most beneficial in these situations.

- You are a procrastinator and need the structure of a course to keep you disciplined.
- It has been a long time since you completed your accounting courses.
- Your university or college program was deficient in providing you with the necessary coursework.
- You got by with memorization rather than learning and understanding.
- You learn best when guided.
- You are an international student whose first language is not English. A review course helps you to equate terms to your language.
- You want to give yourself every possible advantage to pass this exam the first time through.

Don't fall for the 100% guaranteed pass rates. There are usually stiff requirements to meet, such as nearly perfect class attendance and a high percentage of homework completed. Take the time to investigate just how those guarantees work. Remember, it is not the review course alone that will get you closer to your goal; it is your hard work and dedication. There is no magic CPA potion.

CPA REVIEW MATERIALS FOR SELF-STUDY

All candidates should purchase a high-quality, up-to-date set of review materials. These materials must include software. Acquaint yourself with the exam question formats, breadth, and depth of testable topics by practicing the actual concepts tested. Lack of practice time can set you up for failure. Don't let the price be your sole influence. You could receive great value by using manuals and software that cost as little as $50 per exam section. Watch the publication dates. Anything over one year old is probably out-of-date. If a friend offers to give you his materials, do **not** use them if they are more than one year old. You may save a few bucks on materials, but you will be sorry when you get to the exam only to find out that the materials didn't help you learn the concepts that are tested. Why waste your precious time studying incorrect materials? Thoroughly investigate the products available, make your selection, and spend the money! The time and money that you spend investigating and using review materials will pay off in the future. Using materials that are not a good fit for you, or that are old, actually can hinder your studies. Find what works for you.

When you are researching products, consider simple things, such as the look and feel of the product. Is the software product user-friendly? Does the software emulate the look and feel of the real exam? To see how the real CPA exam looks and feels, take the AICPA sample exams at www.cpa-exam.org. Are there enough questions to test your understanding? Does the software contain answer explanations? Can you track your progress and identify which questions you answered incorrectly? Are you allowed to create comprehensive sample exams based on the units or modules you have already studied? If you are using a textbook, do you like the color of the ink, the feel of the pages, and the general layout? Think about the amount of time you will spend with the materials. If the look and feel do not suit you now, it will only get worse as you spend hours and hours with the product. Are the review manuals easy to read? Long, complex sentences are difficult to read and understand. Are the materials offered only online, requiring you to spend time printing them? Printing hard copies can be costly in both time and money. Paper, printer cartridges, and binders are not cheap. If you prefer to read from a book rather than on the screen, ask if hard copies of materials are available.

As mentioned, your review materials **must** contain software. The CPA exam is computer based. You must practice in the form of the actual exam. Studying a text-based review manual in print or on the Internet is very helpful, but you must be able to work the questions as they are presented on the exam. However, don't underestimate the value of text-based materials. Before you can answer a question on the exam, you first must understand the formulas, concepts, and application of those concepts. You can't simply click your way to an answer. Use a combination of products that include practice exams in the form used by the AICPA.

FLASH CARDS

Purchased flash cards give you definitions and lists to memorize. The problem with this type of study aid lies in the fact that you must understand the concepts and be able to apply them practically. The CBT requires candidates to provide in-depth, synthesized knowledge and analysis rather than mere definitions and lists of attributes. Flash cards should serve not only as quick review tools, but to help you understand the material, which happens if you have prepared and summarized the information contained on the cards. You probably will learn more if you prepare the flash cards yourself. Learning occurs through both the preparation and review of the information. Writing information down is an excellent study tool that will help you to retain the information for a longer period. Many purchased flash cards merely list data and definitions. Today's CPA exam seldom asks you to prepare a list or to provide a definition. The emphasis is more on using and evaluating the concepts and formulas. Memorized lists taken out of context leave you with no sense of where, when, and how to use the knowledge. You could invest a great deal of time mastering flash card concepts only to find out at the real exam that you don't know how to apply what you have memorized.

A properly prepared flash card will prompt you to remember concepts and how those concepts are used. Don't look to the cards for a quick fix. There is no substitute for working problems and obtaining knowledge by learning it yourself.

STUDY AID SUMMARY

Numerous types of review course materials are available. The essential characteristics of any study materials are

- Up-to-date materials, no older than eighteen months
- CPA exam focused
- Software using a format that emulates the real CPA exam
- User-friendly—easy to use, easy to read
- Comprehensive—demonstrating all question-format types and giving complete answer explanations
- Materials that include simulation-question formats
- Software that is automatically updated

Take your time to preview a variety of materials. Be wary of high-pressure sales tactics that promise you a 100% pass rate. Be skeptical of review courses that require candidates to pay for all four exam sections up front. It's better to try one section first to see if it fits your learning style. Use a live course format to help motivate you and keep you disciplined. Look for automatic updates when professional standards are changed. Ask about e-mail support; is it generic or customized to your needs? Spending money for materials only to leave them to collect dust is foolish. Find a place to keep your study aids handy and ready for use.

FINDING A SUITABLE STUDY PLACE

The ideal study location is a place that is handy, well lit, comfortable, and easily accessible. Don't waste valuable time driving to a faraway location, such as a library or your office; you may forget most of your materials at home. Your best study area is your home. You do not need an elaborate office area. Something as simple as a card table set up in a corner of your bedroom will suffice. Having a neat home is not your primary goal. Your primary goal is to create a study area where you can sit down and begin working quickly. Make it easy for you to study by keeping everything at your fingertips. Try not to use a place like the kitchen or dining room, where you must pack up your materials after each use. Not only does the packing and unpacking process waste time, it also may serve as a deterrent to your studies. When your materials are easily accessible, you are more likely to study even if you only have a few minutes. It's surprising how much can be learned in just a few minutes. Keeping your study area visible will serve to remind you about the importance of studying. The more visible your area is, the less chance you have of postponing the primary task at hand. Find an area that you can claim as your spot and where you can leave your materials out.

Do you really need a phone nearby? No. Leave your cell phone in another room. It is better to get up to answer the phone when it rings. You don't want to be tempted to use your study time placing telephone calls and checking voice mail messages. Be brave; turn that telephone off and let your calls go directly to voice mail. It's far more important to have a computer nearby where you can work your software questions. Keep in mind that you will most likely need two study places: one to study and learn the concepts, and a second area to practice your software problems. Make sure both are easily accessible and that both areas have proper lighting. Good lighting will help keep you alert and prevent your eyes from tiring quickly. Keep blank index cards near your computer and on your study table. Make it easy for you to prepare your own flash cards. Keep your study area well organized so you don't waste time searching for the proper study aid.

Keeping study materials visible is important. After all, what if you can't sleep at night because you are suffering from exam anxiety? The best cure for insomnia brought on by exam anxiety is to work through it, literally. Get up out of bed and begin answering CPA questions. This is easy for you if your materials are left out in the open, ready to use. You will be amazed at how quickly you will want to go back to bed and sleep after completing a few questions. If you must open drawers or cabinets to find your books before you begin studying, you will waste time. Out of sight, out of mind. A visible study area invites you to study.

Your plan of attack is beginning to take shape. You have selected the exam section dates; you have purchased your study products and readied a study area. Your next step is to develop a personalized plan of what to study based on an assessment of your strengths and weaknesses.

PERSONALLY SPEAKING

Are you scheduled to get married and take a one-month honeymoon in Europe a week before or after the exam? If the answer is yes, you should not schedule the exam during that time. In fact, you should avoid the time period around the big event. Your concentration level is likely to be diminished. Should you hurry the exam process? Yes and no. Remember, the eighteen-month rule becomes effective from the date you sat for the first successfully completed exam section. Take the time to think about your schedule. Customize the CPA journey to your life, not the life of your employer or friends. Don't be afraid to reschedule an exam section. Refer to the CPA Candidate Bulletin located on the Web site at www.cpa-exam.org for the current exam rescheduling rules. Sometimes it's better to reschedule than to take the exam under great pressure. Things do happen. Life is full of interruptions, only some of which we can control. Whatever you do, do not procrastinate. Begin your CPA journey and make it a priority. Then when interruptions occur, at least you have begun the process.

Take the exam as soon as you meet the requirements to sit. Don't always listen to your friends. Make your own plan. Just because I am the director of one of the most successful CPA review programs in the world does not mean that I believe everyone must take a review course. Actually, I chose to self-study for one of the reasons I presented earlier: The review courses were too far away for me to travel to. Today's exam requires that you study and use software to practice the exam question formats. Take a review course if you have been out of school for a long time and/or if you need a disciplined schedule to keep you on point. Self-study sounds glamorous, but it is not easy. It can be a very lonely process.

To complete a review successfully, you must truly be reviewing the material, not learning it for the first time. Sure, there will always be concepts that your college professors did not cover, but you must recognize the concepts that you have not learned and then you must work to learn the material. Because I had not taken governmental accounting in college, I spent additional time on this area. Today governmental and nonprofit accounting counts for twenty points of the FAR section. I couldn't afford to lose a total of twenty points. I knew I needed to earn at least 50% of the allocated points to survive the overall test. When the material is new learning, budget extra time and use it.

Don't just talk about studying; put your plan into action. Many candidates spend more time talking about their plan of attack than executing their plan. Get down to business; it's study time that will help you, not conversations about the process.

The greatest advantage a live review course gives you is the discipline. A quality review program will cover all areas tested. You will be encouraged to study all exam content areas, even if you already know the material. A good review never hurt anyone. The schedule should keep you abreast of new developments concerning both the content and format of the exam. The CBT is an evolutionary process. Exam content, format, and computer-based navigational processes are expected to change in the coming years. A quality review course will keep you apprised of these changes as they affect you.

Regardless of the method of study you choose, the worst mistake you can make is to study out-of-date material. Notice how often I have mentioned this problem. I make frequent references to how current your review materials should be because I hear candidates who earned scores of 72, 73, or 74 go on to tell me that they used a friend's materials, which were two or more years old. They missed those points because of content changes, not because they did not know the material they had studied. Do yourself a huge favor and use current materials. There is a big difference between a score of 74 and 75. A 74 requires you to repeat the exam process. A 75 will make you smile and will allow you to move on to other adventures in your life. Yes, new materials are costly. I always tell candidates to look at it as an investment in their future. Yes, when you purchase study aids, you credit cash, but instead of debiting an expense account, look at it as a debit to an asset account called "investment in your future." You are worth the price of these materials. Your CPA title will benefit you in the future. Your time and self-esteem are too precious to waste by making a poor decision to save money and study old concepts. Give yourself every advantage.

In the discussion of study areas, note that I didn't suggest that the area must be a quiet place. Although Prometric test centers are relatively quiet places, usually other people are taking exams at the same time you are completing yours. I prefer that you get used to the environment and study with some action around you. If small noises upset or distract you, practice studying with earplugs. Although you are not allowed to bring in your own earplugs, the Prometric staff will provide you with a pair if you so choose. Try using earplugs before you go to the test site. Earplugs magnify your internal body sounds, and this may take some getting used to.

Obviously you can study in other places besides your home. If your local library allows you to load software onto their computers, go ahead and try it. A library setting is much like the Prometric center atmosphere. Vary your study locations. When you are learning a particularly tough area, such as deferred income taxes, go to a café, order a gourmet coffee or tea, and stay there until you master the area. You will return home motivated to learn more.

Unless you are a superstar, spread your exam-taking experience out over at least two testing windows. Hurrying to take the exam is dangerous. You can become very demoralized if you are unsuccessful. A little patience and preparation can carry you a very long way. The exam is spread out over testing windows for your convenience. Be smart; use the time you are given wisely.

Carefully evaluate your choice of exam dates, study aids, and study areas. Do everything possible to minimize failure and maximize success by making careful choices. The time you spend in preparation will provide an enormous payback not only when you sit for the CPA exam, but also in the workplace. You will be a more informed and mature working professional.

CPA EXAM TIP:
Establish a visible and accessible place to study. Make it convenient for yourself. Study whenever you have a free moment.

5 ASSESSING YOUR STRENGTHS AND WEAKNESSES

To prepare successfully for the CPA exam, candidates must honestly assess their strengths and weaknesses. Physical, mental, and technical preparedness should be considered. This chapter assists you in assessing all three areas, beginning with the your physical well-being.

PHYSICAL WELL-BEING

It is not necessary to be a famous bodybuilder to pass the CPA exam. What's important is that you take some time to think about what physical attributes can be improved during the study process. Improve what you can, deal with the other problems later. One of the first questions that comes to mind is: Do you smoke? If you do, then physically you are damaging your body. No, this is not a sermon about the perils of smoking. I mention smoking because smoking is not allowed during the CPA exam. For the entire fourteen hours of the CPA exam experience, you must be smoke-free. The longest section is Auditing and Attestation (AUDIT), at four and one-half hours. Is this going to bother you? If it is, begin dealing with the problem now, as you prepare for the exam. Cut back on your smoking or, better yet, go to the doctor for help. Wouldn't it be wonderful if you could quit smoking while you were studying for the big event?

You can't study while you are under the influence of alcohol or other drugs. If you need guidance in helping to eliminate drugs, seek professional help. The pressure and stress of the CPA journey is likely to increase your reliance on chemical substances. Take care of these problems before you begin the study process.

How's your eyesight? Has it been a while since you tested and upgraded your glasses or contacts? Contact lenses are **not** recommended for the study or exam process. Long and late hours of study can cause dry eyes that may make you rub them. Infections can spread from your hands. Get new glasses well before the exam, and practice wearing them when you do your homework. Be assured that you are reading the numbers properly. Staring at a computer screen for four and one-half hours will dry your eyes out. You are not allowed to bring eye drops into the testing area. You must leave such items in a locker located in the Prometric center reception area. During breaks, you may enter your locker and use your eye drops, lip gloss, and take a pill. But no such items are allowed in the examination area.

Are your prescriptions current? Prepare in advance by renewing all prescriptions. Make your doctor appointments before you begin the CPA journey. Later you will be too busy, and you don't want the risk of having an allergic reaction to new medication. Experiment well before the exam dates.

What about that extra weight? Candidates can easily gain five to ten pounds over the preparation period, as chips, cookies, and ice cream seem to be the preferred study snacks. Overeating can make you drowsy. Try eating assorted fresh vegetables and fruits instead. Drink eight to ten glasses of water every day.

It is not necessary that you become a new person to pass the exam, but it is helpful to spend a few minutes reflecting about your physical well-being. If you can easily correct the weakness, do it right away. You will benefit by your actions.

MENTAL STATE

There is no need to get a psychiatric evaluation. Mental preparedness involves clearing your mind by resolving as much conflict in your life as you possibly can. Are you going through a divorce? Do you have a medical problem that causes you discomfort? Does someone you know need your help? Think about the situations in your life that could distract you. Try to resolve these conflicts before you begin the study process. The human brain is ready to help you as long as you aren't constantly sending out signals asking for help. Contemplate postponing one or more sections. Sometimes delaying the exam is a wise idea. Proper preparation requires focus. If you are preoccupied with many thoughts, wait until some of these issues have been resolved. Keep in mind the eighteen-month limitation—you must successfully complete all sections within eighteen months of the day you sat for the first section that you passed.

Child care is often a concern. It's almost impossible to study while children need your care and attention. Work with a family member or trusted friend to establish a schedule of child care that will meet the demands of a lengthy and time-consuming study process. Tell it like it is— you will need a great deal of babysitting assistance. Arrange for day care well before you begin studying.

Attempting the CPA exam isn't going to simplify your life—quite the contrary. The pressures will only fuel any existing fires. Get yourself ready by clearing your mind to the best of your ability. Ignoring mental pressure, or believing that the stress will lift once you begin studying is very dangerous. Face reality, admit your weaknesses, and correct what you can.

TECHNICAL ABILITIES

There is no doubt that your technical ability is the most important element in passing the exam. The required technical knowledge encompasses many areas. Take some time to think back to your college days. Ask yourself if you even remember a discussion of these areas. Use the checklist in

Exhibit 5.1 to evaluate how much you remember. Admit that if you can't recall anything about the area, you must be weak. If you took the course many years ago, more than likely you are weak for two reasons.

1.   The longer the time between the coursework and the CPA exam, the more you are likely to forget.
2.   The content probably has changed greatly over time.

Evaluate your technical strengths and weaknesses individually by exam section, taking into account the possibility that the material might have changed.

Exhibit 5.1: Checklists to Identify Overall Strengths and Weaknesses by Examination Section

Complete the checklists by answering the questions yes or no. A "yes" response indicates a possible strength. A "no" response indicates a possible weakness. Work to correct weaknesses. Believe in your strengths.

Auditing and Attestation (AUDIT) (Four and one-half hours in length)

Topical Area	*Yes*	*No*
Did you take at least one semester of auditing?		
Did your auditing course include coverage of audit sampling?		
Did your auditing course include coverage of reviews and compilations of nonpublic entities?		
Did your auditing course require you to understand the various types of audit reports?		
Were you responsible for knowing the key elements of internal control for the major systems areas of • Revenue recognition and accounts receivable • Purchasing and accounts payable • Investment purchases and dispositions • Payroll accounting • Production and inventory systems?		
Were you required to prepare audit working papers to document the audit procedures performed?		
Did you learn to compute and analyze various ratios and trends?		
Did you learn how to use the AICPA Professional Standards database research tool?		

Financial Accounting and Reporting (FAR) (Four hours in length)

Topical Area	Yes	No

Were you required to prepare the following financial statements:
 	
  • Balance sheet
  • Income statement
  • Statement of Cash Flows
  • Statement of Changes in Stockholders' Equity
  • Statement of Other Comprehensive Income		

Were you required to prepare journal entries?		
Did you learn about derivatives and other forms of financial instruments?		
Were you required to compute the present and future value of money using table factors and formulas instead of using a financial calculator?		
Did you study deferred taxes?		
Do you know how to account for capital lease transactions?		
Did your financial accounting class include coverage of pension accounting?		
Do you remember how to compute earnings per share?		
Did your professor provide complete coverage by teaching all of the material included in the textbook?		
Did you spend time learning the accounting methods for both bonds payable and bonds receivable?		
Do you know how to compute, analyze, and compare certain financial ratios?		
Did you learn how to account for governmental entities?		
Did you learn how to account for not-for-profit entities?		
Were you taught how to use the financial accounting and research system (FARS) database research tool?		

Regulation (REG) (Three hours in length)

Topical Area	Yes	No
Did you study corporation taxation issues?		
Did you study partnership taxation?		
Did you study taxation issues for trusts and estates?		
Did you study taxpayer responsibilities?		
Did you learn how to use a tax research database tool?		
Did you write tax memos to clients?		
Did you complete tax returns and forms online?		
Did you study the AICPA Code of Professional Conduct in your auditing or business law class?		

Topical Area	Yes	No
Did your business law class contain coverage of commercial paper?		
Did you study bankruptcy law?		
Did you learn about real estate and property laws?		

Business Environment and Concepts (BEC) (Two and one-half hours in length)

Topical Area	Yes	No
Did you study microeconomics?		
Did you study macroeconomics?		
Did you study how to legally form, operate, and dissolve both a partnership and the corporate form of business entity?		
Did you study accounting information systems?		
Did you take a finance or a managerial course that included coverage of • Balanced score card • Capital budgeting • Cost volume profit analysis • Regression analysis • Activity-based costing • Variances • Cost of capital		

OVERALL CHANGES BY SECTION

Auditing and Attestation (AUDIT) is always changing. In just five years, about 30% of the content has been revised. Be careful if your audit knowledge is out of date. Admit your weakness. Many college graduates complete only one audit course. Consider yourself fortunate if you took two courses. Even with two courses, areas such as review and compilation services, auditing governmental entities, and assurance and attestation standards are not covered. Statistical sampling is seldom covered in enough detail. The Sarbanes-Oxley Act of 2002 is scheduled for testing beginning in 2005. This is a huge addition to both the Audit and the Regulation (REG) law area.

Candidates may be weak in the Financial Accounting and Report (FAR) section if they have never studied governmental and not-for-profit accounting. Skipping this area could cost you over twenty points. New financial accounting standards are issued frequently. The Financial Accounting Standards Board (FASB) is not shy about changing accounting principles. In recent years we have seen the addition of a new financial statement, the statement of other comprehensive income, a change in segment reporting, and many changes dealing with investments and financial instruments. Candidates who do not know what a derivative is will have great difficulty in passing FAR.

Candidates who take only one income tax class probably have learned only individual taxes. Estate and trust taxation concepts are most often taught in the corporate tax class. Completion of two semesters of income taxation is preferred. The US Congress changes tax laws frequently. If your knowledge is over one year old, you are probably out-of-date. Knowledge of corporate and partnership taxation issues is a must-know! The REG exam also requires the preparation of certain tax schedules that are included in a tax return. Don't fool yourself into thinking it's just individual taxation. It's all types of returns.

Business law issues, usually taught over two semesters, comprise forty points of the total REG exam. Did your college course include a detailed discussion of commercial paper? Negotiable instruments are difficult to understand. Legal concepts have changed the least of any topical exam area. Although there has been little change, some areas have been added. For example, the government regulation of business has been expanded to include environmental and employment laws. Federal securities acts are a must-know. It is difficult to pass the exam without knowledge of the Securities and Exchange Commission (SEC) 1933 and 1934 Acts, including the Private Securities Reform Act of 1995. Property issues now deal with the rights to computer technology, a new area within the last year. Changes abound.

What about the newest exam section—Business Environment and Concepts (BEC)? One semester of managerial accounting is enough for candidates. Very few changes have occurred in the cost accounting area. A solid understanding of such basic issues as variances, process costing, and activity-based costing is sufficient. Two semesters of economics at the sophomore level—one finance principles course and one accounting systems course—is enough.

How will you ever know if you are strong or weak in an area? In addition to the assessment of your strengths and weaknesses listed in Exhibit 5.1, why not attempt some real CPA exam questions? Be cautious, as your question bank must be current. Using current materials, go ahead and preview your knowledge.

KNOWLEDGE PREVIEW

To preview your knowledge, you simply go to an area (e.g., bonds) and work some, perhaps ten to fifteen, multiple-choice questions. Skip around, doing some of the first questions listed in the area and some of the later questions. For example, if your review materials contain forty questions on bond accounting, you might work every fourth question. You may want to go to a bookstore and use the review manuals on the shelves to do your previewing. Of course, when you answer the questions, you can't write in the book. Use a few different manuals to see which one you prefer. The more detailed the answer explanations are, the more effective and efficient your studies will be. Detailed answer explanations help you learn why a particular answer is incorrect. The next time through, you will know how the examiners trick you and what words they use to distract you.

Don't let your knowledge preview scare you. It is natural to forget technical subject matter such as accounting. The whole idea behind CPA exam preparation is to do just that: prepare. If you knew everything already, there wouldn't be anything to improve. Admit your weaknesses and begin correcting them. Don't fear them.

CORRECTING WEAKNESSES

The total extent of any candidate's weaknesses is not evident until he or she begins the study process. It is by listening to lectures, working software questions, and answering questions in review manuals that the candidate will become painfully aware of weaknesses. It is one thing to identify weaknesses; it is another to correct them. The whole focus of the study and review process is to correct weaknesses. Chapter 12, Study Strategies to Improve Your Memory, lists methods to help you learn new areas, correct old habits, and remember material that has been forgotten. Take the time to correct your weaknesses to the best of your ability. Perhaps you will never totally understand foreign currency hedges and translation. However, at least you will have studied the area so that you can define terms, do some accounting, and recite the financial statement disclosure issues. If you ignore weak areas, you might be sorry; areas you ignore always seem to be highly tested. Work to correct your weaknesses and utilize your strengths.

USING YOUR STRENGTHS

Yes, there will be many content areas where you remember the material and can demonstrate, work, and discuss the area. This is wonderful news. It is especially exciting to know that your knowledge remains in your brain, ready for use. Still, candidates seem to continue to study what they know. Stop! This is a major mistake. There is no time to waste studying what you already know. If you know it today, you will know it several weeks from now when you take the test. Candidates like to study their strong areas because it makes them feel good about their progress. It is a comfort zone. Instead, study to correct your weaknesses and use your strengths to build a greater technical knowledge base.

PERSONALLY SPEAKING

Small changes yield big results. When it comes to correcting weaknesses, practice and effort to learn what you don't know will yield huge results. If you work to correct some areas, you will see benefits in other ways. Each time you conquer another technical area, you are not only adding to your technical base, you also are increasing your confidence level by decreasing the number of subjects that you fear. A confident person is willing to take risks. The more confident you are, the more willing you are to take a risk and write down concepts for the graders to grade. I always say you can't win the lottery until you buy a ticket. You can't earn points on an exam section until you begin answering the multiple-choice questions in testlet one. Don't be afraid. Keep on studying. Every weakness you correct is another point for you.

Don't give up too early. I have worked with candidates who ask me a question about a large area the night before they plan to take an exam section. I spend a few minutes explaining some of the basic concepts, the candidates go off to study, and later they come back to inform me that they now understand the area. The greatest payoff comes when the area is heavily tested the next day. If candidates had given up and said that they just couldn't absorb any more knowledge, they would have missed a great opportunity and many points. Some weaknesses take only a minute to correct, while others may take several hours of study. If you have the time, why be lazy? Utilize every minute to make progress toward correcting your weaknesses, and continue to believe in your strengths.

Trying to be the perfect person while you are preparing for a difficult event, such as passing the CPA exam, is a tough task. I can talk all I want about nourishing your body by eating carrots and drinking water, but as I wrote this book, I found I could think more clearly when I ate chocolate-covered raisins and drank gallons of coffee. You don't need the extra pressure of trying to be perfect. Relax and admit your shortcomings. Do your best to cope with the stress.

Technically, the best advice I can give you is to study current materials. Study to learn something about everything. Follow a detailed study plan to correct your weaknesses, not to reinforce your strengths. Study to be your best, not to be perfect. With practice, what you learn today you will remember in the future as you complete each CPA exam section.

CPA EXAM TIP:
Take some time to analyze your strengths and weaknesses. Admit that you are not perfect. Work to correct as many weaknesses as possible.

6 THE MULTIPLE-CHOICE COMPONENT

Ask college students what their favorite exam question format is and the response is usually multiple choice. Why do most students prefer multiple-choice exams? Test takers receive great comfort when answer choices are provided. It seems easier to select from a list of choices than to formulate an answer. Students refer to multiple choice as "multiple guess." Think again. The AICPA Board of Examiners doesn't believe in easy. Today's computer-based test (CBT) may make it easy to click on an answer choice, but selecting the correct choice takes great skill. The purpose of this chapter is to help CPA candidates understand the multiple-choice question format. For help with content, see Chapters 16 through 19, which describe the details of each of the four exam sections.

What could possibly be new about the multiple-choice question design? Aren't multiple-choice questions a familiar format? Yes, some of the details have not changed for more than seventy years. However, the CBT is taking test question selection and scoring processes to new levels utilizing methods such as **multistage testing** presented in distinct **testlets** while tracking **test enemies**. Don't stop now. Read on to learn more about these changes.

MULTIPLE-CHOICE QUESTION PLACEMENT AND SELECTION

Like the pencil-based exam, the CBT presents the multiple-choice question format first. That's, however, where the similarity ends. The format of the CBT is quite different. The overall design of the new exam is to provide the multiple-choice questions first, in individual testlets, and then move into a brand-new question format called simulations. See Chapter 8, The Simulation Component: No Fear, It's Here, for a description of that question format. This chapter focuses on the multiple-choice component.

Where will you find the multiple-choice questions? Multiple-choice questions are found in individual testlets. What's a testlet? In general, a testlet is defined as "a small subset of items in a pool, preassembled to meet sets of content specifications."[1] Each of the four exam sections begins with three testlets of multiple-choice questions. The Auditing and Attestation (AUDIT), Financial Accounting and Reporting (FAR), and the Regulation (REG) exam also include two additional testlets of simulation format questions. During 2004, the Business Environment and Concepts (BEC) exami-

---

[1] Craig N. Mills, Maria T. Potenza, John J. Fremer, and William C. Ward, eds., **Computer-Based Testing**, Lawrence Erlbaum Associates, 2002, p. 96.

nation contains no simulation testlets. Plans are to add simulations to BEC sometime in 2005.

Look at a testlet as just a group of questions. The topics, however, are not randomly selected. The examiners carefully write questions to match the items listed in the content specification outlines (CSOs). The CSOs describe, in outline form, the technical content areas that could be tested. As stated by the AICPA,"The content specifications provide the framework or "blueprint" for testing knowledge and skills on the Uniform CPA Examination."[2]

The current CSOs are available on the primary CPA exam Web site (www.cpa-exam.org). For example, the CSOs for the REG section contain six broad testable areas.

1. Ethics and Professional Responsibilities (15–20%)
2. Business Law (20–25%)
3. Federal tax procedures and accounting issues (8–12%)
4. Federal taxation of property transactions (8–12%)
5. Federal taxation—individuals (12–18%)
6. Federal taxation—entities (22–28%)

The question selection process is directly linked to the CSOs. This means that for the REG exam, each testlet contains questions from all six of the areas just listed. Upon the initial CBT launch, the REG multiple-choice testlets are comprised of twenty-four questions each. The multiple-choice questions cover each of the listed areas within each of the three multiple-choice testlets. This test design requires candidates to be able to switch their focus from one topic to another easily. Careful reading is required. Candidates must differentiate between a tax topic and a law topic. They also must quickly identify the entity type. Is the question referring to a trust, an individual, or a corporation? One question might ask about an AICPA Code of Professional Conduct independence issue. The next question might refer to exemptions for an individual taxpayer; the following question might inquire about the corporate dividends received deduction. On the pencil-based exam, the multiple-choice questions were grouped by topic. Don't expect to find such groupings on the CBT. The FAR section now contains both financial accounting and governmental and not-for-profit accounting topics, a new combination. Candidates must be able to identify the entity type. This is important since for-profit entities utilize different accounting techniques from governmental and not-for-profit entities.

How do you keep your concentration with all that jumping around? Practice with examination software that emulates the CPA exam environment by shifting from topic to topic. Most candidates divide their studies into areas, learning each area separately. At test time, candidates must be

---

[2] *AICPA, Information for Uniform CPA Examination Candidates, 17th edition.*

able to integrate the topics. Most college classes do not integrate topical areas. Don't be caught by surprise—practice the real thing. See how you react. Work to improve any deficiencies. Check your software product. Do the topics match the CSOs? Can you design a test that contains individual testlets? Are all types of topics tested within each testlet? Topical coverage should align with the CSOs since the CSOs guide the question selection.

QUESTION DESIGN AND NAVIGATION

How many exams have you taken using a computer? University and college faculty have been slow to offer computer-based exams. If you have little or no exposure to computerized tests, you must correct that weakness before you arrive at the Prometric test center. No tutorials are available at the centers. Purchase software that closely emulates the new CPA format. View the AICPA exam tutorial and take the sample exams found at www.cpa-exam.org. There is no substitute for the real experience. However, closely simulating the event is very beneficial. What should you notice when you are working the AICPA tutorial?

Exhibit 6.1 presents a screen shot of a multiple-choice question from the AICPA tutorial. The four answer choices are marked with a radio bullet symbol. Expect all multiple-choice questions to offer only four choices and to be marked with a radio bullet rather than the traditional a, b, c, or d choices. Click on your answer choice. If you change your mind, click on your second choice, and the first answer reverts back to being an unmarked item. Note that moving back and forth within a testlet is allowable. Unlike the Graduate Management Admission Test (GMAT) examination, another high-stakes computerized exam, candidates can return to previous questions simply by clicking on the question number or tabbing back and forth. Answers can be changed. Note the "review" feature in the lower left-hand corner. Click on the check mark icon to mark a question for review. You can use the review feature to highlight questions that you have answered or left unanswered.

Exhibit 6.1: AICPA Sample Multiple-Choice Screen Shot

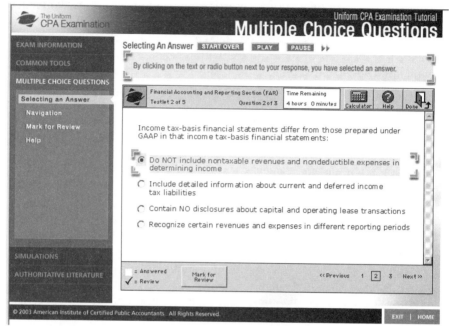

Very important: **Candidates may move back and forth only within testlets**. Once you exit a testlet, there is no returning. All testlets must be worked in consecutive order. For example, since the AUDIT exam contains five testlets, you must complete testlet 1 before testlet 2, and so on. The simulations, always presented in testlets 4 and 5, and are worked last.

Menu Choices

Watch the menu choices. Three menu choices, calculator, help, and done, as shown in Exhibit 6.1, are presented on the top bar.

Exhibit 6.2: Toolbar Only

Spend time clicking on each of the three menu choices. See how the calculator works. It's online. To open the online calculator, double-click on the icon. When you move to another question, the calculator disappears rather than remaining open for use on the next question. Try entering some large numbers to see what happens. The calculator is functional only for up to eight digits. Don't expect to use large numbers. If you must enter a number such as 50,000, be careful that you enter four zeros. There are two ways to enter numbers: Enter directly on the calculator using the mouse to click on the screen, or use the computer keypad located on the right-hand side of the keyboard. Using the keypad is much faster. Be sure to activate the "Num Lock" key before using the keypad. Once you have your answer, you may close the calculator or simply ignore it as it will disappear automatically as you move on to the next question.

What's the "Help?" button for? This menu choice provides details about the exam navigational process. There is no content information here. Candidates should not select this choice during the exam. Use the sample exams and the tutorial to guide you through the process **before** you arrive at the test center.

The "Done" menu choice means just that. You are indicating that you have completed the testlet and are ready to move on to the next testlet. Use the "Done" button **only** if you have answered all of the questions within the testlet. Once you exit a testlet, you are not permitted to go back to complete or change answers. When you select "Done," a prompt will ask if you wish to "Review, Continue, or Exit." If you select "Review," you will remain within the testlet in which you were currently working. If you select "Continue," you will continue on to the next testlet. Clicking on the "Quit" button indicates that you wish to exit the entire examination process. Before the examination shuts down, you will see a prompt that asks if you are sure that is what you want to do. Go slowly here. Be patient and read the screen prompts.

Pretest Questions

Each testlet contains 20% "pretest" questions. What are pretest questions? The AICPA examinations team routinely creates potential CPA exam questions for the purpose of continuous test bank database expansion. These questions are known as pretest questions. Each CPA exam multiple-choice testlet contains a sample of these questions. Candidates cannot determine which questions are pretest questions. This encourages candidates to give equal attention to all questions, regardless of the question nature. Pretest responses are not included in the final score even if candidates chose the correct answer. Pretest questions neither help nor penalize candidates.

"None of the Above"

College students dread exams where "none of the above" is an answer response. This type of answer is not used on the CPA exam. The AICPA psychometricians believe there must be an identifiable answer for each question.

"Test Enemies"

The AICPA examinations team uses the term "test enemies" to describe the situation where the same content is tested in both a multiple-choice testlet and a simulation. The software is designed to catch content crossover on each person's individual test. This control feature helps to allocate the coverage evenly among the CSO areas. When concepts are tested via multiple-choice format, candidates can be assured that the same topics will not also be tested in a simulation. For example, if a multiple-choice question asks candidates to compute the minimum pension benefit obligation, that same concept would not also be tested in a simulation. However, other pension concepts, such as disclosure requirements or the corridor approach, would still be possible simulation topics.

To Guess or Not to Guess?

Are candidates penalized for guessing on the CPA exam? The answer is no, they are not. Select an answer for each question, even if you must guess. Always try to narrow down the choices, to make an "educated" guess versus an outright guess. If you are truly stumped, smile (it helps to relieve tension) and say to yourself: "Wow, I hope that question is a pretest question!" The exam is positively graded. You earn points by answering questions correctly. Deductions are not taken for incorrect answers.

Before the exam begins, take a bold stand. Select an answer choice to use when responding to your "outright" guess questions. For me, it would be the second choice. I like that one. Then go ahead and use your choice each time you must guess. Who knows—one of those guesses could be the correct answer!

Multistage Testing

The CBT is designed using a form of adaptive testing known as multistage testing. The test stages consist of individual testlets. All examinees receive the same level of difficulty on testlet 1. The level of difficulty of testlets 2 and 3 varies depending on individual candidate performance on testlet 1.

There is no internal branching within a testlet. Once candidates begin any testlet, the CBT has already developed the testlet so candidates can move back and forth at will within it.[3] This is quite different from what examinees encounter on other exams, such as the GMAT. Because the computer-based GMAT utilizes internal branching, candidates cannot return to a previous exam question within a testlet.

On the CPA exam, the second testlet may be of the same difficulty level as the first or a higher level. The multiple-choice testlets are stored in the question database at three levels of difficulty.

---

[3] *Computer-Based Testing,* Mills, et al., p. 97.

Difficulty Levels of Multistage Testing

The AICPA examinations team reports that the CBT contains three levels of multiple-choice question difficulty.

1. Easy
2. Medium
3. Hard

All candidates receive the same level of difficulty for the questions in the first testlet. Based on the results of the first testlet, the second testlet may be at an easy, medium, or hard difficulty level. To date, the AICPA has not provided a definition of what constitutes an easy, medium, or hard difficulty level, but it does assure candidates that the difficulty levels have been carefully tested and analyzed, and the proper weights have been applied. The team of psychometricians will see to that. There is a great deal of overlap among the levels. Exhibit 6.3 shows my depiction of how the overlap might occur.

Exhibit 6.3: Testlet Difficulty Overlap

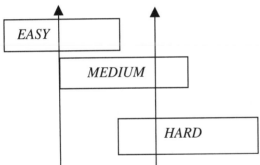

Remember that the first, and only the first, testlet is assured to be at the easy difficulty level. Testlets 2 and 3 vary based on an individual candidate's performance. It is possible for a candidate who performs well on the first testlet to receive a hard level of difficulty on testlet 2. If the same candidate were to perform poorly on testlet 2 at the hard level, testlet 3 may go back down to the easy or the medium level. No matter what the level of difficulty, none of the questions will be a giveaway. Technical knowledge remains the key factor to passing.

MULTIPLE-CHOICE SCORING

Don't let the preceding discussion scare you. Most candidates will be oblivious to the question difficulty level. Most likely all questions will appear to be somewhat difficult. Candidates do not have time to rate the level of difficulty while they are taking the exam. Work the questions, giving each one adequate attention. Move through the exam knowing that some of the questions are pretest questions. If a particular testlet seems to be overly difficult, tell yourself that's okay. You need fewer correct responses to earn the same number of points on a hard testlet as on an easy or medium testlet. Your multiple-choice score is positively tabulated based on the performance of other candidates taking the exam in the same testing window. If you are adequately prepared, both for the exam content and the exam format, you will prevail as long as you manage your time carefully to complete the entire exam. See Chapter 22, Time Management, for hints on how to deal with the time box on the top of your screen.

USE YOUR SCRATCH PAPER

Utilizing a computer-based format presents some challenges that you may not have thought about. Most test takers are accustomed to marking up questions to highlight certain points, delete other points, and perform mathematical computations by hand. This is impossible on a computer screen. Here's where your scratch paper comes in. You will receive four sheets of scratch paper and a Prometric test center pencil. The scratch paper will be bound into a cardboard cover, similar to a menu at a nice restaurant. This prevents you from removing separate sheets. All scratch paper is bar coded and must be returned to the testing center proctor upon completion of the exam section. Additional sheets are available on request but only after you prove you have used all that was given to you. The scratch paper is useful for two purposes.

1. Listing key concepts and formulas that you don't want to forget. As soon as the proctor allows you to begin the exam, go to your scratch paper and prepare a list of key points.
2. Working through computations and sorting data into usable categories.

Divide the first few sheets of paper into three to four columnar sections. When you come to a question that requires a computation, jot down the formula. Then plug the data into the formula and compute the answer. If you can't find your answer response, you have the formula written down in front of you to use for further verification. Perhaps it was just a math error. Maybe you forgot a step. Capturing your thought process on paper saves time by allowing you to quickly review and redo your computations. A methodical approach is best.

Another useful multiple-choice test-taking tip is to write down "a, b, c, d" as possible answer choices. As you read the question, make a pencil slash through the responses that are obviously incorrect. This gives you a visual of the remaining choices and helps you to focus on choosing the one right answer. Sometimes there is more than one correct answer. Your job, however, is to select the one "best" answer. The Auditing and Attestation (AUDIT) section tends to be the biggest tease, by presenting more than one correct choice. The "best" answer will be the response that fits the question. It's the best match for the situation presented in the question. You will improve your chances of selecting the best answer by practicing old CPA exam questions. Be careful, though—make sure your software or textbook questions are current. Remember, your exam performance is compared to the performance of other candidates taking the exam in the same testing window.

PERSONALLY SPEAKING

The computer provides no technical content assistance. When you work the multiple-choice testlets, the professional standards used to conduct research in the simulations will not be enabled. It's just you, seated in front of a computer in the testing center, working the exam with your knowledge and the online calculator. It will not matter at what difficulty levels the AICPA rates your testlets. What matters is that you complete the exam within the allotted time frame to the best of your ability. Worry about what you can control. You control your time and your answers. You do not control the question type or content. I always tell candidates that they have a job to do. Their job is to tackle the single task of answering each and every question. That's it—no grading, no question development, no question critique, and no giving up. You are at the Prometric test center for the sole purpose of providing answers.

Candidates report no problems in navigating multiple-choice testlets. They just wish they could choose the order in which they proceed through the exam. Many would like to complete the simulations first. Why doesn't the AICPA allow this? It's a simple one-word answer: Security! If candidates were allowed to open the multiple-choice testlets, skim them, and then move on to a simulation testlet with the ability to revert back to the multiple-choice questions, they could use the database to research the multiple-choice questions. Since this is forbidden, you have no choice but to work your testlets in consecutive order.

Be prepared to encounter questions that you can't answer. Narrow the choices down and make an educated guess. Close your eyes and think about the key words. Reflect back to your study materials. What was the key word or phrase? Is there a formula involved? Follow the time management techniques offered in Chapter 22. If you do, you should have time to be patient and concentrate. Take a few minutes to think.

Remember, it's a "nondisclosed" examination. If you violate this nondisclosure rule and talk with your friends about what they saw on the exam, you are violating your confidentiality pledge. Don't place much value on their remembrances. Interpretations of what they recall of the question content are often sketchy at best. In the days of the disclosed exam, as a CPA review faculty member, I would wait outside the examination room for candidates to inform me about what they just saw on the exam. The next day, when I received a copy of the actual exam, I was shocked to find that what they told me and what really was on the exam were two very different things. You can't be thinking of what you will report to your friends and colleagues as you take the exam. Your concentration has to be on providing the correct answers. The only way to do that is to learn the concepts. It is now time to get on with the study process.

CPA EXAM TIP:
Answer all multiple-choice questions. The exam is positively graded. There is no penalty for guessing.

7 THE COMMUNICATIONS COMPONENT—FORMERLY CALLED ESSAYS

The communications component comprises ten percent of the total examination points of the Auditing and Attestation (AUDIT), the Financial Accounting and Reporting (FAR), and the Regulation (REG) sections. Upon the initial exam launch in 2004, the Business Environment and Concepts (BEC) section is an all multiple-choice question format. The AICPA plans to add simulations to the BEC section in 2005. As of the date of this publication, the exact timing of when BEC will contain simulations and database research questions is unknown. To keep abreast of CPA exam changes, consult the official CPA exam Web site at www.cpa-exam.org. Candidates must understand the exam requirements and expectations of this area. Ten percent of the total exam score is too much to risk. Increase your total exam score by reading this chapter to learn how writing skills are evaluated on the computer-based test (CBT).

EVALUATION OF WRITING SKILLS

Ten percent of the 100-point total of each of the AUDIT, FAR, and REG sections is graded for writing skills. There are two simulations in each of these three sections. Within each simulation, a "communications" tab prompts candidates to respond in written form to a specific situation. Do not fear this area. There is no need to be an expert in English and grammar. Basic communication skills will suffice. The AICPA has defined six elements that denote effective communication.

1. Coherent organization
2. Conciseness
3. Clarity
4. Standard English
5. Responsiveness
6. Appropriateness to the reader

Now that we know what the AICPA is looking for, it's time to explore how the writing points are earned.

HOW POINTS ARE EARNED

Points are awarded for writing well. The six elements just listed constitute effective writing. Following the six elements sounds easy enough as long as you understand what each element requires. Let's begin with element 1, coherent organization. The overall organization of your answer should guide the reader through the response. A third-grade English teacher might say: "In paragraph one, say what you are going to say. In the middle paragraphs develop and support the statements. Use the final paragraph to summarize what you said." Coherent organization refers to the same concept. Key elements are support and summary. Pretend you are telling a story. Your first step is to set the scene using an introductory paragraph. Then convey the facts of your story. Use examples and support what you say with the practices of the profession. When you have said enough to make your point, summarize the conclusions in the final paragraph. Use prose writing rather than business writing. This is very important. Prose writing utilizes full statements with no abbreviations and no bulleted or numbered lists. This may go against what you know is used in the business world, but you are not in the business world. During the exam, you are in the AICPA's world. It wrote the exam, and you must follow its rules. Please: **no abbreviations and no bulleted or numbered lists.**

Write using paragraphs, as demonstrated in this book. Indent each paragraph a few spaces. Remember, you are typing your response directly into the exam simulation. Watch the address; usually the response is required to be in a "memorandum" form, with To:, From:, Date:, and Subject: clearly indicated.

Be concise. Use short sentences rather than long-running sentences. Use the language of the profession, but, at all times, think about to whom you are responding. If you have been asked to respond to a client about a difficult accounting issue, be sure to explain any accounting terminology. Define terms the reader is not likely to know. Clarity is an element that the AICPA will look for; avoid using slang or jargon.

Think standard English, which requires the use of proper punctuation, capitalization, and grammar. You are graded for grammar and spelling. The good news is you have spelling assistance. A spell-check function is available for use. You must, however, activate the function. It's not automatic.

Be responsive. Focus on the question requirements. Address what is asked. Write about the topic. Don't go off on tangents. Staying on topic is very important. To earn points, candidates must respond to the question requirements. For example, if, on the FAR exam, you are asked to write a memo to clients about how they should recognize revenue for their type of business, don't write about accounts receivable or expense allocation. If you address topics that are not part of the question, your answer is considered to be "off topic" and the response is not graded.

Don't try to show off. Use simple words that readers are likely to understand. A bookkeeper isn't going to understand the latest references to Internal Revenue Code sections or Financial Accounting Standards Board (FASB) pronouncements. Keep the FASB statement numbers to yourself.

Explain the topic using language that is appropriate for the level of the recipient. Writing that is appropriate for readers takes readers' backgrounds into account. For example, a different response is required for a child versus an adult.

Your first order of business should be to "key word" the communication response on your scratch paper. Take some time to reflect about the question requirements. Jot down some of the key phrases and words that apply to the situation. Develop your discussion and support responses first. Then go back and write the introduction and the conclusion.

Use examples to support your statements. Be careful to state the examples in complete sentences rather than in an abbreviated form. Avoid the temptation to present a journal entry in the middle of your answer. For example, if you were explaining a situation where inventory had been sold and the client used a perpetual inventory system, you might be tempted to write

Upon sale of the inventory the following journal entry is made:

Cost of goods sold	DR	
Inventory		CR

This journal entry would be considered an incorrect response. Remember to use prose writing rather than business writing. A prose response to this situation might be

> *On the date that the inventory is sold and title to the goods has been passed to the customer, a journal entry is made to record the sale. An expense account called Cost of Goods Sold is increased and a current asset account Inventory is decreased.*

Sound test-taking skills require that candidates take the time to proofread written responses. Candidates often overlook this very important step. Under time pressure, it is easy to omit key words such as "not" and "the." It only takes a minute to read your response. Avoid making silly mistakes. Proofread and use the spell-check function each time you make a correction.

COMMUNICATION GRADING PROCESS

The communication components, like the essays of the pencil-based exam, continue to be graded by human beings, although a machine-graded process may be used to identify incorrect grammar and spelling. A "holistic" approach is used. Holism is defined as a theory that believes the whole is greater than the sum of its parts. By using a holistic grading approach, the graders read the answer and assign a score based on the incorporation of all six elements rather than awarding one point per element. The graders receive extensive training in applying the holistic grading method. They assess candidates' writing skills at levels ranging from weak to very good. A hypothetical grading scale developed could be

Overall assessment of writing skills	Points awarded
Very weak	1–2
Weak	3–4
Average	5–6
Good	7–8
Excellent	9–10

Weak writing includes these problems.

- The writer did not specifically address the question requirements.
- The writer wrote about the question rather than directly presenting arguments, examples, and support to answer the question.
- The writer presented irrelevant topics.
- The writer jumped from one thought to another without providing a connecting link.
- The writer used abbreviations.
- The writer used bulleted and/or numbered lists.
- The writer did not spell-check or proofread, leaving more than one error.
- Punctuation, capitalization, and grammar errors were noted.
- Not all sentences were complete; several fragments were noted.
- Sentences were too long, discussing several ideas within one sentence.
- Separate paragraphs were not used for each main idea.
- The answer was lacking an introduction and/or a conclusion.
- The use of slang, jargon, and technical terms was prevalent throughout the response.

Very good writing includes these strengths.

- No irrelevant information was given. The response was tailored to the question and provided a concise, clear answer.
- The answer was coherent with principal ideas presented in the first sentence of each paragraph. The remaining sentences developed and explained the ideas.
- The passage did not contain any ambiguous or misused words.
- The vocabulary matched the recipient's level of understanding.
- No abbreviations or bulleted or numbered lists were used.
- The essay was relatively free of spelling, grammar, punctuation, and capitalization errors.

The best answers are simple, short, and address the question. Even a very good writing sample may contain some mistakes. The graders are not looking for perfection, as they understand the time pressure to complete the exam. Mistakes are tolerated to a certain degree. However, candidates should try to make it as easy as possible for the grader to award points.

Depending on the quality of writing, candidates who attempt to prepare a response that addresses the question requirements should at least earn one point. Will the ten percentage points be allocated evenly between the two simulation questions? Not necessarily. The AICPA says it does not plan on sharing the point allocation with the public. Therefore, we cannot assume that the ten points are allocated evenly between the two communications tabs. For example, depending on the examination, one communications tab might be worth six points and another might be worth four points. Because candidates cannot know the point values, they should carefully prepare written responses for both communication tabs as if each tab were worth many points. We know each tab is worth less than ten points, but we are operating under a cautious testing environment. We want to earn points.

Remember, the CPA exam is positively graded, with points earned for providing correct statements. Negative grading requires the ability to deduct points for making incorrect statements. Candidates should practice writing to earn points. They should never think about how many points are being deducted. Points are always earned, not deducted.

Now that we are clear that candidates should plan to earn the maximum number of communication points, it's time to think about how candidates earn these precious ten points.

TEST-TAKING TIPS TO MAXIMIZE POINTS EARNED

Proofread your answer. Most people think proofreading involves simply reading your answer. That's only half the task. To make proofreading a beneficial process, candidates should follow a system. First, before you proofread, click on the "spell-check" tool bar and check your spelling. It's a waste of time to proofread before you spell-check. Second, reread the question requirement and reflect a moment. What did the question require? After you have formulated a response in your head, go back and read over your answer. Did it address the question requirements? Did you stay on topic?

Proofread slowly, looking for incorrect verb tenses and missing or incorrect punctuation. Remember, grammar check is not enabled. You are responsible for noting grammatical errors. Watch the punctuation. If you used a question, use a question mark at the end of the sentence. Watch the possessive. If you are unsure about the proper use of punctuation, rewrite the sentence to avoid the reference to the possessive. Look for missing words. It would be a terrible mistake to omit a little word like "not" because this omission could change the whole meaning of your answer. If during your proofreading exercise you add to your answer, don't forget to go back and spell-check another time before moving on. You may have accidentally misspelled a word when adding new information.

The graders can't read your mind. If you think a point is important, then you had better write it in your answer. Yes, you must be concise, but you also must support and develop your points. There is no benefit to keeping the concepts in your head. Write them down. Don't be afraid of saying something incorrectly. Points are not deducted for incorrect statements. You'll earn points by stating relevant concepts. Don't be timid and don't give up. Keep on fighting to earn those points. In the end, you won't be sorry that you took your time to write a good response. It could be the difference between a score of 74 and a score of a 75.

Be confident in your abilities. You may not have won a writing award, but you know how to communicate. You are careful to follow the rules. This fact alone can help you earn more points than the person who has the detailed knowledge but who can't write in a very basic, straightforward manner and who doesn't follow the exam rules.

HOW MANY POINTS ARE AWARDED FOR CONTENT VERSUS WRITING SKILLS?

You might be surprised to learn that the majority of the points earned in the communication component are awarded for writing rather than content. It's how you write it, not what you write. As long as you address the question and write about the topic, you will earn points. You may make an incorrect content statement, such as saying that accounts receivable are usually a long-term asset. However, if you write it using the appropriate grammar, sentence structure, capitalization, and punctuation, you will earn points. Follow the rules, say what you know, write carefully, and remember to proofread. Those writing points are out there for you to earn. Go for the ten points allocated to the communication component!

PERSONALLY SPEAKING

I hope you believe that the communications component is your friend. This is an area where you can easily earn points. There really isn't a right and a wrong answer. It's all in how you present the answer. However, a candidate of mine made one huge mistake in the very first testing window of the CBT. She copied and pasted research information into her communication response rather than into the appropriate tab within the simulation. Read the question requirements carefully. Most likely the question will state that your answer is to be your written response. You are not to open the research tab on the menu and search for paragraphs out of the professional research databases to support your answer. The communications response is all free-form. You write the entire answer. The professional research database tools are to be used when completing questions that specifically require that you go to the research tool and paste support into the boxes that are provided. As of the publication date of this book, the research component is only a copy-and-paste function. No edit privileges are allowed. The communications component, on the other hand, is to be all free-form response.

Please spend the necessary time to proofread your response. It takes so little to make your chances of earning points much more likely. I know, I don't care to proofread what I write, either. I know you are under time pressure. Of all the time-saving techniques available, however, don't think about skipping the proofreading routine. It is a necessary and very beneficial step. Write about the topic, write carefully, and proofread your response. By doing so you will maximize your chances to earn points. Do the easy things to help yourself. At the end of the testing window, when your score arrives, you will be pleased that you followed these simple techniques. You will be a CPA!

CPA EXAM TIP:
Your communication response must be on topic. Address the concept, do not just state the concept. Clearly identify a thesis statement. Develop and support main ideas. Avoid the use of fragments, bullet points, numbered lists, and run-on sentences. Use spell-check and proofread.

8 THE SIMULATION COMPONENT: NO FEAR, IT'S HERE

Three of the exam sections contain five testlets. The first three testlets utilize the multiple-choice format, and the last two testlets utilize a "simulation" format. What is a simulation? As stated on the CPA exam Web site (www.cpa-exam.org), "A simulation can be defined as an assessment of knowledge and skills in context approximating that found on the job through the use of realistic scenarios and tasks, and access to normally available and familiar resources." To the CPA candidate, a simulation represents a series of questions that are similar to mini case studies. What makes the simulation format unique is that the questions are tied to a company profile. In the Auditing and Attestation (AUDIT) section, for example, the type of company, a service industry versus a manufacturer, will affect the answer response. This chapter describes the similarities and the differences among the simulations used in AUDIT, Regulation (REG), and Financial Accounting and Reporting (FAR).

SIMULATIONS IN GENERAL

Don't fear the simulation question format. Many of the questions are nothing more than queries requiring candidates to respond by selecting the "best" answer from a drop-down box. Overall, simulations consist of a series of tabs. The first tab is always the direction tab, and the last tab is always the resource tab. Exhibit 8.1 demonstrates a tab format for the FAR section.

Exhibit 8.1: Sample Tab Arrangement for FAR

Directions	Situation	Treatments	Cumulative effect	Journal entries	Financial statements	Written communication	Research	Resources
		✏	✏	✏	✏	✏	✏	

There are two types of tabs.

1. **Informational tabs** provide information that may or may not be important to solving the questions
2. **Work tabs** require candidates to provide an answer

The work tabs are marked with an icon that looks like a pencil. When your open a simulation testlet, all of the pencil icons are white. After you open a work tab and provide any kind of an answer, right or wrong, complete or incomplete, upon closing the tab, the pencil will turn blue. It is very important to understand that a **blue pencil does not indicate that the work tab is complete. A blue tab just indicates that some work has been done.**

In the preceding example, there would be a pencil by everything but the directions, the situation, and the resources. Do not confuse the **Resources** tab with the **Research** tab. The Resource tab shows selected information that might be helpful when formulating answers for the work tabs. The Resources tab contains no gradable points; it is not the same within each simulation or within each exam section. In other words, candidates do not know what information is under the tab until they click and look. The **Research** tab, on the other hand, represents a question type that requires candidates to use database tools to locate a supporting source and then copy and paste that information. Chapter 9, The Research Component: How Many Hits? discusses how to complete the **Research** tab. Every simulation contains a research requirement (pencil icon).

Another common work tab is the **Written Communication** tab. This is similar to any essay format; candidates are required to prepare a well-written response. Chapter 7, The Communications Component—Formerly Called Essays, presents ideas about how to prepare a relevant and well-written communication response.

In total, the two simulation testlets represent 30% of the total exam section's points. Although most candidates fear the simulation exam test questions, several of those who have taken the computer-based CPA exam report that the simulations are very easy to follow. Again, as mentioned several times in this book, all candidates should work the sample exams and the AICPA tutorial before they arrive at the Prometric test center. See the tutorial and the sample exams on the primary CPA exam Web site.

The communication tab represents 10% of the three exam sections that contain simulation questions. If candidates master the communication component, as discussed in Chapter 7, then they must earn only 20% of the total exam points by completing the rest of the simulation requirements. The research tab is 6–7% of the total exam. That leaves us with about 13 or 14 total points. Split those 13 to 14 points between two testlets, and you have on the average 7 points for each simulation. This is not enough to get all upset about. However, there are points to earn. It will be difficult for candidates to pass an exam section if they complete only the communication and research tabs of the simulations.

What's the key to solving simulations? To complete the simulation question format successfully, candidates should be well versed in the content of the examination and should have practiced working this type of question on the CPA exam Web site. Content and practice are the two key factors.

Candidates will use the same tactics to learn the content for the simulations as they did for the multiple-choice questions. Study the material in a well-developed review manual and you are on your way to passing. Practice the AICPA sample exams. The AUDIT, FAR, and REG sections each contain one sample practice simulation. Many vendors offer practice simulations. But don't expect a practice simulation to be exactly like what you will see on the exam. Be confident, learn the material, and you will be able to earn over half of the simulation points. Certainly you will earn the ten points allocated to the communications component. Candidates have a very good chance of earning the research points. There is no need to tremble and be fearful. Your content knowledge will carry you through. Knowing something about the unique features of each simulation type is also helpful.

FAR SIMULATIONS

Some of the types of tabs used in the FAR simulations were presented in Exhibit 8.1. Take some time to read those tabs again. Think about what each might require you to do. The tab "Journal Entries" indicates that you must type in the journal entry. This is easy if you have already studied to prepare for the multiple-choice questions. You must know the **same** content and the **same** concepts for the multiple choice and the simulations. Does the Financial Statements tab mean you should stand ready to prepare an entire statement, such as the statement of cash flows? No, it is highly unlikely that you would be required to complete an entire statement. You should, however, be prepared to complete a statement section—for example, the operating section of the statement of cash flows.

Could there be other tab requirements on FAR simulations? Yes, there could be. It would be exhausting to sit and worry about all the possibilities. Learn and review the content. The simulations will take care of themselves. Practice the unique features. An orange box indicates work to be completed. When you click on the orange box, the box turns yellow. This means the cell is ready to accept information. Type in your answer—it's that simple.

When you need to use the calculator, simply click on the calculator icon. If you want to use an EXCEL-like spreadsheet, click on the "Sheet" icon on the title bar. Note the phrase EXCEL-like. The spreadsheet does not contain all of the functions of EXCEL. For example, some of the present value wizard functions are not part of this spreadsheet tool. Don't be caught by surprise—work the sample exams to see the differences.

Speaking about present value, you may be required to reference present and future value tables to compute answers. Don't worry, you can find the tables under the Resources tab. The examiners provide you with the information you need to complete the question. It is just a matter of practicing the format.

REG SIMULATIONS

Again, the REG simulation contains two work tabs that are common among all simulations—the communications tab and the research tab. What other types of work tabs might there be? Most likely within at least one of the two simulations, you will have to complete a portion of a tax schedule. Candidates who are unfamiliar with various key tax forms, such as schedules A, B, C, and D, should review the forms before taking the exam. An orange box indicates what work must be completed. Enter answers in all orange boxes of each schedule. You will not be asked to complete an entire form.

AUDIT SIMULATIONS

The AUDIT work tabs almost always consist of some type of report or auditor communication that an auditor would complete in a routine engagement. This is usually the research component. Don't fear the communication component of each simulation in AUDIT—just study the AUDIT concepts. The trick in the AUDIT simulation is to be sure to read the company profile and examine the financial statements. These information tabs provide key information to use when solving the work tabs. For example, the audit risks for a service industry are different from a retail industry. There are little or no inventory issues in a service industry—the big risk is labor-related and revenue recognition. Put yourself in the client's business and think before you respond. Think specifically about what it is that the client does.

The AUDIT exam does not test just audit issues. It also tests review and compilation engagements as well as attestation engagements. After all, the AUDIT exam is the longest of the four sections—it is very comprehensive.

As of the publication date of this book, the AUDIT exam does not require candidates to prepare paperless audit work papers and documentation. The AICPA hopes to add such detail to this area in the future. Don't get too comfortable with the exam as it is. The new computer-based exam is a work in process. The AUDIT section is especially subject to change. Stay tuned for further developments. Visit the Web site often. Likely additional products will be brought to market to help candidates learn more about the simulation questions. Wiley is planning to publish a simulation guide soon.

PERSONALLY SPEAKING

Candidates report that completing the simulations is an adventure. It is fun, and usually requires easy to medium-level knowledge. The great fear of the simulation format was overexaggerated. Candidates who took the CPA exam shortly after the launch date of April 5, 2004, had few examples to work before the exam. Now most vendors sell sample simulations as part of their product. According to the early exam candidates, they could answer the questions easily just by practicing the sample exams on the Web site, www.cpa-exam.org, and studying the content. Yes, there were some early screen freezes and other unforeseen problems. However, most of these issues were quickly cleared with the help of the Prometric proctors. Remember, a candidate's work is saved every sixty seconds. Even a power outage won't keep a candidate from completing the exam. Every test site is required to have auxiliary power available.

I can't stress enough the power of practice! When candidates call me to report problems, it almost always comes back to the fact that they had not worked the AICPA sample simulations. There are a few tricks to completing the simulation work tabs. Spend time working the simulations well before you begin your CPA exam studies, then again during your studies, and of course the day before your arrive at the Prometric test center. Ignore my words of advice, and you will be sorry. The practice simulations are free and readily accessible. No excuses—work the sample simulations and you will benefit greatly. You will be one step closer to successfully completing your goal of being a CPA.

CPA EXAM TIP:
Work the AICPA sample exam research requirements found at www.cpa-exam.org **before** you go to the Prometric test center. The search functions do not operate exactly as they do in practice.

9 THE RESEARCH COMPONENT: HOW MANY HITS?

The AICPA defines research as the ability to locate and extract relevant information from available resource materials.[1] To the CPA candidate, research may cause a great deal of trepidation and fear. Candidates commonly ask what research tools are used, what topics are researched, and where they can obtain tools to practice the research techniques. If you have no previous experience using the professional research tools that the AICPA has chosen to utilize, don't despair. This chapter identifies the research tools, provides guidance on obtaining practice software, and gives you tips on how to conduct your searches. As of this book's publication date, all CPA examination sections except the Business Environment and Concepts (BEC) section contain at least one research question. Upon the initial launch of the computer-based CPA exam, the BEC section contains only multiple-choice questions. Candidates, beware: Simulations and research questions are scheduled to become part of the BEC section as early as 2005. Before you sit for BEC, be sure to check the central Web site for the computer-based exam at www.cpa-exam.org. Changes do occur. The publisher of this book, John Wiley & Sons, provides CPA exam candidate updates at www.wiley.com/cpa. Stay informed; check the AICPA and Wiley Web sites before beginning your studies.

RESEARCH TOOLS

The three exam sections utilize these professional research tools:

- **Auditing and Attestation** (AUDIT): The AICPA Professional Standards
- **Financial Accounting and Reporting** (FAR): The Financial Accounting Research System (FARS)
- **Regulation** (REG): A form of a tax research database, similar to but not identical to databases offered by such tax giants such as Commerce Clearing House (CCH) or RIA Checkpoint by Thomson.

A section of each simulation is devoted to testing the candidate's ability to utilize the listed databases. Most universities and colleges now incorporate use of one or more of these databases into their accounting curriculum. Candidates who are unfamiliar with any of these research tools should begin

---

[1] *The CPA Exam Alert (January/February 2003): AICPA, "Skill Definition for the Revised CPA Exam," p 3.*

by practicing the simulation component of the AICPA sample exam found at www.cpa-exam.org. No one should set foot in a Prometric test center until he or she has spent considerable time practicing the navigational format of the various search routines. Each of the research tools is different, and each of the search routines is different. For example, the FAR research routine requires candidates to copy and paste only one paragraph to satisfy the research requirements. AUDIT, on the other hand, requires candidates to paste multiple paragraphs. Many AUDIT research questions expect candidates to rearrange the order of the paragraphs. The REG search function requires candidates to enter an Internal Revenue Service (IRS) code section and code subsection.

Knowing one search routine is no guarantee that you can perform other search routines. It is very dangerous to make any assumptions about proficiency in this area. You must practice the AICPA simulations to see how the search routines have been adapted. Let's say you have worked in public accounting as an auditor and have used the AICPA Professional Standards while performing everyday duties. Could you safely skip the practice exam, relying on work experience? Most definitely not! You should take a trial run using a search function to see how to rearrange the paragraph order and how to copy and paste. The functions do not operate exactly like the original products. For example, in the FARS search tool, there is **no** back button. The "history" button serves the same function. Take no chances; spend some time with the AICPA sample exam.

REQUESTING FREE SOFTWARE

How do you request the free database search software? Go to the main Web site of the CPA exam (www.cpa-exam.org) and click on the link that allows you to order the free Web-based research tools to practice using FARS for the FAR exam and the AICPA Professional Standards for the AUDIT exam. Currently there is no practice software available for the REG exam.

To request the free software, you must have a valid "notice to schedule" (NTS). Remember that an NTS is given to candidates only after the state board of accountancy has issued an authorization to test (ATT). Access to the practice tools is granted for six months. Candidates should request only what is needed. For example, if you plan to take AUDIT within the January/February testing window and FAR in the October/November testing window, request AUDIT now. Do not request the FAR until your exam date is closer.

Understand that the navigational procedures may vary slightly between the exam and the practice tools received from the AICPA. The AICPA sample exam offers the best look at the functionality of the research tools. You must work these sample exams to become familiar with the unique features of each of the search routines for REG, FAR, and AUDIT.

REG RESEARCH

The work tab of the simulation is entitled "Research." The search utilizes the IRS Code. The book icon is entitled "Code." Each REG research requirement begins with a set of directions. The search requirement is then listed in **bold** wording below the directions. Two orange boxes appear below the requirement, asking the candidate to enter the IRS Code section and the IRS Code subsection. Exhibit 9.1 shows a sample research requirement.

Exhibit 9.1: Sample REG Research Requirement

Sample Directions: Use the research materials available to you by clicking the CODE button to research the answer to the following question. Find the code section that addresses the question, and enter the section citation in the boxes below. Give the most precise citation possible. Do NOT copy the actual text of the citation.

Sample research requirement: **Jennifer, who is single, has a salary of $30,000 for the year. She has itemized deductions of $15,000, all attributable to a personal casualty loss when a hurricane destroyed her residence valued at $45,000. What code section and code subsection permits Jennifer to deduct the personal casualty loss on her personal tax return?**

Section	Subsection
§	( )

In the exhibit example, you would click on the upper icon called "Code." A search screen then appears asking for a search phrase. You should enter a phrase in the search box that best matches the situation described in the requirement. Here the situation is a personal casualty loss. Try entering "casualty loss." All hits for "casualty loss" will be highlighted in blue. Then slowly scroll through the hits, looking for the best code section. Unlike the AUDIT and FAR searches, you are not searching for a particular paragraph. You are researching for one code reference and one code subsection. Once you find it, write the code section down on your scratch paper. Then close the research "Code" area by clicking on the "X" in the upper right-hand corner. The research screen from Exhibit 9.1 will then reappear. Enter the code section and subsection into the orange boxes. Why not hit the copy and paste function? Some candidates have experienced problems with this function. Take the easy way out—simply write down the IRS Code references and type them into the question.

Do not drill deeper into the code references. Many of the searches cite additional references, such as paragraphs and subsection references of subsections. This is **not** necessary. Keep it simple. Enter only the IRS Code section and code subsection.

As of the publication date of this book, candidates have experienced problems accessing the code on the sample exam. If this happens to you, try the sample exam on a more up-to-date computer, perhaps at work or at your local library. Once you access the code search function and try the sample exam question, you will see it's easy. The most difficult part is identifying the search phrase. Study using reputable CPA review materials and the search phrases will become second nature to you. You should be able to quickly identify the issue; as you practice and learn the concepts required to answer the multiple-choice questions, you will see references to the key IRS Code sections. It is these Code sections that are entered into the research box.

FAR RESEARCH

The work tab of the FAR simulation is entitled "Research." Exhibit 9.2 shows a sample research requirement.

Exhibit 9.2: Sample FAR Research Requirement

Sample Directions: Use the research materials available to you by clicking the STANDARDS button to find the answer to the following question in either the Current Text or Original Pronouncements. Highlight and copy the appropriate citation in its entirety from the source you choose. Then click on the box below and paste the citation into the space provided below. Use only one source.

Sample research requirement: **What are the steps to conduct a test for impairment of goodwill?**

```
┌─────────────────────────────────────────────────────────────┐
│                                                             │
└─────────────────────────────────────────────────────────────┘
```

You are expected to paste **only one** paragraph into the box shown in the exhibit. If you attempt to paste another paragraph into the box, the first paragraph will be deleted automatically.

Once you understand the particular exam requirement, you must establish a search phrase. Be sure to enclose the phrase in quote marks so as to avoid having to scroll through numerous irrelevant hits. For example, a candidate entering "goodwill impairment" will receive many irrelevant hits because the search tool highlights a hit each time the word "goodwill" is found in the standards and every time the word "impairment" is found.

Each hit is highlighted in blue. Typing the phrase "goodwill imparement teset" into the search box results in zero hits. Why? The words "impairment" and "test" were misspelled. In all of the search functions, spelling errors result in inaccurate or zero hits. Candidates who struggle with spelling should open up the "Written Communication" tab within the simulation, type the word or phrase, run spell-check, and write down the correct spelling. Be sure to delete the research phrase from the communication memo before you exit.

A candidate typing the phrase "goodwill impairment test" into the search box would see a display of paragraph 57 of an accounting standard. Upon reading the paragraph, you note that goodwill impairment is the topic but the discussion focus is on changing events and circumstances rather than the actual steps to conduct a goodwill impairment test. Take a deep breath—your search worked! It has brought you to the standard where goodwill impairment is discussed. Be patient and continue scrolling. Here the issue is more detailed and specific than the question requirement. Since your hit is more specific and you are looking for something more basic, scroll up! Go up to the more general areas; scroll down for more specific issues.

The hard part of any search routine is identifying the proper search phrase. Get clues from the question requirement. Most of the CPA exam research requirements are written to be very basic. Let the question guide you—use the words and phrases given in the question, and be sure to spell the words correctly.

Order the free FAR search tool from the AICPA. Practice and you will be perfect. However, don't assume that the AUDIT routine works like the FAR routine. AUDIT requires the pasting of **more than a paragraph**.

AUDIT RESEARCH

The research requirement of the AUDIT exam is not usually under a tab entitled "research." The work tab could be found under a specific topic, such as "Auditor's Report." You will know it is time to research when the tab requirement looks like the one in Exhibit 9.3.

Exhibit 9.3: Sample AUDIT Research Requirement

Sample Directions: During the fieldwork on Q Company, the client asks you to perform an audit of the financial statements for the current year only. You have now completed your fieldwork and find that you can issue an unqualified opinion. It is noted, however, that Q Company has a going concern issue. Q has adequately disclosed the going concern issue in the notes to their financial statements.

Use the research materials available to you by clicking the STANDARDS button on the title bar to prepare the proper auditor's report. Click on the box below and paste the appropriate paragraph(s) as needed to present the appropriate auditor's report. Use the controls provided to reorder or delete paragraphs you highlight. **You should NOT edit the model paragraph(s) in any way.**

Independent Auditor's Report

(Addressee)

Don't blow it! Be sure to paste **all** of the necessary paragraphs. Do not attempt to add the addressee or the last day of fieldwork. You must copy and paste paragraphs only. Do not spend time trying to edit the paragraphs. Simply paste the paragraphs in, and then make sure the paragraphs are in the proper order. In the example in Exhibit 9.3, the going concern paragraph must be the last paragraph. When you pasted paragraphs into the gray box, the going concern explanation might not have been entered last. Rearrange the order using the red arrow buttons that will appear on the bottom of the screen.

Avoid overpasting paragraphs. There is a limit as to the number of paragraphs that you can enter. If you enter more than the capacity, the first paragraph you pasted will disappear.

Again, just as in the REG and FAR search routines, you should beware of spelling errors and you should enclose your search phrases within quote marks. When answering the sample question in Exhibit 9.3, you might consider using the search term "going concern." The use of this phrase would result in many more hits than searching for "unqualified auditors opinion." The second search phrase guides you directly to the area of unqualified audit reports. Since the auditor wishes to issue an unqualified opinion, it is easier to locate this section of the standards first. Then use the scroll function to go up or down to find the going concern treatment. Be patient—scrolling takes much less time than using the search phrase function.

To paste the second paragraph, you must click **below** the gray box, not within it. This may sound like a simple statement, but practice clicking to see how the copy and paste function works. It's a tragedy to waste precious exam time by making several unsuccessful attempts to paste additional paragraphs.

There is no substitute for practice. Get on the www.cpa-exam.org Web site and work the sample exams. Don't fear the search routine. Exhibit 9.4 highlights ten search tips. Follow the search tips, remain relaxed, and you will prevail.

Exhibit 9.4: Top Ten Research Requirements Search Tips

1. There is no "back" button. The history button provides the same functionality.
2. There are no "edit" privileges allowed in any of the research requirements. Do not waste time attempting to edit.
3. Misspellings are not tolerated and will result in irrelevant or zero hits.
4. Searching for subsequent hits within a document requires scrolling. Be patient and scroll.
5. Use quote marks around search phrases to reduce the number of irrelevant hits.
6. The REG research requires entering the IRS code section and subsection. Do not drill further into the various code references.
7. The AUDIT research function requires candidates to rearrange paragraph order. Practice using the up and down buttons on the sample exam.
8. The FAR research function usually requires the pasting of only one paragraph. Search for the most relevant paragraph.
9. Obtain free access to the FAR and AICPA Professional Standards. Practice search routines.

10. **Work the sample exams several times before going to the Prometric test center**. Understand how these tools work, as search tools on each of the exam sections work differently.

PERSONALLY SPEAKING

Of all of the changes made to convert from the pencil-based CPA exam to the computer-based exam, candidates were most worried about solving the research component. Now that the exam has launched and candidates have completed the exam, most candidates say that the research component does not present a major stumbling block to exam success. Many candidates report they actually have fun searching for the answer. They report completing the Research tab requirement is easier than answering the multiple-choice questions. Do not worry about the research. Obtain the free AICPA database tools for the AUDIT and FAR sections. Think about tax terminology as you study the taxation area. Practice the sample exam search routines, and remain confident.

Consider purchasing a guide to simulations. As of the publication of this book, John Wiley and Sons is considering such a guide. For further details, check the www.wiley.com/cpa Web site.

Problems arise only when candidates omit practicing the sample exam. Many candidates waste precious time trying to figure out how to paste an additional paragraph into the AUDIT research tab. Practice going to the bottom of the first paragraph you pasted, click directly **below** the first paragraph, and you have got it. Ignore the sample exam, act like a know-it-all, and you will encounter problems. The research requirement is easy. Knowing the content well enough to answer the multiple-choice questions and to solve the other simulation requirements is a much greater challenge. Practice and you will indeed be perfect in solving the research requirements.

CPA EXAM TIP:
To avoid wasting too much time searching, work the Research tab last within each simulation. Answer the easier types of questions first. Do not exceed your allotted time for testlet 4. Testlet 5 has some easy questions waiting for you.

10 CPA EXAM GRADING

The CPA exam is graded positively. This chapter explains the grading process. Candidates should understand how a positive approach is applied to arrive at the final exam score for each section. Candidates who understand the grading process are better prepared to respond to varying question formats. An understanding helps to decrease exam fear. Informed candidates increase their chances of passing. This chapter does not cover the details of the rescore and appeal process. This information is presented in Chapter 25, Regrouping after an Unsuccessful Attempt.

WHO GRADES THE CPA EXAM?

The American Institute of Certified Public Accountants Board of Examiner's Advisory Grading Service grades each exam section uniformly and fairly. Yes, it is a fair process. Graders are carefully selected and well trained. The AICPA applies strict quality control checks that include additional reviews if needed. Immediately upon completion of a section, the Prometric test center transmits each candidate's exam results to the AICPA offices in New Jersey. Tight security is used to prevent loss of data during transmission.

WHAT IS A PASSING SCORE?

A score of 75 represents a passing score. Does this mean that a candidate must answer at least 75% of the questions correctly to pass? No, it does not. The scores reported to candidates upon completion of each exam section do not represent the percent correct. Simply stated, a score of 75 reflects the examination performance that is representative of a person who has the necessary knowledge and skills to practice as an entry-level accountant. Because CPA candidates receive different test forms with different test questions, the percentage of questions a candidate needs to answer correctly to earn a score of 75 may differ from one test to another. For example, if two candidates sit for the same exam section, on the same day, at the same Prometric test center, at the same time, each candidate will receive different exam questions. Although all questions are drawn from the same set of candidate specifications, the test forms and questions vary. The AICPA utilizes a large database of questions to generate various exam forms. An equivalent score of 75 on different exams is maintained through a psychometric procedure known as equating.

College students are pleased when a professor announces that the exam score has been curved. Equating is a much more involved process than simply adding curve points. Equating is a psychometric procedure that requires detailed analysis of exam questions both before the questions are included in the database and after the questions have been utilized. Don't worry; trust the AICPA to perform the analysis and apply the equating techniques. Know that the process is well documented and carefully applied to give candidates the maximum benefit. Use this information only as a reminder that adjustments are made for questions that appear to be of a higher level of difficulty. The reported scores are numeric representations of your examination performance. Some professors believe that a raw score (total number of questions correct out of the total number of questions given) as low as 50% may equate to a reported score of 75. Don't spend time guessing what raw score may equate to a certain reported score. Spend your time studying the exam content to do the best that you can. Don't worry about other exam candidates. You will be alone in the exam, working on the computer all by yourself. Your success does not depend on other candidates' results. Your success depends on how well you respond to your questions. There is no need to be perfect or even 75% correct to pass the exam. You have room to make mistakes. You have room to misunderstand some concepts. Go easy on yourself when you encounter rough patches where you are unsure of your response. At the end of the exam, know that your score is calculated fairly. A score of 75 or higher will make you happy. A score of 74 or lower will require you to regroup and work to improve your knowledge base. Does this imply that the CPA exam is a pass-or-fail exam?

Some states and jurisdictions think the CPA exam is a pass-or-fail exam. The state of New York, for example, has passed legislation to report CPA exam scores as pass or fail. Candidates will not receive a numerical score. Most states have elected to report numeric scores using a scale of zero to 99. No, you won't earn a score of zero. To earn a score of zero you simply show up, turn the computer on, and submit your examination results without answering anything. It won't happen to you. Has anyone ever earned a score of 99? Yes, it does happen. Candidates who do earn a score of 99 have a chance to win a special award from the AICPA, the Elijah Watt Sells award. At the time of publication, details were not available as to how this award would be determined under the computer-based format. It doesn't matter. What really matters is that you successfully complete the exam. Awards are just the icing on the cake. Those three little initials after your name represent the real reward.

WHAT INFORMATION IS MADE
AVAILABLE TO THE GRADERS?

The CPA exam graders have no access to candidate data. Information such as candidate name, gender, age, number of previous exam attempts, educational background, and work experience are all retained at the state level and/or in the national candidate database by the National Association of State Boards of Accountancy (NASBA). The CPA exam graders see only your candidate number. Your grade is based solely on the answers you provide during the examination.

IS THE EXAM MACHINE GRADED?

The AICPA emphasizes that humans will continue to grade the exam. Obviously, some sections, such as your multiple-choice answers, are machine graded, as are the drop-down box type answers you provide in the simulations. In fact, there is a major advantage to the computer-based exam grading process that was not always used under the pencil-based model. If you submit an incorrect response within a computational question, you will earn points based on carry-through of your incorrect data. For example, if you are asked to complete a spreadsheet response showing the computation of a company's gross profit, you will earn some of the points even if your first element, net sales revenue, is incorrect. It is not graded as all or nothing. You are awarded points by carrying through the incorrect sales amount. This is comforting. Single mistakes won't affect an entire problem.

Yes, humans grade the communications component of each simulation. Machine grading is applied to verify grammar, spelling, and punctuation. Humans grade the communications component, review the overall process, and determine the final grade. Be sure to read Chapter 7, The Communications Component—Formerly Called Essays, for more information about how the communication responses are graded.

THE EXAM IS GRADED POSITIVELY
RATHER THAN NEGATIVELY

Most college students are conditioned to negative grading, where exams are worth a total of 100 points. Points are deducted from the 100-point total every time a student provides an incorrect response. The CPA exam is graded using the opposite approach. Each exam section is worth 100 total points. However, when candidates begin, they begin with a score of zero. Points are earned by responding correctly. The equating process calls for a varying point allocation. Some testlets may contain questions that in relation to other testlets are considered to be easy. Other testlets might be rated at a medium or hard level. The average candidate is oblivious to this process. Most candidates believe all questions are difficult. Remain determined to do your best. Don't waste valuable time analyzing the level of difficulty.

Is the CPA exam a hierarchical exam where candidates are asked to exit the exam if they perform poorly? No, all candidates receive the same number of questions in each testlet, and all candidates are given an equal amount of time to complete the exam. If testlet 1 of the Auditing and Attestation (AUDIT) exam contains thirty multiple-choice questions, there will be thirty questions in testlets 2 and 3. All candidates are given four and one-half hours to complete the AUDIT section, no matter what level of question difficulty they encounter. The reported score has been adjusted for the difficulty level. Fewer correct responses of a medium to hard difficulty level are required to earn the same amount of points earned by answering a testlet categorized as easy. In other words, candidates who correctly complete a testlet categorized at the medium or hard level of difficulty can earn the same amount of points with fewer correct responses. Don't fret about this. Know that your grade is primarily dependent on content knowledge. Learn the content to earn a score of 75 or higher. Count on the AICPA to grade your exam fairly in relation to other CPA exam candidates.

PERSONALLY SPEAKING

Don't grade your exam. The AICPA hires a staff to perform this function. Silly as this may sound, candidates have reported to me that during the exam they spent time tabulating their score. First of all, this is impossible. You don't know if you responded correctly, and you are not told the point values. You have no idea at what level of difficulty the questions you are currently working with have been rated. Second, this is the wrong focus. You have a job to do. During the exam, your job is to answer all of the questions to the best of your ability. You are not the paid grader. You are the exam taker! Complete your job. It's a huge mistake to think that you can gain some idea of your grade. Wait until your receive your score. Some candidates who thought they were knowledgeable enough to grade themselves gave up and did not complete the entire exam section. Much to their surprise, when the score was released, they had answered far better than they had thought. Had they not given up early, they would have passed. What a waste of time and effort! I know it's tempting to compute a score. Drop the idea. Use your precious exam time to proofread, rework questions, and check your responses. Complete the tasks that are assigned to you. Your job is to answer the questions, not to grade them.

Why do I say the exam is graded fairly? I have been involved in helping CPA candidates for over twenty years. The grading process I have observed is fair. I believe this will continue under the computer-based exam. The passing score has been set to distinguish candidates who are qualified to practice from those who are not. This means that the AICPA has invested a great deal of time and money to establish passing scores at a level that represents the knowledge and skills entry-level CPAs must demonstrate to ensure that the public interest is protected. Determining passing scores on licensure exams requires expert professional judgment. The AICPA has identified practice experts, who meet as a panel. These panelists are trained to be consistent in their understanding of the requirements of an entry-level accountant. The panel uses a candidate-centered approach to establishing the CPA exam passing score. In candidate-centered methods, the focus is on looking at actual candidate answers and making judgments about which sets of answers represent the answers of qualified CPAs. There is no way CPA candidates have enough information to calculate their own score. Trust the procedures. Know that they are fair. Work on improving your content knowledge; it takes knowledge within each exam section to pass. Do your job. The AICPA will do its job.

CPA EXAM TIP:
Order free AICPA software to use as a practice tool for the AUDIT and FAR research. See www.cpa-exam.org for details.

11 DEVELOPING YOUR PERSONAL STUDY PLAN

It's time to get down to the business of studying. Just talking and reading about the exam does not give you the technical edge. Chapter 2, Content and Overall Exam Format, explains what concepts are tested. Using the techniques in Chapter 5, Assessing Your Strengths and Weaknesses, you have determined your weak areas. Now prepare to be successful by devising a plan to learn the concepts. The first step in developing a personalized study plan is to analyze each day of the week to find the time to study.

SCHEDULE YOUR ACTIVITIES

A plan is a detailed method by which a project is completed. In preparing for the CPA exam, you must divide up the overwhelming amount of technical material into bite-size chunks and then prepare a plan that gives you study time to learn the concepts tested. Finding time to study is easier said than done. Begin to find study time by listing how you spend your time each day. Use a chart, like the one in Exhibit 11.1, to write down your daily activities. Prepare a different chart for every day of the week. Sample charts for a workday, for example a Monday, may look like Exhibit 11.1. A sample chart for a weekend day might look like Exhibit 11.2. Take note of the times when you can study. During the week, the most obvious study times will be early morning before work, during the lunch hour, and late evenings after work. Notice how much more study time is available on a weekend. Now force yourself to use the time to **study**. It's very tempting to waste time on a weekend, just because there seems to be so much extra time. This is why you prepare a plan. Establish the plan and stick to it.

Exhibit 11.1: Sample Weekday of Activities

Day of the Week: *Monday*

Time	*Activity*
6:00 a.m.	Wake up at 6:15 a.m. *TIME TO STUDY*
7:00 a.m.	Shower, eat breakfast, get ready for work, housework, drive kids to school
8:00 a.m.	Leave to catch train to work; arrive at work at 8:30 a.m.*
9:00 a.m.	WORK
10:00 a.m.	WORK
11:00 a.m.	WORK
Noon	Lunch hour *TIME TO STUDY*
1:00 p.m.	WORK
2:00 p.m.	WORK
3:00 p.m.	WORK
4:00 p.m.	WORK

<u>Time</u>	<u>Activity</u>
5:00 p.m.	WORK
6:00 p.m.	Leave work at 5:10 p.m. and travel home on train*
7:00 p.m.	Cook dinner, eat dinner, spend time with family
8:00 p.m.	*TIME TO STUDY*
9:00 p.m.	*TIME TO STUDY*
10:00 p.m.	*TIME TO STUDY*
11:00 p.m.	Get ready for the next day. Go to bed 11:15 p.m., to get seven hours of sleep.

* *See Chapter 12, Study Strategies to Improve Your Memory, for tips on how to study while you are doing household chores and commuting to work.*

Exhibit 11.2: Sample Weekday of Activities

Day of the Week: *Sunday*

<u>Time</u>	<u>Activity</u>
6:00 a.m.	Wake up at 6:15 a.m. *TIME TO STUDY*
7:00 a.m.	Shower, eat breakfast, get ready for church, read the paper
8:00 a.m.	Church
9:00 a.m.	Church, travel back home, visit with family
10:00 a.m.	*TIME TO STUDY*
11:00 a.m.	*TIME TO STUDY*
Noon	Eat lunch
1:00 p.m.	*TIME TO STUDY*
2:00 p.m.	*TIME TO STUDY*
3:00 p.m.	Watch football game, wash clothes*
4:00 p.m.	Watch football game, run to the grocery store*
5:00 p.m.	Continue washing clothes and other household chores*
6:00 p.m.	Go out to dinner with family and friends
7:00 p.m.	Family dinner
8:00 p.m.	Pay bills, get mail ready for the week, e-mail friends
9:00 p.m.	*TIME TO STUDY*
10:00 p.m.	*TIME TO STUDY*
11:00 p.m.	Get ready for the next day. Go to bed 11:15 p.m., to get seven hours of sleep.

* *See Chapter 12, Study Strategies to Improve Your Memory, for tips on how to study while you are doing household chores and commuting to work.*

Plot out your day, listing times beginning early in the morning to late at night. Allow for about seven to eight hours of sleep. You can't afford to be lazy. You may have to abandon optional activities, such as playing on the softball team, watching television, and taking naps, to make time to study. You may even have to postpone volunteer work until you pass.

After you list your daily routine, you must stand back and examine how you use your time. Obviously, you cannot cancel work every day or you will be too poor to sit for the CPA exam. However, why can't you study during your lunch hour?

Use your schedule to find time to study during the week. Yes, some evenings may include fun activities, such as bowling, exercise, school events, and church meetings. Prepare a separate schedule for every day of the week. Then examine your schedule and find times to study. This may mean canceling some of the fun activities.

Most accountants stick to a predictable schedule of activities. Notice that the schedules do not include much time for phone calls, watching television, surfing the Internet, or shopping at the mall. These activities are considered fun things that you can do **after** you pass the exam. For now, keep your extracurricular activities to a minimum.

FINDING TIME TO STUDY

Does a person need a full hour to eat lunch? No one ever said passing the exam was going to be easy, and certainly no one ever pretended that you could prepare without sacrificing something that you enjoy. Make the commitment to pass; find the time in your schedule to study. Where can you find time?

Try the morning. Chapter 12, Study Strategies to Improve Your Memory, suggests that you listen to recordings of lectures about law, economics, information technology, and audit topics. Most people learn these topics by remembering words rather than formulas. Repetition is key. You also must find some time to sit down and work questions to test your retention and understanding of the material. Determine when you will study, and make studying a habit.

It takes about three weeks of constantly doing something to make it a habit. If you set your alarm to wake up forty-five minutes earlier to study before you go to work, you could form a morning study habit in a very short time. Five, forty-five-minute morning sessions each week gives you a total of almost four hours of study time a week. Exhibit 11.3 presents a suggested study plan.

Exhibit 11.3: Suggested Study Plan

Study Time	Minutes of Study per Day	Total Study Time per Week
In the morning, before you go to work or school	45 minutes per day, 5 days a week	3.75 hours
During your lunch hour	45 minutes per day, 4 days a week (go out to lunch with your friends on Friday)	3.00 hours
Evening time after work	2 hours, 4 nights per week	8.00 hours
Saturday morning	3 hours 15 minutes	3.25 hours
Sunday evening	3 hours	3.00 hours
Total study time		21.00 hours

Organized people who deliberately make time to study can easily find twenty-one hours per week outside of work to study. Notice that Friday is a light day, with no studying during lunch or in the evening. Adjust the plan to fit your life. For example, if you make the decision to continue bowling, you might give up a weeknight and study for three hours on three evenings instead of two hours for four nights. If you must attend a family event on Sunday, add three hours of study time to Saturday so as to free up the entire day on Sunday, or exchange Sunday study time with Friday evening. Sticking to the plan requires flexibility. However, just spending time looking at the material while you tick off the minutes spent is not going to help you.

REAL STUDYING

Real studying means that you are using time to learn topics, not just wasting time staring at your review manuals. Real studying means you will spend about 25% of your study time reading and about 75% of your study time doing. Whatever you do, don't confuse staring at the material with actively studying to learn the material.

It is easy to determine if you have wasted study time or used your time wisely to learn and retain information. Simply try to answer the sample questions. Use test software to create a simulated exam, or try to work some questions in a review manual. If you can answer the questions correctly, you will know that you learned the material. If you are unable to answer the questions correctly, you've wasted time.

HOW MUCH STUDY TIME?

How much time should a candidate study? The answer depends on a number of factors.

- **How much time do you have before your scheduled exam date?** If there are five months, you don't need to study as much each day as you would if there were only three months left.
- **How much do you know?** If you recently graduated from college and took all of the courses discussed in Chapter 5, you probably know a great deal. You are current and need to study less than the person who has been out of college for five to ten years.
- **How quickly do you absorb technical material?**
- **How current are you in the particular area?**
- **What activities do you perform on your job that may help you learn an area?** If you prepare corporate tax returns, you will be well versed in this area and will require less study time for the Regulation (REG) exam section. If you audit for a public accounting firm, your audit skills will help you absorb the audit examples more quickly than if you have never been an auditor. With work experience, Auditing and Attestation (AUDIT) should be a section that you will feel confident taking with less study time.
- **How many exam sections must you take?** If you are just beginning your CPA journey, you have more time than a person who has successfully completed a section. Remember, the eighteen-month rule requires that candidates who have passed one section to complete the remaining three sections within eighteen months of the test date of the first section that candidates pass.

It is impossible to say exactly how much time a person must study. The schedule of twenty-one hours per week is about the average time a person can carve out of a very busy weekly schedule. Keep in mind that if you attend a review course, the hours you spend at the review course should count as study time. The basic rule is to study as much as you can to learn what you need to learn. Don't let time be the driving force. When preparing your study plan, let the number of topics you must learn and review be the driving force.

Quality study time does pay off. Spending all of your spare time studying is not a lifestyle that you want to keep up forever. The good news is there is no need to execute this study schedule forever. Take one exam section at a time. Study hard, sit for a section, and then take a short break. Reward yourself with a minivacation from the rigors of study. Then select another exam section, and go for it again. It won't take as long to prepare for the Business Environment and Concepts (BEC) section as it will for the Financial Accounting and Reporting (FAR) section. AUDIT is the longest CPA exam section, and it is very comprehensive. BEC is the shortest, but this section tests a wider range of subjects. A person who prepares tax returns for a living should need far less time to prepare for REG than to prepare for AUDIT or FAR. Personalize your study plan to fit your background, your strengths, and your weaknesses. See Chapters 16 through 19 for a detailed description of each exam section. Use this information to help you prepare your study schedule.

PREPARING A STUDY PLAN BY TOPICS

Examine your review materials. Divide up all materials by exam area, then further divide them into concepts tested within the exam section. The subtopics can be called chapters, modules, or units. For simplicity, we will call them modules. Count up the number of modules you should study and review. If your materials contain twenty-four modules and you have twelve weeks to go before the exam, you should study two modules per week to complete all twenty-four modules. Notice that it is assumed that you can and will complete two modules per week, right up to the exam date. If you skip a week of study, you must increase your studies during the next week if you want time to take practice exams and have not already included them in your schedule. Make sure to schedule a few extra days.

Obviously, two modules per week for twelve weeks is a pretty tough schedule. It is probably unrealistic to assume that there will be no major interruptions. Don't set yourself up for failure. The plan for success allows for interruptions by periodically finding extra time to catch up. In other words, budget time to catch up by leaving some holes in your personalized study plan. When you reach the catch-up date, if you are already caught up, reward yourself by taking some time out for fun.

Once you determine how many modules you must study per week, take some time to consider the mix of subjects that you must learn.

SUBJECT MIX

If you plan to take more than one exam section within a testing window, mix up the exam sections and the subject matter in your study plan. Schedule a tough subject with an easy one. Mix the fun topics with the dry and difficult areas. For example, if you plan to study three modules per week, don't select three difficult FAR topics for the same week. Help yourself stick to the plan by picking one difficult area, one area of medium difficulty, and one easy and fun area. An example of a mix of material might be

- **Difficult:** FAR—Pensions
- **Medium difficulty:** FAR—Fixed Assets
- **Easy:** FAR—Inventory

Take a pretest of the concepts to determine if the area is difficult or easy for you. Once you determine the subject mix for the week, take a look at how you will accomplish the plan. Begin the week with the difficult area, by further dividing the pension area, for example, into three topics.

1. Pension definitions and terms
2. Pension calculations
3. Pension footnote disclosures and financial statement presentations

Early in the week, study the terms during your commute to work. During your lunch hour, review the terms and begin learning the formulas for the computations. The wise candidate will study for a short time period, not more than an hour. Studying for a long stretch of time greatly decreases your retention rate and your efficiency. People absorb things more quickly and easily in short time periods and by dividing the material into bite-size chunks of information.

BITE-SIZE CHUNKS

Research studies show that people learn more quickly when the material is divided into small, manageable study areas. Bits of information are easier to study. Gain confidence working with bite-size areas and noting that progress was made. Another advantage of studying small areas is that this method allows you to utilize a building-block approach. We all know we can't divide until we master the areas of addition, subtraction, and multiplication. Accounting, like math, keeps building. Use previously mastered techniques to help you learn new accounting information. For example, to understand how to account for liabilities, you must know how to compute net present value. Once you know how to compute present value, bond and lease accounting will be much easier, since the areas begin with the computation of net present value. Prepare your study plan by blocking out several short time intervals throughout the day to study. Your careful planning will reap big rewards by not only giving you several breaks, but also by improving your long-term memory. Your retention rate will be much higher when you study over short periods rather than long ones.

TO THINE OWN SELF BE TRUE

"To thine own self be true" is an old fashioned way of saying be honest and see things as they are. Be honest when you develop your study plan. If you must travel to see relatives for the weekend, you shouldn't schedule a difficult area for review, unless your relatives allow you to study during the day and then plan a relaxing evening for you. Take a realistic look at your upcoming week. For a busy week, schedule light study, say ten hours; schedule as many as twenty hours of study during a quiet week.

Schedule open time to accommodate sickness, family crises, and overtime at work. It's inevitable that problems will occur. Once every five to six weeks, schedule a week with no study. This is your catch-up week. It is best to take at least two to three days off work to catch up. Use your vacation time for study.

BOOK YOUR VACATION NOW

Plan to take some time off work to prepare for each exam section. Use your vacation or take an unpaid leave of absence. The last thing you need is an argument with your boss about getting time off to take the exam. Whatever you do, don't plan to work during the day and then sit for an exam section in the evening. Sure as can be, that workday will turn out to be ghastly, and the bad day could carry over to affect your exam performance. Your work will be worthless, as your mind will be on the studying that you wish you could do. If only bosses would realize that passing the CPA examination is a major professional hurdle for which most candidates need some help. Help yourself by arranging to take the time off work several months in advance of the actual testing date.

BUDGET TIME FOR REVIEW

Don't forget to budget time to review previously studied material. Schedule the entire week and the weekend before the exam for some review. Use purchased course software to create self-tests. Look for review manuals that contain sample exams. Review questions and index cards that you wrote as you discovered difficult areas. Skim your notes. For each area, work every fourth multiple-choice question. Work some simulations using CPA exam software. Pay attention to how you answer the communication component. Meet with your study buddy and quiz each other out loud or by exchanging lists of your favorite CPA questions. Remain focused on the CPA exam. Be happy that by developing and sticking to a detailed course of action, you managed to create time for review just before the exam.

APPRECIATE THE PLAN

Don't ever underestimate the value of planning. Generally accepted auditing standards require audit planning because planning is critical to auditors' performance in accomplishing their goals. The time you spend planning will benefit you later by helping you meet your goal of passing the CPA exam.

Candidates often spend more time planning New Year's Eve parties than they do preparing a study plan to accomplish a lifetime goal as prestigious as passing the CPA exam. Look at your study plan as a road map to the end of the CPA journey. Each topic that you learn, study, and review means you are that much closer to reaching your destination. A detailed study plan lets you see just how much more you have left to accomplish. A plan serves as a reminder that you must study early and often. If you slack off even one day, you must pay in the future by carving time out of an already jam-packed schedule.

PERSONALIZE THE STUDY PLAN

There is no magic amount of study time. Personalize your study plan by thinking about your weak areas and how much time you have each day to study. Don't be overly ambitious. A person simply cannot study for ten hours a day and be effective. Look for small bits of time to learn the bite-size chunks of material. As the days get closer to the exam, you will be surprised at how much better prepared you will be if you established a personalized plan to meet your personal goals. Don't forget an important rule: Study what you don't know, not what you do know. Have some confidence in your ability to retain information. There is no time to waste. Use your time and your abilities wisely. Make the sacrifice.

GIVE UP ACTIVITIES

There is no doubt that during your CPA exam preparation you will have to give up some things that are fun to do. You may even have to sacrifice and give up helping with the lawn work or the cooking and cleaning chores. You just can't do what you were doing before. You can't squeeze time into an already-too-busy schedule. Take a careful inventory of all of the activities you are involved in and give up something to make room for study time. Who knows? After the exam is over, you might discover that your new streamlined plan allows you time to return to school to get another degree, spend more time with your family, or just plain spend time reading and relaxing.

DESIGN A PLAN TO SUCCEED

Designing a plan to succeed is so much more fun than designing a plan that on paper looks great, but after one to two weeks, you haven't accomplished a thing because the plan does not fit your lifestyle. If you are not a morning person, by all means, don't schedule early morning study times. Plan to spend the late evening hours studying. Incorporate all of the topical areas into your plan. Mastering some areas and leaving other areas untouched could be dangerous. The AICPA Board of Examiners has a way of testing the areas that you didn't study. Spend time on all subject areas to do your best at learning something about everything. Believe that your plan will be a guide to success. Believe that you can pass the CPA exam.

DON'T WASTE TIME—COMPLETE THE JOB

Don't be lazy. You must perform and study every day. There is no slack time. The suggested study plan in Exhibit 11.3 requires you to begin studying several weeks before each exam section. If you want a less intense schedule, begin earlier and study less each week. If it's been a long time since you took an exam or studied accounting material, you may need to begin a month earlier, to provide for extra time to learn and review the material. If you find yourself not completing the assignments on time, you should make extra time in your day to study or study Friday and/or Sunday to always stay on target. When you fall behind, you will find it very difficult to catch up. Make studying a habit by making studying one of your daily chores.

Exhibit 11.4: Sample Study Plan: Twenty-One Study Hours per Week
Schedule for Eight Study Weeks

NOTE: This study plan has been prepared for the Regulation (REG) exam section. It is assumed that the candidate has purchased current CPA Review materials from a reputable provider. The materials should contain a software package to use as review.

Assumptions:

- Friday and Sunday are free days (no studying required) as long as you have completed your "to do" list for the week.
- Saturday study time is six to seven hours. This time may be spent in a CPA Review course or self-studying.
- Study weekday mornings, Monday–Thursday, for 45 minutes
- Study weekday lunch hours, Monday–Thursday only, for 45 minutes
- Study 2½ hours on Monday, Wednesday, and Thursday evenings.
- Study Tuesday evening for 1½ hours.

Your study week looks like this

Study Time	Monday	Tuesday	Wednesday	Thursday	Saturday
Morning	45 minutes	45 minutes	45 minutes	45 minutes	3 hours
Lunch Hour	45 minutes	45 minutes	45 minutes	45 minutes	
Afternoon					3 hours
Evening	2 hours	1 hour	2 hours	2 hours	
	30 minutes	30 minutes	30 minutes	30 minutes	
Total	4 hours	3 hours	4 hours	4 hours	6 hours

Your study topics look like this.

Week	Monday	Tuesday	Wednesday	Thursday	Saturday
1	• Individual taxation; Basic concepts • Work the AICPA tutorial at www.cpa-exam.org (if this is your first exam section)	• Continue individual taxation	• Continue individual taxation • Work the AICPA sample examination for REG at www.cpa-exam.org	• Continue individual taxation • Review various individual taxation tax forms and schedules (see Chapter 18 for a discussion of the most likely tested schedules)	• Complete individual taxation review
2	• Work practice questions on individual taxation • Begin corporate taxation; basic concepts	• Continue corporate taxation	• Continue corporate taxation	• Continue corporate taxation	• Complete corporate taxation
3	• Work practice questions on corporate taxation • Begin partnership taxation	• Continue partnership taxation	• Complete partnership taxation	• Begin trusts and estates taxation	• Complete trusts and estates taxation
4	• Review tax return preparer's responsibilities	• Review tax topics; complete taxation sample exam	• Review taxation sample exam and learn from mistakes	• Begin contracts	• Complete contracts
5	• Begin sales	• Complete sales	• Review insurance	• Review secured transactions	• Begin bankruptcy and debtor-creditor relationships
6	• Complete bankruptcy and debtor-creditor relationships	• Begin commercial paper	• Complete commercial paper	• Begin professional responsibilities and code of conduct	• Complete professional responsibilities and code of conduct
7	• Begin SEC Acts	• Continue SEC Acts	• Complete SEC Acts	• Review agency	• Review employment laws
8	• Begin property	• Complete property	• Review trusts and estates	• Complete a review of law topics by generating a practice exam; review results	• Complete an entire practice exam; review results

This schedule does not include a catch-up week or extra time to complete an overall review of all materials studied. Use Fridays and Sundays to remain on track when the tasks have not been completed by the designated time. A study plan is a personalized document that must be tailored to your needs and to your time schedule. If you need to take several review tests, allow time for doing so. Plan to budget additional time to learn new material that was not covered in your academic studies. Spend time plotting your personal needs. Then forge ahead and execute the plan. Stick to the schedule each week. You will retain the information longer when you study for a short time each day. Remember, it is impossible to pull an all-nighter to review for the CPA exam. Don't even think about it. This is the big league. Take your studies seriously—view the task as a job that you must complete. Yes, it's work. However, the rewards for completing this job (passing the exam) are huge!

PERSONALLY SPEAKING

I can't tell you how much fun I gave up the summer that I wrote this book. At the beginning of the summer, my golf game was improving because I had some time to golf almost every day. Then, when crunch time arrived, I had to give up even the simple things such as meals with my family and Sunday golf. I had to work around the clock. I am a procrastinator who always works better under pressure. Don't think this works for the CPA exam. You will be assured of running out of time. The CPA exam waits for no one. No matter how much you would like to postpone the date, it arrives. Yes, you are allowed to reschedule, but depending on the timing, doing so may become costly. Plus, if you reschedule a section, you may not meet the eighteen-month deadline to complete all four sections. That is why it is so critical to establish a detailed plan and stick to it. Make the sacrifice each day to meet the end goal. In the end, you will be able to say you really did do the best that you could.

I kept pushing to finish this book so that I could get some sleep, take some time to see my daughter's soccer games, and visit my son at college. I can take time for the fun things only when I have accomplished my work goals. When it comes down to it, you have options. You can always give up the plan and not become a CPA. I could have given up on writing this book or on taking the CPA exam. In the end, I would never have accomplished a dream that I always had. I often dreamed of being a CPA and of authoring a book.

CPAs like to be organized. Preparing a study plan keeps you organized. Use a bright highlighter to ceremoniously check off what you have studied. Use incentives to reward yourself. When I was studying for the Certified Internal Auditor's (CIA) exam, I could afford to take a week off from work and fly to Florida to study on the beach. It was great. Each morning I would wake up early, study until noon, sit in the sun from noon to 3 p.m., shop until 5 p.m., and go back to studying after dinner. If I didn't accomplish the modules I wanted to, I wouldn't allow myself to go have fun. My reward for accomplishing my daily goals was to do something I enjoy.

Your incentive could be something simple, like going to a movie, taking a bubble bath, or hitting golf balls at the driving range. Maybe you want to shoot some hoops or attend a play or opera. You can go only if you accomplish your goal. You must stay home if you don't. Allow time for fun, but not at the expense of achieving your goal.

I speak with both successful and unsuccessful CPA candidates. With almost no exceptions, those who pass have made sacrifices to achieve their goal. A recent e-mail from an unsuccessful candidate summed it up simply by saying: "I failed the exam because I failed to give up anything." She went on to explain that during the months she took the review class she didn't take time to study. She didn't take the time to study because she said she had no time. After the exam, she realized that she would have passed if she had sacrificed a few activities to make time to study. Sacrifice for the important matter at hand—passing the exam. Successful candidates realize that they have no time to lose. Every minute of study makes a valuable contribution to the goal.

Let's say you use the example time allotment of studying twenty-one hours per week. What should you do when you have completed the necessary weekly modules in only sixteen hours of study time? You're fully prepared for the topics listed that week and you spent five hours less than you budgeted for. This is the fun part. You get to choose what you want to do. Here are four good options

1. Use the extra time to go back to a previous area and review it.
2. Use the extra time to move forward to get ahead in other areas.
3. Use your software to generate mock exams to test your time management skills and your long-term memory.
4. Reward yourself—go have some fun and spend some time with your loved ones!

You pick the option. You worked hard to stick to the plan and it paid off. What you do with the extra time is up to you. Because you have a plan that details what you must do to achieve success, you can pause along the way. It's all part of the plan. Trust your study plan. It will guide you to success. Believe that you can pass the exam by learning one concept at a time over the course of several days and weeks.

CPA EXAM TIP:
Be realistic when preparing your study plan. You can't do it all. Passing the CPA exam requires sacrifices. Be prepared to make the choice to study. Be prepared to give up some fun activities.

12 STUDY STRATEGIES TO IMPROVE YOUR MEMORY

Are you studying to remember the material, or are you simply studying to pass the time? Of course you want to remember the concepts when it comes time to use them. Most candidates don't really know how to study. As a college student, you might have studied for the moment. The kind of person who studied for a day or all night and then dumped the material out on the exam the next day has far less retention than the person who learned the material over the course of time and then reviewed the day before the exam. This chapter gives you proven study strategies that not only help you assimilate the material, but also help improve your long-term memory. Not all study techniques work for everyone. Review the suggested techniques and select the study strategies that will help you.

PROVEN STUDY STRATEGIES

Study to learn and retain. Chapter 5, Assessing Your Strengths and Weaknesses, demonstrates how to determine your strong and weak areas. Chapter 11, Developing Your Personal Study Plan, helps you prepare a study plan to fit your life and to meet the deadline of the CPA exam. How do you go about studying the material that you have identified? Use a variety of study techniques, and practice, practice, practice.

BREAK THE MATERIAL INTO SUBTOPICS

Divide the material into bite-size chunks. When eating, a person who quickly gulps down a meal is subject to an upset stomach; the person who eats slowly, taking time to chew several times, has a much easier time digesting a meal. Subtopics are easy to study for a few minutes at a time. Research shows that people absorb concepts more quickly when they break the material into small themes. Before you can compute the amount of interest expense paid on a particular bond, you first must understand how to compute the amortization of the premium or discount. Take baby steps first, then start walking. Before you know it, you will be running. In other words, take the time to understand the foundation first.

Refer to your study plan. If you are taking a CPA review course, the material should be subdivided for you. If you are self-studying, divide the material into chapters or modules as shown in your CPA review materials. Recall that your college accounting, auditing, and tax texts contain too much material, are probably out-of-date, and are class focused instead of CPA exam focused. Try not to study from your texts. Use CPA review-oriented materials that are less than twelve to eighteen months old.

People learn best when they break the material apart. A bite-size chunk is a portion of the material, not the entire area. For example, bonds are tested on the Financial Accounting and Reporting (FAR) exam section. The area of bonds is very broad. Are we talking about bond investments or bonds payable? Let's say bonds payable. Now we can further subdivide bonds payable into nine concept areas.

1. Bond terminology and definitions
2. Determining the present value
3. Accounting for bond issue costs
4. Bonds issued between interest payment dates
5. Bonds issued with detachable warrants
6. Accounting for convertible bonds
7. Amortization of bond discounts and premiums using the straight-line method
8. Amortization of bond discounts and premiums using the effective interest method
9. Retirement of bonds

Studying the concepts one area at a time will allow you to master topics in a shorter period of time.

STUDY OVER SHORT TIME INTERVALS

Do you really need a large block of time to learn something? Most candidates believe they do. Here's what typically happens. All week long you say you will postpone your studying until Saturday, when you will have a big block of time. Saturday comes around, and you wake up and say you will study as soon as you run errands. At the dry cleaner's you run into a friend and go out for lunch. Then after lunch, on the way to the library, you decide your car is dirty. After you wait in line at the car wash, you decide it's almost time for dinner. Your day has been consumed without you ever having studied. Wait a minute. Why didn't you study in your car while you were waiting in line at the car wash? In less than fifteen minutes you could have learned the terms that pertain to bonds. Why didn't you tell your friend you planned to study today, and you will lunch with him or her for thirty minutes as long as he or she spends another thirty minutes quizzing you? If you make no sacrifice, you will accomplish little. Even if you spend the whole day studying, is it possible to really stay focused the entire time? Most studies show that fifteen to thirty-minute study intervals are far more productive than large blocks of time.

This story demonstrates that if you had divided the material into bite-size chunks, you would not have wasted so much time. You could have studied between errands. In fact, your errands could have served as a study break. You don't need an entire block of time. Once you break the old habit of believing that you must have several hours to study, you will find you have more study time. You will be less likely to procrastinate and more likely to jump in and learn.

Should you worry about dividing the material? No. You really don't have the time to analyze the entire CPA exam content. If you purchase reputable CPA review materials, the material will be broken down into enough subheadings. Check your review materials for topic subdivisions. The more subtopics you see, the better.

Where do you find short bits of time? This list suggests how to carve short study intervals out of your normal day.

- In the morning, when you are drinking your morning beverage, try reading CPA materials instead of the newspaper.
- Throughout the day, whenever you sit down, read CPA materials instead of a book or magazine.
- Whenever you are in a line, use the time to study—lines at the school waiting for your children, lines in the subway, lines at the car wash, and any other line.
- During your work commute, why not study on the train or subway? You can even study in your car driving to and from work via audio recordings. Be careful not to read and drive at the same time.
- In the evening, study when you go to bed. Get used to putting yourself to sleep with your study materials. Not only will you go to sleep more quickly, you also will retain the material longer, as your mind will be clear, ready to absorb the information.
- When performing routine workouts, such as using workout machines, jogging, or bicycling, you can study. You don't have to use this time for practicing problems or reading. Use it to listen to recordings of the material. Recordings are especially useful when studying law and audit topics, two exam topics that rely heavily on words rather than computations and formulas.
- Study during lunch. Passing the CPA exam takes sacrifice. Give up thirty to forty minutes of your lunch hour. Pretend you no longer have a lunch hour. Now you have a quick brown bag lunch that takes ten minutes to eat, and you can spend the rest of the time studying. You can also use money you save on lunches for CPA study materials.
- When you are in the passenger's seat en route to the mall or to see the relatives, study. If you happen to be driving, listen to recordings.

These are just some of the many ways you can find time to study. Take a moment and think about your typical workday, then list your normal routine. Once you write down your daily activities, you will see where you might find time to study. Break yourself of the habit of believing that you can study only on a day off from work. Start new habits. It only takes about three weeks to form a habit. After three weeks, you will have a new habit of taking time out of your day to study every day. Your confidence level will increase each day as you learn more material. You can be proud that every day you are one step closer toward your goal of becoming a CPA.

WRITE IT DOWN

The age-old image of schoolchildren writing each spelling word ten times is a good model to follow when you are struggling to absorb and remember a difficult technical concept. Let's say you have trouble remembering the formula for computing the amount of revenue from an installment sale contract. The formula is quite involved. Write it down. Use pen and paper or type it on the computer. Performing the repetitive task will help you. Take a break and write the formula down over and over again. Make an index card of the formula and put it in a pile that you will review once a week. Review it often.

Having trouble grasping a topic? Draw two columns. In one column write down what you know. In the other, write down the question areas—in other words, what you don't know. Ask your review instructor, a friend, or your accounting professor for tips on the question areas, but be sure the person you ask is technically competent and up-to-date on the topic.

SAY IT OUT LOUD

You learn by hearing. What better voice to hear than your own. Wouldn't it be wonderful if in the middle of the Regulation (REG) exam, you hear your voice reminding you about the elements of a contract? Talk to yourself. Repeat concepts out loud and often.

Prepare your own tape recordings. Record yourself describing the financial statements prepared for each fund type of a governmental entity. Later listen to the recording on your way to work or to the mall. Sort the laundry, do the dishes, and listen to yourself repeating the concepts. After a while you will be able to fast-forward the tape over the sections that you could repeat in your sleep. The Financial Accounting and Reporting (FAR) sections will seem much easier if you know the elements of the governmental financial statements. You will remember these relatively obscure bits of information for a longer period of time if you prepared your own study aids.

Give your index cards, book, or notes to someone else and let the person quiz you. Answer the questions out loud. Your long-term memory will improve greatly by repeating concepts out loud.

TAPE IT TO THE BATHROOM MIRROR

It's time to learn the two basic financial statements. You must know the elements of a classified balance sheet and a multiple-step income statement.

Tape the model to your bathroom mirror. Every morning, when you brush your teeth, read the model. As you are putting away your toothbrush and toothpaste or combing your hair, look in the mirror and recite aloud what you have just read. One week of grooming with CPA exam concepts and you will have memorized many concepts. Is it time to replace the model? Tape another example up to study the next week.

PREPARE A SUMMARY

Some areas require the preparation of a summary. The four steps to internal control is a good example of several concepts that are important to learn for the Auditing and Attestation (AUDIT) exam. Spending time to summarize the process helps reinforce the main ideas. See Exhibit 12.1 for a summary example. Review your summary and make several copies of it. Place copies in strategic places, such as the bathroom, car glove compartment, work desk drawer, your briefcase, nightstand, or near your favorite chair. Whenever you have a free moment, review the summary sheets. You learn as you prepare the summary. You will recall the concepts when you review them and when you complete practice quizzes.

Exhibit 12.1: Four-Step Approach to Internal Control

1. **Obtain and document an understanding of internal control**

    Why is the auditor understanding the internal control process?

    - **To plan the audit** by determining the nature, timing, and extent of tests to be performed
    - **Required by GAAS**
    - Identify **potential misstatements**
    - Consider factors that affect the **risk** of material misstatement

    *What is **internal control?***

    - A **process** established by the board of directors, management, and other personnel, designed to provide reasonable assurance that management achieves three objectives.

        - Reliable financial reporting
        - Effective and efficient operations
        - Compliance with laws and regulations

    *What must the auditor **understand?***

    - The five internal control components

        1. Control **E**nvironment
        2. **R**isk Assessment
        3. Control **A**ctivities (performance reviews, information processing, physical controls, and segregation of duties)
        4. **I**nformation and Communication
        5. **M**onitoring of the Controls

- **Direct** relationship between the **internal control components** and the three **management objectives** listed above

*What is the auditor doing during the **understanding?***

- Understanding the **design** and whether the controls have been **placed in operation**—is the client **using** controls?
- Document by flowcharts, narrative memos, questionnaires, and/or decision tables

*NOTE: Understanding the controls does not mean evaluating the **control effectiveness**—control effectiveness is evaluated by performing tests of controls*

2. **Assess control risk**

   - Definition of control risk: The risk that the internal controls will not prevent or detect a material misstatement in the financial statement (FS) on a timely basis.
   - Auditor hopes to keep control risk low and assess control risk **below maximum**.
   - Definition of assessed level of control risk: The conclusion reached as a result of assessing control risk.
   - Assessing control risk is the process of evaluating the effectiveness of an entity's internal control in preventing or detecting material misstatements in the FS. **Control risk should be assessed in terms of the FS assertions.**
   - **Assessing control risk at below maximum** involves

     - Identifying specific controls relevant to specific FS assertions that will be likely to prevent or detect material misstatements in those assertions **and**
     - Performing tests of controls to evaluate the control **effectiveness**

   - Control risk can be assessed below maximum for all or some of the financial statement assertions.
   - Controls can be related either directly or indirectly to a FS assertion. The more indirect the relationship, the less effective that control may be in reducing the control risk for that assertion.
   - The auditor must assess control risk at **maximum** when three conditions occur.

     1. The client is not using any controls. Therefore, it would be **ineffective (overkill)** to perform tests of controls.
     2. In the unusual case where performing tests of controls would be more expensive **(inefficient)** than performing substantive tests. Skip the tests of controls. Remember, tests of controls are optional.
     3. The auditor cannot relate (link) the client's controls to one or more FS assertion.

   - If the auditor must assess control risk at maximum, the control risk is high and detection risk must be kept low. As detection risk decreases, the auditor should

- Increase the amount of substantive testing
- Perform the tests closer to the balance sheet date
- Use more effective audit procedures (obtain more outside evidence)

3. **Perform tests of controls**

- Definition of tests of controls: Tests directed toward testing the **design** or **operation** of the internal controls to determine if the controls are operating **effectively**.
- Four techniques used to perform tests of controls

    1. Observation (best for segregation of duties)
    2. Inspection
    3. Inquiry
    4. Reperformance

- Tests of controls must be related to one or more FS assertion
- Tests of controls are optional. However, if the auditor wants to assess control risk below maximum, the auditor is **required** to perform tests of controls. Why? The auditor must provide proof that the controls are operating effectively.
- **Control effectiveness** is tested using three questions

    1. **How** were the control procedures applied? Were the control procedures applied in the proper manner?
    2. **By whom** were the controls performed?
    3. Were the necessary controls **consistently** applied?

- Tests of controls are usually performed at **interim**. Test again at year-end only if circumstances or personnel have significantly changed.
- Does the auditor test all internal controls?   No, the auditor will test only those controls that relate to items the auditor uses in performing audit procedures.

4. **Reassess control risk**

- Based on the results of the tests of controls, the auditor makes a final assessment of control risk.
- If controls are not operating effectively, the auditor assesses control risk at **maximum** and documents the following two items:

    1. The **understanding** of the internal controls and
    2. The **conclusion** that control risk is assessed at **maximum**

- If the tests of controls prove that one or more controls are operating effectively as related to one or more FS assertion, the auditor can assess control risk at **below maximum** for that assertion and must document the following three items:

    1. The **understanding** of the internal controls
    2. The **conclusion** that control risk assessed **below** maximum **and**
    3. The **basis** for the conclusion (the fact that the controls are operating effectively)

- **Recall:** The auditor may assess control risk at **maximum** for some FS assertions, and **below maximum** for other FS assertions.
- The auditor does not rely entirely on internal controls because even the very best controls may break down due to the following **inherent limitations:**
  - Misunderstandings
  - Mistake in human judgments
  - Carelessness
  - Mistake due to human failure such as simple error
  - Collusion
  - Management override

PREPARE LAST-MINUTE STUDY PACKETS

You are fearful you will forget some very important concepts. Fear greatly decreases your ability to perform. To alleviate fear, prepare a last-minute study packet. Purchase four pocket folders, one for each exam section, to store your last-minute study packet review materials. Place summary pages, last-minute lists, and troublesome formulas in the folders. Review the appropriate packets the night before each exam section. Review the packet one more time in the morning before you travel to the Prometric test center.

PREPARE YOUR OWN FLASH CARDS

Purchased flash cards are convenient and easy to use. However, there is no substitute for preparing your own. Purchase colored index cards. Pick a different color for each of the major sections within an area. Begin each index card with a heading so it is clear what you are talking about. For example, an index card acquainting the CPA candidate with the different funds used in accounting for governmental entities would say: "Five Governmental Funds." Be specific to help you remember. If you just wrote "governmental funds" you would not be helping your mind to recall that there are five funds. Then list the funds on your card. You have learned because you wrote it down. You will be reminded every time you study the card and every time you repeat the concepts out loud.

The color-coding of the cards is important. You can shuffle them, drop them, or combine them, but if they are color-coded, you will never forget what they pertain to. The color association also helps you to recall information faster on the exam. For example, select a different color for each of the five broad areas of the Business Environment and Concepts (BEC) section: one for economics, finance, information technology, managerial accounting, and business organizations.

Make index cards only of information you do not know. Writing out a concept that you can recall is a waste of time. Too many cards can overwhelm you and cause you to lose valuable study time. Believe in yourself. If you know the concept today, chances are you will remember that concept a few months from now. Periodically take practice quizzes to test your long-term memory, preferably using a computer-based format.

Prepare the index cards from the questions. If you answer a homework question incorrectly, ask yourself if you have learned the concept and will retain the concept for later use. If the answer is yes, you will remember, do **not** prepare a card. If the answer is no, you won't remember, make the index card by using the information in the question. See Exhibit 12.2 for a sample flash card of a business law concept that is always part of the REG exam.

Exhibit 12.2: Sample flash card and its application

Assume you were answering this law question about coinsurance.

> Clark Corporation owns a warehouse purchased for $150,000 five years ago. The current market value is $200,000. Clark has the warehouse insured for fire loss with Fair Insurance Corporation and Zone Insurance Company. Fair's policy is for $150,000 and Zone's policy is for $75,000. Both policies contain standard 80% coinsurance clauses. If a fire totally destroyed the warehouse, what total dollar amount would Clark receive from Fair and Zone?
>
> a. $225,000
> b. $200,000
> c. $135,000
> d. $150,000

You are totally clueless about the formula. You go to your review materials and see how they explain the answer. To make a flash card from the question, you would

- Define what a coinsurance clause is.
- List the formula to compute the dollar amount to be received by the insured.
- List any special comments that you need to recall in this situation.

Your index card should look like this

HEADING:
Amount to be paid when coinsured

DEFINITION:
Insured party agrees to maintain insurance equal to a specified % of property value. If insured does not carry specified %, insurance company pays a proportionate amount.

FORMULA to determine proportionate amount:

$$\$\$ \text{ Recovered} = \text{Actual loss} \times \frac{\text{Amount of insurance}}{\text{Coinsurance \% x FMV property at time of loss}}$$

Back of Card

SPECIAL NOTES:
Formula does not apply when property is completely destroyed.
$$ Recovered when property is 100% destroyed is the lower of the market value of the property on the day of loss or total insurance carried.

QUESTION(S):
Page 67, # 4
Page 33, #16

Test the card by working the question. The fire **totally destroyed** the warehouse so the above **coinsurance clause does not apply**. The insurance companies will each pay their proportionate share of the market value of the property on the day of the loss. Don't apply the coinsurance formula. Use a simple apportionment formula. Total insurance carried was $225,000 ($150,000 by Fair plus $75,000 by Zone). Current loss on the day of the fire was $200,000. The answer is b. or $200,000. There is no need to apportion because the question asked what amount would the insurance companies pay in total. Let's keep it simple—the total insurance was $225,000. No insurance company is going to pay you more than the property was worth ($200,000). Don't waste your time—compare the value of the property on the day of the loss with the insurance. If there is enough insurance to cover the total loss (yes, there was $225,000 of insurance), the maximum the insured (Clark) can receive will be the market value of the property on the day of the loss.

Review the reasoning used in this response. Learn to talk to yourself to reason out answers. Use your common sense to understand the concepts, not just memorize the concepts. Clark shouldn't be making money on a fire. Clark should not receive more than the property is worth.

Your review materials should also contain an example question where you would apply the loss. Try this CPA law question.

> In 2004, Pod bought a building for $200,000. At that time, Pod purchased a $150,000 fire insurance policy with Owners Insurance Company and a $50,000 fire insurance policy with Group Insurance Corporation. Each policy contained a standard 80% coinsurance clause. In 2008, when the building had a fair market value of $250,000, it was damaged in a fire. How much would Pod recover from Owners if the fire caused $180,000 in damage?
>
> a. $ 90,000
> b. $120,000
> c. $135,000
> d. $150,000

Time to apply the coinsurance formula. Apply the formula because the damage of $180,000 was less than the fair market value of $250,000. Plug your numbers in as follows:

$$\$\$ \text{ Recovered} = \text{Actual loss } \times \frac{\text{Amount of insurance}}{\text{Coinsurance \% x FMV property at time of loss}}$$

Actual loss $180,000
Amount of insurance from Owners $150,000
Coinsurance % Owners 80%
FMV at time of loss $250,000

$$\$\$ \text{ Recovered} \quad = \quad \$180,000 \quad \text{x} \quad \frac{\$150,000}{80\% \text{ x } \$250,000}$$

Answer is: c., $135,000

The coinsurance formula is almost always tested. Don't leave home without knowing the concept. Now you know your flash card worked. At the bottom of the card, jot down questions to use to test and review your knowledge. Two weeks from now, go to the referenced page number of your review materials and work the question number listed. The aim is to still remember how to apply the concepts.

LINK THE CONCEPTS TO REAL-LIFE SITUATIONS

Build on what you know. Link what you are learning to your real-life experiences. Once a year you file your individual tax return. Look at the tax form when you study the tax area. Think about the schedules you prepare for the external auditors. These schedules are what the auditors audit and what they include in their documentation as audit evidence. You are a professional, so think professionally. Just because you are now studying for the CPA exam doesn't mean you should forget about what you have learned. CPA candidates tend to regress to the old college model where they study massive amounts of information over a short time period, using only the information from class notes and textbooks. Now you are a professional. The CPA exam is a professional exam. Use what you have learned from real-world experience to help you visualize and recall information. Linkage allows you to digest the information in bite-size chunks. Build examples using your real-life experience.

USE MNEMONICS WITH CAUTION

Mnemonics is the use of letters to form a word that you will use later to recall concepts. For example, a common mnemonic to remember the five components of the internal control process is "MARIE." The memory device works like this:

M: **M**onitoring the internal control process
A: Control **A**ctivities
R: The entity's **R**isk assessment
I: **I**nformation and Communication system
E: Control **E**nvironment

One letter corresponds to one of the five internal control components. Mnemonics is helpful when you are first learning information. But you must realize its limitations. All you have learned is the list. Today's CPA exam no longer asks candidates to prepare lists. Today's CPA exam expects candidates to be able to analyze and react to information. It would be terrible if all you could remember was "MARIE" and you couldn't recall what the mnemonic meant or how it was used. Employ mnemonics with caution.

DRAW AN EXAMPLE

Graphs, pictures, diagrams, and charts assist you in analyzing the information. Timelines are useful visuals to map out what is happening when. Graph what happens to the carrying value of the asset over time or what happens to the depreciation in the early years. Pictures help you remember; a complicated AUDIT topic such as control and detection risk can be diagrammed and easily analyzed for effects. Exhibit 12.3 diagrams the audit risk model.

Exhibit 12.3:   Example of an audit risk diagram when control risk increases

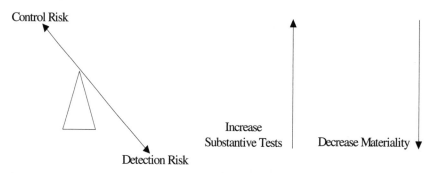

Control Risk

Increase
Substantive Tests

Decrease Materiality

Detection Risk

Exhibit 12.3 reminds you that whenever control risk increases, detection risk decreases. When detection risk decreases, substantive tests must increase and materiality must decrease. A picture is easier to remember than words. The opposite occurs when control risk decreases. Look at the triangle in the middle of Exhibit 12.4. It represents a seesaw—when one end goes up the other must go down. If control risk goes down (decreases), then detection risk would go up (increase). Now substantive testing would be decreased and materiality would be increased. Now all items are opposite. It takes many words to remember all of this, but one small diagram shows it all.

Exhibit 12.4: Example of an audit risk diagram when control risk decreases

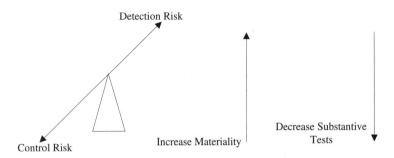

Detection Risk

Control Risk

Increase Materiality

Decrease Substantive Tests

BOND WITH A STUDY BUDDY

Try studying with a coworker, college friend, or review course acquaintance. A study buddy can help you stick to your study plan. A study buddy works, however, **only** if you study. When you meet your buddy at the library only to spend the evening gabbing about the latest office gossip, the strategy is not working for you. Here's how a study buddy situation works.

- Meet at a quiet place where you can each study on your own and later convene to discuss topics out loud. Library meeting rooms, your office at night or weekends, or a bookstore café are good places.
- Make a pledge to each other to be on time for the arranged study sessions. This gives you an excuse to leave your home and go study.
- Decide on a subtopic to study. If tonight's session is managerial accounting, bring the relevant materials with you.
- Determine the subtopics to study. Divide the topics into thirty-minute time chunks.
- Go off and study the assigned topics individually.
- Reconvene at the established time. Work questions in your review materials one at a time. Go over the answers together. Assist each other to figure out and research answers to tough questions.
- Periodically test each other by selecting a few questions for your buddy to complete. Exchange questions, go off to a quiet corner, and spend the correct amount of time preparing an answer. Grade each other's answers. Discuss the AICPA unofficial answer compared to your buddy's answer.
- Take a few minutes to complain about how difficult this exam is. Moan and groan about its breadth, depth, and difficulty. Go ahead; get it off your chest. It is far better to complain to your study buddy

than it is to complain to your family, friends, and coworkers. Your study buddy really knows how you feel.

• Before you leave, agree on the meeting time, place, and subject matter of the next study session. Tell your study buddy that you believe in him or her. Reinforce the idea that this exam is passable.

Study partners help to keep you on schedule, motivated, and encouraged. Two heads can solve a problem quicker than one. Dump your study buddy if he or she doesn't keep the schedule, isn't supportive, isn't serious, or won't share information that helps you. Don't continue a relationship with a lazy person. The exchange of information should be rich and equal. Limit the number of people in your study group to three. Any more and you will need schedules just to keep track of the study group. Keep your study process simple.

REVIEW OF STUDY STRATEGIES

What do all of these above study techniques have in common? They give you the opportunity to study at a minute's notice. Your study materials are handy. They encourage you to study using small amounts of time to improve your long-term memory. They eliminate the guilt of not studying by allowing you to use every free moment to get something done. Consider using all of the described strategies. The variety will help keep you interested in the study process. Too many candidates think of studying as something to do when they want to punish themselves. Tell yourself that studying is fun. It can be if you change the methods used frequently. Studying is also rewarding. When you find you actually know answers, you will be so excited. Understand that all of the sacrifices and the time spent studying pay off. To give this exam your best, you must utilize every spare moment of time. There is much to learn—get excited about it!

TAKE THE TIME TO SLEEP

You can't study, read, write, or retain information when you are tired. Sleep is important throughout the study and exam process. If you find yourself waking up in the middle of the night with exam anxiety, simply switch on your night-light, grab the study sheets that are conveniently sitting on your nightstand, and study yourself to sleep. The best cure for insomnia is reading CPA materials. They will put you to sleep more quickly than anything sold on the market today.

TRY KEEPING IT QUIET

You like noise. You study in the middle of the family room while the television is blaring, your teenagers or roommates are talking on the phone, and the dog is barking. Try studying in a quiet place. Studies show you will learn the information more quickly and retain it longer. There won't be much background noise at the Prometric test center. It's a good idea to get used to a similar environment now. Try to simulate the actual test atmosphere.

JUST KEEP GOING

Don't give up. Expect ups and downs in the study process. You may think the road to the CPA exam is linear. In actuality, it is full of bumps, hurdles, and ups and downs. The quickest method to dig out of a rut is to sit down and study. Stop feeling sorry for yourself. Don't tackle the difficult areas if you are down. Select an area that you enjoyed studying while in college. Begin with an easy, fun area. The minute you get back to your original plan, your guilt and fear will go away. Squelch your fears with action. Hard work and determination will help you feel better. Look at Exhibit 12.5 and admit that your preparation is going to be up and down. Recognize that after every downturn there also can be an upswing.

Exhibit 12.5: The journey to prepare to pass the CPA Exam

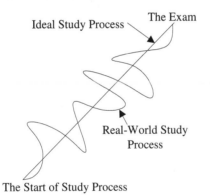

In the exhibit, the squiggly line represents your performance. The straight line shows how the ideal world would prepare for the exam. Exam preparation just isn't a linear process. It is like a golf game. You see the hole and you attempt to drive the ball. The best plan would be to drive the ball straight to the hole, yet your game plan seldom turns out like that. Eventually you get to the green and putt in for the finish. Your journey was anything but straight. The ups and downs you experience are part of the game. Accept the hooks, sand traps, water holes, hurdles, and the rough, but never give up the game or the plan. Keep on trying. Your hard work will be rewarded at the finish line.

PERSONALLY SPEAKING

My biggest challenge is to motivate CPA candidates to never give up. Accountants are a unique group of people. We are dynamic, fun-loving, and extremely detailed. We can absorb great amounts of technical information, and numbers have never bothered us. We are anything but bean counters. We are often overly critical of ourselves. It's time to give ourselves a break. Understand the problems you might encounter. Accept the ups and downs. Talk to yourself. Listen to the CD recording that accompanies this volume. Perfection is not your goal. You only want to learn enough to pass. A score of 75 on each exam section allows some room for mistakes, misunder-standings, and misapplication of concepts. You only have two choices. You can give up now, and you will never be a CPA or you can continue to work toward the dream of accomplishing your goal. The choice is yours. Keep the dream alive—continue to study.

CPA EXAM TIP:
To help you remember important informa-tion, tape the examples to your bathroom mirror. Each day, review the information as you brush your teeth. Don't waste a minute of time.

13 COPING WITH FAMILY, FRIENDS, AND COWORKERS

Studies have attempted to prove that successful people succeed only when they receive a great deal of support from the people around them. Although this may be true, it can be dangerous to expect total support throughout your CPA exam preparations. If you begin the exam preparation process with the expectation of receiving little or no support, you will be pleasantly surprised and appreciative when someone does something nice for you. If you expect everyone around you to continually bolster your spirits, you will live in a constant state of disappointment, spending more time unhappy and focusing on the reasons why no one seems to care about your journey to become a CPA. You begin to wonder why no one understands that you are preparing for the longest and most difficult examination of your life. Get a grip—this is **your** goal, not their goal. Likewise, when you successfully complete all four exam sections, this will be your achievement, not theirs. Communication is the most important component of any relationship. Begin by communicating with those involved.

FAMILY

There is no one like family. They can make you feel as if you are the most important person in the world. Then again, they can make you feel lower than you have ever felt before. No one is any better at laying on the guilt than family. Family situations tend to run in extremes—loyal and supportive today, aloof and uncaring another day. Are they really acting aloof and uncaring, or is it just your perception of their actions? When people are stressed, they tend to overstate the situation. Whenever you feel your family is not providing the necessary support you require, stop and ask yourself, "Is it them or is it me?" Have you communicated with them lately? Have you asked for support? Spend some time explaining what passing the CPA exam means to you and what it could mean to them. A CPA earns more money and can count on greater job stability.

Perhaps you are just so stressed out that no level of support would please you at this time. If that is the case, take a break from studying and from your family. It's time to take a walk, jog, or drive somewhere, but by all means, take some time to be alone and to relax. Think about what your family is going through. They feel your stress and they want to support you. Your family may seem to be acting distant, but their aloofness may just be the result of leaving you alone so that you can accomplish your goals. Stay calm and do not overreact. Give yourself a day to cool off and to allow your family members to realize that you need them. If by tomorrow things don't look better to you, call a family meeting and ask what **you can do** to improve the quality of your family life. Don't blame them for your problems and stress. If they ask you to give up on becoming a CPA, explain to them how achieving the CPA designation will most likely make life better for everyone in the family. Remind them that the study process doesn't last forever. Let them know of your plans to complete all four sections within eighteen months. They will give you more space and time to study if they know there is a time frame within which you must pass all four parts. Try to schedule a break in between exam sections, so you can plan an event where you and your family can be together without the stress of the exam hanging over your head. A day trip to the zoo, an outing to a movie or play, or even a picnic in the park could serve as a reminder that you do indeed love them and want to spend time with them. Your family cares; they just need a gentle reminder of the intensity of your goal. Try to keep family matters as calm and uneventful as possible. How can you do this? At least one family crisis is bound to happen during your exam preparation.

When a crisis or problem arises, keep it in perspective. You did not create the problem just because you are preparing for the CPA exam. Things just happen. Avoid the guilt trip and by all means avoid pointing fingers and placing blame on yourself or others. It is a waste of your time to think or say: "You know I don't need this. I am too busy and I have to study for the CPA exam. Why did this have to happen now?" A family crisis is not the time for you to be self-centered. Focus your attention on dealing with the aspects of the situation that you can control. If you can't control or change anything, then realize you must accept what has happened and move on.

Give troublesome situations some time. Things may look very bleak today, but the next day may be beautiful. You are very fortunate to be part of a family, however large or small. Don't begrudge family members your support. Give your family some time where the words "CPA" or "exam" are not mentioned. They need a break from the stress and pressure too. The type of person who strives to become a CPA is often a family member who is looked up to and depended on. Be thankful that you've earned such a high level of respect from your siblings and parents. Do what you can to help with the family situation, then revert back to your focused study plan.

Resist the urge to reschedule an exam section. Just because you can sit for the exam one section at a time and rescheduling an exam section is fairly easy and inexpensive to do (around $35), don't take this option lightly. If you have already passed a section, the eighteen-month time clock has begun ticking. Remember, candidates are allowed to sit for an exam section only once within each testing window. You don't have an unlimited amount of time to pass. Consider asking relatives for assistance. You may find that they are very happy to take over for you—they just don't know what you need until you ask. Stress or no stress, you must continue to study. Lack of study will stress you out more. Whatever crisis you encounter, continue with your studies.

Establish a structured study plan and communicate the plan to your family and friends. Include family time in the plan. Most family members will endure the process better when they know a certain amount of time will be set aside for them. Even if the time is only four hours per week, it is their personal time with you. Now be careful—you must stick to the plan and you must make your family the central focus during their established time. Make the promise of time and keep it.

When it's time to enjoy family and friends, do just that—enjoy them. You should clear your mind periodically. Plan activities that will get you away from your study environment and help you rejuvenate. Who needs reminders of the hard work ahead? Plan a candlelight dinner at home. Don't worry about the food—carryout food, gourmet food, or hot dogs and boxed macaroni and cheese, the candlelight will make you all focus on each other. When it's family time, make it worthwhile. Simple gestures can make a big impact by creating a great moment. Laughter is a fabulous stress reliever. Find a funny movie, play games that make you laugh, or read a funny book.

Keep in mind that your family and friends are feeling the stress, too. During your scheduled family time, allow your family and friends to choose the fun activity. It is time for them to control the plan. A change of pace will provide you with a fresh outlook. Let those around you know that you realize that they are making sacrifices to help you achieve your goal. Be grateful for any support you receive. A simple thank-you will mean much to those who have assisted you.

Be honest to yourself and to your family. If family members are taking on additional tasks to give you time to study, then you had better be studying and making sacrifices, too. When you decided to become a CPA, did you give up the weekly bowling or golf outing? Are you pretending to work on CPA preparation software when what you are really doing is playing games on the computer? Are you really studying, or are you surfing the Net? Yes, you do need time to relax, but are you taking too much relaxation time for yourself? Every week take the time to reflect on what you did right, on what kept you studying. Also reflect on what you did wrong, what kept you from meeting your goals. Stick with the techniques that helped to keep you focused; change the incorrect, unproductive behavior. Learn from your mistakes.

When it is time to study, involve family and friends in the process. They can quiz you using index or note cards. They can read materials to you while you drive. Their involvement will give them a greater understanding of the depth and breadth of the material that you must learn. After a few hours of studying with you, they will become much more supportive because they will quickly see the difficulty of mastering so much technical material. There is never an ideal time to sit for a CPA exam section. There will always be distractions, crises, and family misunderstandings. It will always seem as if you don't have enough time. Manage your time to the fullest and stick to your study plan.

FRIENDS

Friends can hurt you or help you. Allow friends to give you support. When dealing with your friends becomes more draining than fun, think about changing friends. A friend is someone who helps and understands. A friend should never keep you from meeting your goals.

Friends are the great distracters. You choose your friends because you enjoy being with them. The real struggle is to set your priorities and stick to them. If your friends have never experienced something as all-encompassing as preparing for the CPA exam, they really won't understand what you are going through. Tell them you need their help to keep you focused. It is no exaggeration that studying for the CPA exam probably will take more time than you have. Yes, friends can help by quizzing you, but this may end up in a fun outing instead of an afternoon of study. It is easy to become distracted, so during your crunch times, avoid frequent meetings with friends. Make sure your friends understand just how difficult it is to pass the CPA exam. Show them the statistics: The first-time passing percentage for each section is between 25% and 32%. Over two-thirds of the candidates fail each section.

Schedule get-togethers in advance. Avoid spontaneous invitations. Looking forward to spending time with your friends can serve as an incentive to you to accomplish your goals. Be realistic—you will not have a great deal of time to devote to your friends. Good friends will understand and will admire your dedication.

Communicate more through e-mail. However, when you are busy studying, don't take the time to open your e-mail. Avoid phone conversations since they can easily eat up valuable time and often lead to spur-of-the moment plans to go have some fun. Why spend time in your car talking on the phone when you could be listening to CPA review recordings? Establish a set time each day to answer e-mails from friends. Don't exceed the set time. Use some of your scheduled open time to return phone calls to friends. Again, use only the established amount of time. Build time into your study plan for family and friends with the understanding that such time frames must be controlled.

Don't let the exam preparation process get you down. Studying for each exam section involves sacrifice, but the process does not continue forever. Limit your fun time now and enjoy your new status as a CPA later. Ask your friends for support to help you concentrate on the task at hand. Good friends will be there for you.

COWORKERS

Should you tell your boss that you are studying to pass the CPA exam? It depends. Look around—are most of your superiors CPAs? If the answer is yes, your boss is more likely to support you in your endeavors. If the answer is no, you might want to keep your exam preparation a secret for the time being. In most cases, your colleagues will eventually figure out that you plan to sit for the exam. Although you can schedule exam times for evenings and weekends, coworkers often know more about you than you think. Why be so secretive about your plans?

Your boss is a human being and could become intimidated by your plans. Your boss's greatest fear may be that you are learning more than he or she is. To retaliate, your boss may consciously or subconsciously assign you more overtime tasks, overlook you for a promotion, and just plain make your life tough. Frustration and negative feelings are not going to help you.

Assess the situation and ask yourself if your boss could be threatened by your exam preparation. This usually occurs when the boss is not a CPA. In this case, delay your announcement as long as you can be assured of getting the personal time that you need to complete your plans. Do not lie to your boss. Don't tell you boss that you are not studying to pass the CPA exam if you are. CPAs maintain a high level of integrity and should not bend the truth. Be up-front and honest if your colleagues confront you. You have made the commitment to bettering your future, and you plan to achieve your goals. Power rests in the ability to control the situation. You don't have to act like your boss or coworkers. Don't mimic their bad behavior. Rise above the petty jealousies, the stupid misunderstandings, and the misplaced trust. You are going to become a CPA by sticking to your plan of study.

FRIENDLY ADVICE CAN HURT YOU

So friends or coworkers are CPAs. They eagerly advise you about how they studied to pass the exam. Should you listen? Usually the answer is no. The CPA exam continues to change, and the changes are not always as obvious as the big change from a pencil-based exam to a computer-based exam. For example, in 2004, when the computer-based exam launched, the Business Environment and Concepts (BEC) section did not contain any simulations. The AICPA plans to add simulations to this section sometime in 2005. Question format changes are not the only expected change. Content changes occur six months after a technical pronouncement has been implemented. The exam utilizes a large database of questions. The communication components that a friend or colleague encountered may not be what you will see.

Advice about recent review courses and materials may be relevant. However, before you commit, take the time to check out such recommendations personally. Your particular learning style affects how you learn. What works for one person might not work for you. For a comprehensive update of exam changes, consult the Wiley Web site www.wiley.com/cpa at least once every three months.

Your friends are different from you. Each of us is an individual, and as such, each person should individually design and stick to his or her own study plan. In other words, tailor your study plans to fit you by helping you to correct your weaknesses. We all come from different backgrounds and have experienced a variety of learning models. You must tailor your preparation process to what works best for you. It takes a personalized study plan to be successful.

STICK TO YOUR PLAN

You spent time developing your study plan, and you are well aware that the more closely you follow the plan, the better chance you have of successfully completing each exam section as planned. Desire alone will not lead to achievement. Will your exam scores be determined by how many sporting events or movies you attended this year, or by how much time you spent preparing for the exam? You know the answer. You know what you must do. Remain committed to your plan of attack. Study and learn the concepts. Practice what you have learned.

If your boss is driving you crazy, all the more reason to stick to your plan. Passing the exam will give you greater job mobility. Spending time complaining about your boss to your family and friends isn't productive. Use that time to study and learn exam concepts. Pass the exam and improve your situation. Do something about the things that you can control. Ignore what you cannot control.

PERSONALLY SPEAKING

If you look for a distraction, you will find one. Let's say that you have a problem gambling or spending too much money shopping. If you avoid visiting casinos or shopping malls, you won't have the opportunity to spend money. The same situation applies to family, friends, and coworkers. If you allow them to distract you, they will.

My family is generally very supportive. I have noticed, however, that when I spend too much time requesting or demanding support, they become turned off by my attitude. Most people want to help you because it is their idea, not yours. Let them help out but remember to say thank you and to tell them how much you have been able to achieve because of them. In any situation, humility will serve you well. Who likes a braggart or a big shot? I have achieved much in my life, and you will, too. We could not have accomplished what we have without the help and support of those around us. Being humble and thankful does not mean you have turned into a meek weakling. No, you have matured to the level of understanding that most people never reach. You are confident in your abilities. You understand that the assistance from others has benefited you greatly. You alone are just that—lonely. You need the people around you, and it is wise to show appreciation.

I am bothered when CPA review candidates drive to class, walk in the door, pick up the lecture materials, and leave before class even begins. Why pay for expert lecture assistance when you don't plan to use it? Think about what you are doing before you make your decision to leave class. One evening I overheard a CPA candidate tell her friend that she had to leave class early because she had to watch her team play in the World Series. Since when is baseball tested on a CPA exam section? Her reasoning was that she thought her team would lose the game, and she wanted to see the last game of the year. Think about what she was doing—her priority was watching a baseball team lose. It had nothing to do with her goal of passing a CPA exam section. When the exam results are released, is she going to think about her losing team, or will she focus on why she didn't pass that particular exam section? Ten years from now, is anyone going to remember that World Series game? Ten years from now, are you going to be earning more, working less, and receiving greater respect because you are a CPA? In the scheme of life, passing the CPA exam will have much more of an impact on your life than watching a baseball game. She was so close to avoiding the distraction—she had come to class. She was in the right place to learn. Think about the consequences of your actions. Think about what you are doing before you make your decision. Will your choice hurt you or help you?

I have assisted thousands of CPA candidates over the last fifteen years. Do you know who my CPA heroes are? My heroes are the people who have worked and worked to pass the exam—the people who took an exam section more than once before they passed. I fondly remember the candidate who attempted the exam a total of fourteen times. He had received approval to sit for the exam based on economics and finance courses with only a few lower-level accounting classes. He was taking the exam without having learned the material. Imagine taking a CPA review course to learn the material for the very first time. A CPA review should primarily be a review, not new learning. At first I thought he was lazy and was not taking time to study. Then I realized the real problem: He was learning the material for the first time. I remember his brother coming to a review session to ask how he might assist his sibling in the study process. His parents promised him an international trip when he passed. Despite the number of attempts, this candidate finally did pass all four sections. He turned all of his previous failures into one great big success named "CPA." Today he is a successful CPA with a great deal of confidence. I am sure that if his family had given up on him, he, too, would have thrown in the towel. His family was there for him in a very positive way. In my mind, he will always be a CPA hero. He made a plan and stuck to it.

I recall another candidate who has taken the exam too many times to mention. When he calls or e-mails to discuss the exam, I ask myself: What can I say to help him understand that he must make the commitment? He always allows himself to become distracted somewhere during the study process. His excuses range from the birth of a child, an irrational boss, and a sick wife, to just not having enough time to study. After nine years of attempting to pass the exam, his business is suffering because he has not become a CPA. He has lost large clients because he cannot perform attest work for them without a CPA license. Don't misunderstand me; he is one of the nicest men in the world, but he will not pass an exam section until he focuses on the task of practicing and studying. Several candidates have encountered stumbling blocks and still survive. There has never been a totally calm time in my life, and I would guess that you probably could say the same thing. Commitment is personal. His commitment to passing the exam is just not there.

A CPA candidate in her mid-forties approached me one evening during the class break. She looked drawn and pale, a look not unique to a person undergoing the exam preparation process. She was seeking advice—the following week her mother was being admitted to a nursing home. The family could no longer care for the mother at home because her Alzheimer's disease was advancing and most of the time she was not aware of her actions. The CPA candidate was feeling a great deal of guilt, not only about studying for the exam, but also about moving her mom to a home. She said she would miss class the entire next week to help her brothers and sisters admit her mother. Upon further inquiry, I found out the candidate had five siblings, and all five were going to be there to admit the mother. I asked a simple question: "Will your mother know if you are there?" The candidate quickly replied no because her mother got very disorientated when she was with more than one person at a time. I suggested that the CPA candidate attend class this week and visit her mother the following week after she had time to settle into her new surroundings. Her mother probably would appreciate a visit at a later time, and then perhaps she would have a good day and be able to communicate with her.

That special CPA candidate came to class for the rest of the sessions. She fought hard to concentrate, visited her mother at a later date, and went on to pass the CPA exam. Her courage and determination serve as reminders that it is up to you to assess and control the situation to the best of your ability. At first, the CPA candidate's siblings were unhappy with her decision to complete the CPA review. Later, when she was the only person who could visit the mother during the day, they realized that their sister had made a great decision that allowed her to contribute to the family at another time, in another way.

Stick to your study plan and believe in yourself, because in the end, it will be you who can change things. You will be far less stressed by doing what you ought to do to achieve your goal. You will have no reason to feel guilty if you do what is right. That student kept studying and visited her mother at times that were different from what her family thought she should do. She did not act selfishly or badly. She acted responsibly. She achieved her goal of becoming a CPA and was a good daughter all at the same time.

The decision is yours: Remain committed and pass, or make excuses for not studying and lose sight of your goal. Family and friends are gifts. Friendship is a special gift that allows us glimpses of our best selves. Practice how to recognize and nurture your best self. Ask for help to meet your goal. It's easier to become a CPA with the assistance of your family, friends, and coworkers. Treasure the support you receive to reach your goal.

CPA EXAM TIP:
Passing the exam is your goal. Don't expect your family, friends, and coworkers to support you 100%. Treasure the support you receive. Don't be a complainer—complaining won't help you learn.

14 REVISING YOUR PERSONAL STUDY PLAN

Why include a chapter on revising a plan that was well planned and completely scheduled several weeks ago? It is human nature to procrastinate and put off doing things that one just may not enjoy. Who enjoys sacrificing fun times with family and friends? After about three to four weeks of study, many CPA candidates will realize that their exam section is booked for a few weeks away and that they have not yet accomplished what they thought they would. This chapter helps CPA candidates revise their personal study plan to adjust for a loss of time.

HOW DID THE TIME FLY BY?

Time waits for no one and keeps on marching whether you are ready or not. People lose track of time for many reasons. They may have procrastinated (the most common problem), or they may have experienced a family crisis, such as an illness. It is not frivolous to assume that people will need to adjust their study plans at least once before their scheduled exam section. Life is complicated, and time flies by. Accept the fact that you have to adjust your plans, and don't waste time lamenting about lost time. Once you reflect on your current situation, you can begin to make a new study plan.

REFLECTING UPON YOUR CURRENT SITUATION

Where are you now? You might be working many hours of overtime. Maybe you just recovered from an illness. Begin by asking yourself if the things that caused you to postpone your studies have been resolved. If you were completing a college class, and the class is now over, you will have much more time to study. Accept the fact that circumstances have caused you to fall behind. Take action to adjust the current situation.

Increase your study time from twenty-one hours per week to thirty hours per week. If you cannot control the problem that caused you to fall behind in your studies, perhaps it is time to admit that maybe you should wait to sit until the next testing window. However, when you are evaluating your current situation, be honest and be very critical of yourself. For example, don't kid yourself into believing that a few hours of overtime per week caused you to fall behind by several weeks. That just shouldn't happen. Admit that you didn't utilize your time wisely. You blew it. Now you must give up every spare minute to study. It's time to make the super sacrifice.

MAKE A SUPER SACRIFICE

A super sacrifice requires you to spend less time eating and sleeping and more time studying. A super sacrifice requires that you give up **everything** that has been fun. Now you must study every day, including Friday and Sunday. You must study in the morning, study during every lunch hour, and study in the evening. You must give up all leisure activities—no time for sports activities, no time for charities, and no time for you.

The super sacrifice may affect you monetarily if you must take time off work to catch up. If you have used your vacation days, consider taking time off without pay. It's too late to fool around. You must use every spare minute of time to learn the material.

ADJUST HOW YOU STUDY—LEARN BY DOING

In the past, you spent about 25% of the time reading material and 75% of the time practicing the concept application. Now there is almost no time to read. Adjust your study time to 10% reading the material and 90% working CPA exam questions. By spending 90% of the time practicing questions, you are combining learning with doing. You must learn by your mistakes. For example, by completing the next Financial Accounting and Reporting (FAR) multiple-choice question about derivatives, you can learn what a derivative is.

> Derivatives are financial instruments that derive their value from changes in a benchmark based on any of the following except
>
> - Stock prices
> - Mortgage and currency rates
> - Commodity prices
> - Discounts on accounts receivable

You did not take the time to read the material. What knowledge can you gain by studying this question? You read the answer explanation and see that the fourth choice was the correct answer. Here's what you have learned.

- Derivatives are financial instruments.
- Derivatives derive their value from changes in a benchmark.
- Typical benchmarks used are stock prices, mortgage rates, currency rates, and commodity prices.

Since the fourth response was the answer, it means that discounts on accounts receivable are not acceptable benchmarks for deriving the derivative value. If you have time, you would prepare an index card for these concepts.

You move on and attempt to complete the next question.

> Which of the following is not an **underlying**, according to SFAS 133, the derivatives accounting standard?

- A credit rating
- An interest rate index
- A security price
- All of the above could be underlyings

This is a confusing question, as you hardly know what a derivative is, let alone what an **underlying** is. That's okay. Move on to the answer explanation, where you read this.

The fourth answer option is correct, since the basic definition of an underlying, according to SFAS 133, is any financial or physical variable that has either observable changes or objectively verifiable changes.

Prepare an index card by writing out the definition of an underlying. Then list examples of an underlying as a credit rating, an interest rate index, and a security price. Think about the three examples. What do they all have in common? They all change, hence the observable changes, and they are all objective changes that are easy to verify.

If you had taken time to read all about derivatives, it is doubtful that you would remember much from your reading. By attempting to answer the question, you are thinking about the concept, reading the concept, and then reinforcing the concept by writing out the index card. Later, as you travel to work or to the mall, take the time to review the index card. You are learning by doing rather than reading. Taking action and doing serves as a powerful learning method. Chances are you won't quickly forget the concepts that you have read, written, and practiced.

Let's try one more derivative question.

Which of the following is **not** a distinguishing characteristic of a derivative instrument?

- Terms that require or permit net settlement
- Instrument that must be "highly effective" throughout its life
- No initial net investment
- One or more underlyings and notional amounts

Who knows what the answer might be? When you read the answer explanation, you see the answer is the second response. The answer explanation goes on to say that as specified in SFAS 133, derivative instruments contain

1. One or more underlyings and one or more notional amounts
2. No initial net investment or smaller net investment than required for contracts with an expected similar response to market changes
3. Terms that require or permit net settlement, by means outside the contract, and delivery of an asset that is substantially the same as net settlement

SFAS 133 makes no mention of the fact that an instrument must be "highly effective." The important concept to learn from this question is that derivative instruments contain the three factors just listed. Again, prepare an index card. Write it out. Learn by doing.

When time is running out, you must become an efficient and effective learner. You must learn by doing rather than by reading. You should also remain calm.

REMAIN CALM

Tell yourself that if you panic and begin to doubt yourself, you will not learn anything. Anxiety and fear do not motivate. They cause you to become distracted and lose focus. With little time left to study, you must use every minute of spare time to absorb a concept. Don't fret about what you don't know. Continue with your work, conscious that you must learn everything you can in the time that is left. Proceed to learn as much as you can in the time that is left. Attempt to learn something about everything.

LEARN SOMETHING ABOUT EVERYTHING

Even though time is passing, allocate time in your study plan to study all of your weak areas. Forget about mastering the material; perfection is not a requirement to pass the exam. Correct those weaknesses you can, and forget about what you are having difficulty learning. If you believe you are weak in a major area, such as corporate taxation, take some time to try to learn something about the topic. Learn enough to be dangerous, to answer some questions, and to make educated guesses on other questions. Use your study time wisely.

USE YOUR STUDY TIME WISELY

Go back to Chapter 11, Developing Your Personal Study Plan. Study your daily schedule. Yes, you will find time by sacrificing your fun. It's not only about finding more study time. What's important is to use all of your study time wisely. Count the number of days remaining to your exam date. Count the number of modules or units that you must complete. Prepare a brand-new study schedule using the remaining time. This is it: the study schedule that you now must adhere to. You must stick to this new study plan, and you must study more efficiently.

Quickly review the areas you know. Work questions, learn from the questions, and move on. Vary the topics that you study. When you are fresh and alert, study the difficult material. As you tire, shift to your strong areas. When you find your mind wandering, take a short break by walking around the house and reading lists, definitions, or formulas out loud. Get your blood flowing by walking, but don't waste the time. Leave no time for pleasure—study as you walk, work questions until you fall asleep, and always do more than you think you can. When you are tired, give in and get some sleep.

IMPORTANCE OF SLEEP

Overwhelmed, frustrated, anxious CPA candidates often sacrifice sleep for study time. Giving up sleep for study can be dangerous. The more tired you become, the grumpier and the more anxious you become. To absorb technical material, candidates must have adequate sleep. Your body needs sleep, so don't deprive yourself. The less sleep you get, the duller your brain becomes. Keep your brain sharp—get a good night's sleep!

CONTINUE TO BELIEVE

Even though time is short, you still can absorb more concepts, formulas, and knowledge. Continue to believe that you have the ability to learn more and continue to believe that you can pass the CPA exam. Don't ever lose sight of the end goal. You **can** pass the CPA exam. You **will** pass the CPA exam. Stay in the game for the fight. You will never know if you can pass until you try. When you try, you will want to give it your all and do the very best that you can under the circumstances. Keep on studying, using every available minute of the day. Go for an overall knowledge of each area tested. Remember, overall knowledge is not perfect knowledge. Go easy on yourself—study what you can to correct as many weaknesses as you can. You will run out of time. You will not be perfect. These are just facts of life. However, these facts do not alter your chances of passing. You can and will pass long before you have perfected each and every formula, definition, and theory. You will pass by doing your best with the knowledge that you possess. It can be scary if you let it be. Fight the urge to give up your goal of becoming a CPA. Preparing for the exam is not easy. There will be challenges. Continue to believe that you can pass each and every exam section one section at a time. Continue to prepare to the best of your ability.

Personally Speaking

I always fall behind schedule, even when it's something simple and fun like packing for vacation or preparing for a party. Why does this happen? For most accountants, it happens because of several reasons. Our jobs are demanding and often require overtime. We are perfectionists who spend too much time in the beginning of any project just making sure everything is perfect. Then, as time goes on, we run out of preparation time. It's bound to happen. Realize that this is normal. Accept the fact that you'll probably need to adjust your study schedule more than once. Don't waste time worrying or attempting to place blame. Adjust and learn by doing.

Should you consider the option of rescheduling your exam section? I suggest that you think long and hard before you decide to reschedule. Most accountants are much better prepared than they think. Don't work toward perfection. Sooner or later you **must** take the exam. The longer you postpone a section, the greater the chance is that you will never accomplish your goal. If you have completed a section, the eighteen-month clock is ticking away. You have only eighteen months from the day you sat for the first exam section that you passed to complete all four sections. Remember that you are allowed to sit for a section only once within a testing window. Don't risk the chance that you won't have time to pass all four sections within the eighteen-month time frame.

To utilize the learn-by-doing technique, your review materials must contain detailed answer explanations. The right answer must be listed along with an explanation as to why the other answers are incorrect. Always check the materials before you purchase them. The more detailed the answer explanation, the better.

I ran out of time to study for both the CPA and the CIA exams. Somehow I managed to pass both exams. I did it because I never gave up. I kept adjusting my study plan to obtain the most knowledge in my weakest areas right up until the first exam day. I kept on studying to learn something new. I kept on reviewing to bring back what I might have forgotten. In the back of my mind, I kept telling myself that I did not know at what knowledge level a person passes the exam. Therefore, I proceeded in confidence, admitting that I wasn't perfect. Yes, I have weak areas. However, I will do the best I can to learn everything I can, and I will perform to the best of my ability on all exam areas. I will do my best because it's all I know how to do.

Exhibit 14.1 uses the letters of the alphabet to create the ABCs of Life. I keep these ABCs in mind when I feel depressed or overwhelmed. The letters and phrases serve as reminders that I am living my life by doing the best I can. I don't make excuses for mistakes. I just always keep trying to do my best.

Exhibit 14.1: The ABCs of Life

To achieve your dreams, remember your ABCs.

*A*void negative people, places, and things.
*B*elieve in yourself.
*C*onsider things from all angles.
*D*on't ever give up and don't give in.
*E*njoy life today; yesterday is gone, and tomorrow may not come.
*F*amily and friends are hidden treasures; seek them and enjoy them.
*G*ive more than you planned to.
*H*ang onto your dreams.
*I*gnore those who try to discourage you.
*J*ust do it, baby.
*K*eep on trying.

*L*ove yourself first and foremost.
*M*ake it happen.
*N*ever lie, cheat, or steal—always strike a fair deal.
*O*pen your eyes and see things as they really are.
*P*ractice makes perfect.
*Q*uitters never win and winners never quit.
*R*ead, study, and learn about everything important in life.
*S*top procrastinating.
*T*ake control of your own destiny.
*U*nderstand yourself in order to better understand others.
*V*isualize it.
*W*ant it more than anything.
*X*celerate yourself.
*Y*ou are a unique creation of God; nothing can replace you.
*Z*ero in on your target and go for it!

SOURCE: Author Unknown; Revised by Ms. Alice Brown, friend of the author.

Revise your plan and then stick to it! You can't allow distractions to affect you. Sooner or later, you must make the study sacrifice. The sooner, the better, as you will be brought closer to your overall goal of passing all four sections within eighteen months. Get going and keep going. There is no time to waste!

CPA EXAM TIP:
Don't make excuses for why you have not met your study goals. Stop talking and get studying!

15 HOW WILL I EVER PASS? PRACTICE MAKES PERFECT!

Feeling overwhelmed? Time is running out, you have much more to study, and you can't recall the material you studied a few weeks ago. Your mind is a jumble. It would be easy to give up. You can't remember the last time that you had some fun without feeling guilty. You are frustrated and miserable. Stop and review your options. Yes, you could give up. Then you would have some free time for a few weeks before you realized you had stopped short of even attempting, let alone achieving, your goal. The second option, keeping up the fight, is still doable. It's time to enter "crisis mode." You can still pass. Take control of the situation. Begin by talking to yourself and continuing to believe.

YES, I STILL BELIEVE I CAN PASS

Although that might sound like you're Peter Pan calling for Tinkerbell, it's not a bad analogy. After all, it seems it would take one small miracle for you to pass. That's what you think. How do you know what it takes to pass? Have you ever been employed to grade the CPA exam? Have you ever taken an exam where you only needed a score of 75 to pass, and probably even a raw score of two to ten percentage points less than that? You don't know anything about the level it takes to achieve a passing score. It's time to stop thinking about what you can't control and get a grip on what you can control. The AICPA controls the grading of the exam, so forget about that. You can control your attitude by remaining positive. Yes, you still can pass the exam, by taking one section at a time. With a positive attitude, you can go on and adjust your study plan to help correct your major weaknesses, forget about everything but studying, and sit for one exam section. Now that your attitude is corrected, move on to adjusting your study plan.

ADJUSTING YOUR STUDY PLAN

Seems like you've done this before. In Chapter 11, Developing Your Personal Study Plan, you prepared a study plan to fit your needs. Then, in Chapter 14, Revising Your Personal Study Plan, you realized that you were no longer on target and you revised the plan. Now it's time to make an adjustment. There is not enough time to revise and apply your plan. It's time to adjust. When you are three to four weeks away from the exam, revising the study plan probably won't help. Adjust the plan to do what you can and forget about what you can't accomplish.

Take some time off work to study. Maybe you are feeling ill. After all, you probably **are** ill from worry and stress about the CPA exam. You could accomplish so much in just one to two days of uninterrupted study. Use some vacation time. Find extra time somewhere, somehow. Sit down with your support group and explain to them that it's crunch time. Ask for their patience in bearing with you. There are only a few days or weeks left. Give up the fun. Stay home on weekends and study; stay in on your lunch hour and study while you eat. Study all of the time.

What should you study? Adjust your study plan by analyzing the areas of greatest concern. In other words, what haven't you studied, and how much is it tested on the CPA exam? Let's say you have not even opened a review manual to study governmental and not-for-profit accounting. Assess its importance; it's twenty points of the Financial Accounting and Reporting (FAR) section. Is the area important? Yes, twenty points are important. If you scored a perfect score on the intermediate and advanced financial accounting areas, you would earn eighty points, and you could kiss your worries about government and nonprofit entities away. The chances of scoring perfectly on topics as diverse and detailed as those areas are about like the chances of winning the lottery when the pot is over $100 million. Yes, governmental and not-for-profit accounting is important. You must do something about it.

First, assess your entry-level knowledge. Do you know anything about governmental accounting? If the answer is yes, then you don't have to spend as much time on the topic as you would if you didn't know anything. Keep in mind the requirement to pass—a candidate must know something about everything. A candidate does not need to master everything. Go for the points you can learn without using all of your remaining time on one topic. Using your review manual, go to the governmental chapter(s) or module(s), and spend a short time reading. Important areas would be the five governmental funds, the two proprietary funds, and the two main types of fiduciary funds. The overall funds represent the big picture. It is also necessary to know the names of the financial statements prepared for each fund type. Candidates must possess a general knowledge of the types of information included and the names of the financial statements. After you have briefly reviewed the broad overview, go to the multiple-choice questions to learn the details. Try to answer the questions. Expect your answers to be wrong. That's okay—you will learn from the answer explanations. In fact, some professors say that candidates remember the questions they missed better than the questions they answered correctly. When you get a question wrong, you actually take some time to think about it.

For a demonstration of how to learn from an answer explanation to a question, consider the following question.

QUESTION:

Which of the following is correct regarding the Budgetary Comparison Schedule required by governmental accounting standards?

I.   The Budgetary Comparison Schedule may be either in the budgetary format or in the format used in the Statement of Revenues, Expenditures, and Changes in Fund Balances.

II.   The Budgetary Comparison Schedule may be presented as a Budgetary Comparison Statement, considered part of the basic financial statements subject to audit.

   a.   I only.
   b.   II only.
   c.   Both I and II.
   d.   Neither I nor II.

Let's say that because you have never taken a full governmental accounting course, your governmental accounting knowledge is very weak. This is true of over 70% of the CPA candidates. So now what? You don't have time to go back to college to take the course, and you don't have a great deal of study time to devote to learning all of the special requirements of governmental accounting. After all, the area is only worth 8 to 12% of the total points tested on the FAR section. What should you do? You should learn from the question answer.

First, try to make a very good guess as to what you think the answer should be. What do I mean by a "very good guess?" A "very good guess" implies that you will make every attempt to reason out the answer based on facts given in the question, based on your current knowledge about the topic, and using common sense. In the preceding question, it is clear that you must know the various methods of presenting a Budgetary Comparison Schedule for a governmental entity. Oh, that's news to you—you just learned after reading this question that a Budgetary Comparison Schedule is **required** for governmental entities. This is one point you might not have known before you read the question. After reading the question carefully, let's say you guessed answer a. Upon checking your answer response, you see that the correct answer is c. Don't be concerned about missing the question. You are simply practicing. You can miss many questions during practice. It's not the real event. Use practice time to learn. Not only have you learned that a Budgetary Comparison Schedule is required for governmental entities, you also have learned that there are three acceptable methods of presenting the schedule:

1.   In a budgetary format
2.   In the format used in the Statement of Revenues, Expenditures, and Changes in Fund Balances
3.   As a Budgetary Comparison Statement, which is part of the basic financial statements that are subject to audit

Have you learned all that you should know about the governmental Budgetary Comparison Schedule? No, there are other points of knowledge, such as the fact that if the budget has been revised, both the original and the revised budget must be presented. There is always more to learn. However, you have used your time wisely—by practicing the questions, attempting to correctly answer the questions, and learning from your mistakes, you have increased your knowledge level. If there's time, you could make note cards listing the points that you just learned. Preparing note cards helps you to focus and to remember the points for a longer period of time. Note cards are also very useful as a review tool just before you sit for the exam. Will you remember what you have learned? If you say, "Yes, I won't forget," then you should not make a note card. However, if you think you will forget, take the time to write out a card to review just before the exam. Of course, if it is two days before the exam, you don't have enough time to prepare a note card, let alone review it. Be confident and believe that you will remember enough of the details when the time arises.

Studying by learning from the answer explanations is called the crisis study mode. You spend less time reading about the topics and more time working questions. Normally, of your total study time, you would spend about 25% reading and 75% of your study time practicing. When you are in crisis mode, spend only about 10% of your study time reading chapter discussions. The 10% reading is just to get a brief overview of the topical area. Then, jump in and go directly to the practice questions to see what you can learn quickly.

The crisis mode of studying is not the ideal, recommended method. However, it has been proven to work as long as candidates do not get frustrated. Keep an open mind and let the concepts sink in. In crisis mode, it is important to remain calm. Learn and remember what you can, and forget about what you can't remember. There is no time to worry about what you don't know. Remain confident that you have learned something and that when it comes time to use the knowledge on the exam, you will do your best. It's all a frame of mind. You still have the power to control the exam because you are conditioned not to allow the things you don't know to get you down. You realize that you don't need to be perfect to pass the CPA exam. You accept the fact that you will be less than perfect. There is room for error.

UNDERSTANDING AND APPLYING THE CRISIS STUDY MODE

The overall goal of the crisis study mode is to do what you can. Correct your major weaknesses by working the questions. You skip the reading and jump to the doing. To use the crisis study mode most effectively, you must not panic. Keep your mind on the task at hand and don't think about what you don't know. Walk into the actual CPA exam as confident as if you had spent years studying and reviewing the material. Tell yourself that you did the best you could. Now you are going to use what you know to answer the questions to the best of your ability.

Liken the crisis study mode to a person who has just won a contest at the grocery store. The winner is given ten minutes to fill a grocery cart with everything he or she can put in the cart. What's your plan?

First, you would analyze the layout of the store. Meat is the most expensive grocery item, so plan to go directly to the meat section. Your family is allergic to turkey, so you plan to avoid that area of the meat department. Produce is also expensive, but it is very perishable. You could freeze the meat for later use, but if you don't eat the produce right away it will spoil, so you skip the produce area. Cereal is also expensive and usually has a long shelf life. However, you know your family only eats certain kinds, so before the event, you scope out the store and note where your favorite cereal is. Notice how you are analyzing the situation as it fits the contest and your individual needs. This is how you make a successful plan when studying in the crisis mode.

Now the time comes for the contest to begin. Do you walk or run down the aisles? You hurry, but you are careful not to run so fast that you might slip. You proceed directly to the meat section, grabbing some expensive items along the way. After all, you want to make the trip worthwhile. You don't look back and worry about the food items you missed. You just keep going to the meat department. When you reach the meat coolers, you use your planned knowledge to get the maximum benefit. You select steaks and other expensive cuts of meat.

In the crisis study mode, study what will benefit you the most. Forget about the knowledge you already have. Study what you don't know, not what you already know. Correct as many weaknesses as you can. Get maximum points from the situation. When it comes time for each exam section, continue to believe that you can succeed. Remain calm and do not panic. Earn points along the way from what you remember of your carefully applied study plan and from your crisis study mode approach. A calm person can apply the knowledge so much more accurately than a frantic person. You wanted steaks because you enjoy the taste, but they are expensive and something you couldn't afford to buy. You corrected the weakness in your budget by throwing steaks in the grocery cart instead of hamburger. You can afford to buy hamburger. You remained calm. Study what you don't know. Fix what you can in the time you have. When the real exam comes around, you will have both hamburger knowledge (knowledge you learned a long time ago) and steak knowledge (your newly acquired knowledge). Believe that you can pass. Use everything you've got to do so.

PRACTICE MAKES PERFECT

Michael Jordan, one of the greatest basketball players ever to play professional basketball, practiced his game until the day he retired. Why is it that a pro like him found it necessary to practice his skills continuously? If you were to ask him, he would tell you he did not want to forget. He would talk about how when he first retired briefly to try baseball, his basketball skills declined. He would also tell you that he wanted to do his very best. He saw basketball as his job, even if it was an enjoyable job; he still found it necessary to practice to remain at the top of his profession. He wanted his moves to be second nature and just happen. Without practice, his body would not have known how to move automatically to respond to a situation. Take a hint from someone who understands the value of practice. Practice your test skills so that you will respond naturally to the questions. Your brain will just do what it needs to do.

Think about how you have learned important skills in your life. How did you learn to ride a bicycle? You didn't spend time reading about it in a book. No, you got on the bicycle and practiced. At first you started out slowly, maybe with special devices to help you, such as training wheels. It wasn't easy. You wobbled, you fell, and you hurt yourself. Wasn't it worth it? In the end, you learned an important skill that gave you freedom as a child. Today, even if you haven't ridden a bicycle in years, you can still get on one and ride. Don't waste time reading about accounting. Spend time working the problems and practicing. Don't spend an inordinate amount of time on concepts that you know. Instead, quickly review these topics, practice a few questions, and don't let the self-doubt creep in. You know it today; you will know it in a few days or a few weeks. You are in crisis mode. Your time is very valuable. Make the most of it. Practice rather than read!

READING VERSUS PRACTICING

Many candidates spend too much time reading about CPA exam topics and too little time working the questions. Be aware of this problem and limit your reading time to no more than 25% of your total study time. If you are taking a CPA review, your reading time may even be cut to 10 to 15% because you're spending time in class hearing and learning the testable concepts. As a result, you should spend less time reading. Studies have shown that reading is one of the least effective techniques for learning. **Working the problems is the most effective study technique.** Do the work and you will remember. The closer you do the work to the exam section date, the less chance you have of forgetting the concept. Beware, though—you can't pull an all-nighter for the CPA exam. You must begin the study and practice process well before your exam test date. Merely reading topics is not nearly enough—it's a dangerous process that often leads to forgetfulness. Again, the most effective study technique is that of **working the problems.** Do the work and you will remember the concepts. Spend time reading and you might remember the concepts, but chances are you will forget what you read quite quickly. With so much material to study and so little time left before your exam testing date, use the most effective technique. Be a Michael Jordan. Be a professional and practice, practice, and practice some more. Practice as much as time allows.

HOW MUCH PRACTICE?

The phrase "Practice makes perfect" is a tease. CPA candidates don't need to obtain a state of perfection. CPA candidates know that they can be less than perfect and still pass the exam. How much time you should practice depends on many factors, such as how much time you have, what you do for work, how long ago you graduated from college, and what you recall from college learning experiences. There is no set length of time to study to ensure that you will pass. The suggestion is simple: Practice every minute that you have to spare. Make practice a priority. Schedule practice into the study schedule. Practice by using bite-size chunks of time. Work questions to assess your ability, and then continue to work questions until you correct as many of your weaknesses as you can. When you arrive at the Prometric test center, don't rush into things. Take a deep breath, manage your time, and control your mind. Avoid making silly mistakes. You are in control even when you must guess at the correct answer selection. After all, you don't need to be perfect to pass—a score of 75 will do just fine.

Don't underestimate the value of learning by practicing. So what if you attempt a question during your studies that you cannot answer? By going to the answer explanation in your study materials, you can learn just what you did wrong. Over the years the exam has changed from one of memorization to a critical thinking, analytical exam. Memorizing old CPA questions will no longer help you. You must know the concepts and understand them well enough to apply them. Practicing will help to crystallize the concept in your brain. It's almost like brainwashing oneself. What you are doing can certainly be said to be washing your brain and cleaning up the concept application by practice. When you practice, you will find out for sure if you really know how to use what you have learned. When in doubt, find out! Go work the questions and find out what you don't know. Work to correct your weaknesses.

PERSONALLY SPEAKING

Yes, the crisis study mode can produce positive results. However, avoid this mode if you can. Using this method takes a lot of guts. You have to be a confident person who won't allow self-doubt to creep in. Many well-prepared candidates fall apart shortly before the first exam section because they lose control of their emotions. Self-doubt creeps in and takes over.

Those people who have used the crisis study mode are more apt to succumb to self-doubt because they know they used an approach that was less than ideal.

I passed the exam without a review course. I basically studied for one week and used my guts to get through, but it wasn't easy. I studied hard in college and learned the material well. I used a reputable set of review manuals, so I had guidance and knew what the big areas were. Because I was working very long hours in public accounting, I just ran out of study time. I had to use the crisis study mode. Frequently that little doubting voice would start to talk to me. I had to say, "Go away, I am doing my best. I believe I can pass." The worst part was controlling the self-doubt at the exam. It's hard to believe that you can pass when you are stumbling over the material and guessing at answers, unsure if you have answered even one question correctly.

I knew that many people had studied more than I did. My best friend from college, then a first-year law student, had self-studied two to three hours a day. The colleague I rode to the exam with had taken a review course and seemed to have studied everything. The first day of the exam, I saw a woman who in college had always outperformed me. Did I have a chance? I believed I could earn at least 75 points, and this would put me over the top. I told myself my friends and acquaintances could earn a higher score than me, but in the end there was room for all of us to pass. When I didn't know something, I first tried my educated guess using what I knew and using my common sense. When in total doubt, I moved on to make an outright guess. I never stopped believing. If it sounds easy, think again. After the first day of testing, I ran back to my hotel room and called my husband. I was crying so hard that he couldn't understand a word I said. I wanted to go home and give up. My husband was very supportive and talked me out of it, reminding me that I had no way of telling how I performed. He encouraged me to keep going so I could learn more about the exam. Then, if I had to go back, at least I would know what I was facing. Boy, did I ever need that advice! I stopped crying and started to review my material for the next day. I kept on fighting.

I passed three out of four sections. I scored 75 points in two sections, getting as close as I could and still passing. Just think: If I had given up, I would have had to start all over. I scored in the 90s in Auditing and At-testation (AUDIT) because I was an auditor and used my practical knowl-edge to write good communication responses. I scored a 68 in Law or what is now known as Business Environment and Concepts (BEC). I knew that by using the crisis mode I was cutting something short. Six months later, I re-turned to pass Law.

Try your best to avoid using the crisis mode. If you find yourself in a position where it means you either give up or use the crisis study mode, you know what to do. Get going, apply the crisis techniques, do the best you can to correct your obvious weaknesses, and enter the test center still believing that you can pass. Solidify your learning by proving what you know and, more important, what you can remember. Practice until you almost become perfect. I believe that you can do it. Now prove to yourself that you can do it!

CPA EXAM TIP:
Don't expect to reach perfection. Being perfect is not a requirement to pass the CPA exam. Work to correct what you can. Continue to believe in yourself.

16 THE ART OF AUDITING AND ATTESTATION

The Auditing and Attestation (AUDIT) section of the CPA exam is the longest and the most subjective exam section. Here the candidate must not only possess a great deal of conceptual knowledge, but also must apply that knowledge to a wide variety of client situations. Of the four exam sections, the AUDIT section tests what is done in practice—the practice of public accounting. Get ready to think for a very long time: four and one-half hours.

AUDIT: THE TIME CHALLENGE

Arrive at the Prometric test center at least thirty minutes before the exam begins. Wow—that means you will be at the test center for over five hours. Such a long time frame makes time management and endurance a challenge. Fight the urge to rush through this exam. Pace yourself and use at least fifty minutes for each of the five testlets. Use all of your allotted time. Why hurry home only to think of a key concept that you could have remembered during the exam if you would have just taken some time to sit back and reflect? Use all of the four and one-half hours of time. Take at least one five-minute break between testlets three and four.

When you utilize the full amount of time, you can say that you really tried to do your best. Leave early, and you may hate yourself when you receive a score of a 73 or 74. You will always wonder if the extra fifteen or thirty minutes would have helped you. You probably could have earned the additional one to two points by spending time proofreading your communication responses. Use the full amount of time to read those tricky multiple-choice questions. Tricky multiple choice?

TRICKY MULTIPLE-CHOICE

Are the AUDIT multiple-choice questions really that tricky? "Tricky" may not be the correct word. Many of the questions are very thought provoking. The AUDIT exam tests real-world experiences, which requires candidates to apply their knowledge rather than just recite knowledge. It's not just rote memorization. Most CPA candidates do not have experience as public accounting firm auditors. At best, a candidate may possess one to two years of experience. Any kind of audit experience helps. Even an internship as an auditor gives a candidate an edge. People with experience can visualize the audit documentation, the client forms and systems, and the report types. If at all possible, postpone taking the AUDIT exam until you gain some real experience in public accounting or in corporate finance. It will help greatly. If you do not work in public accounting, don't despair. Any type of office work will help you to learn systems. If you don't have any work experience, you still can pass this section—it just takes a little more work.

THE KEY TO PASSING AUDIT

Successful completion of the AUDIT section requires candidates to apply knowledge rather than merely repeat knowledge. The AUDIT multiple-choice questions are the most difficult of all four exam sections. The difficulty arises for three reasons.

1. Except for the statistical sampling and the computation of analytical procedure ratios, candidates are not using a formula or algorithm. Candidates are relying on words to answer the question.
2. Many of the AUDIT questions have more than one correct answer. However, examiners ask candidates to identify the "best" answer. Sifting through the answer responses looking for the best answer can be challenging.
3. Several questions require candidates to know the definitions of numerous words and phrases and then to apply these concepts, definitions, and phrases, to real-world situations.

You can do nothing to address the difficulties caused by reason 1. Most of the AUDIT questions are not numerical in nature; that is a fact. Recognize this fact and change your study habits accordingly. Using different study techniques for the AUDIT multiple-choice questions leads us to reason 2: Candidates must work to find the "best" answer.

The best answer is the one that gives auditors the most assurance. It's the answer that makes the best case for the situation. Auditors just know the reason is good, just because they have audited and understand the concepts. To reach the level where you can select the best answer, you must spend considerable time practicing all of the content areas. This is one reason why the study time for AUDIT is longer than the Regulation (REG) and the Business Environment and Concepts (BEC). Not only is more material tested, there are more variations to choose from.

Reason 3 is difficult for most candidates. Most candidates sitting for the CPA exam have never worked as an auditor for a public accounting firm. How can you compensate for this deficiency? Practice, practice, and practice some more. Work as many multiple-choice questions as you can. Don't go back to your old college textbook. Read and practice with current—no older than six months—material. The AUDIT content can change. Don't choose the first answer you see. Choosing the best answer takes time. For example, consider this AUDIT multiple-choice question.

Which of the following most likely would give the most assurance concerning the valuation assertion of accounts receivable?

a. Tracing amounts in the subsidiary ledger to details on shipping documents.
b. Comparing receivable turnover ratios to industry statistics for reasonableness.
c. Inquiring about receivables pledged under loan agreements.
d. Assessing the allowance for uncollectible accounts for reasonableness.

Wow, what a rich question! First you must recognize the key words in the question. "Most likely" is very important. Write "YES" on your scratch paper to remind you that you must select an answer that represents something the auditor would very much like to do. Valuation is the major concern here. Recognize that valuation is a "financial statement assertion." Now recall your knowledge. There are five financial statement assertions.

1. **Presentation and disclosure:** Deals with presenting the account on the proper financial statement in the proper section and requires that the client prepare the proper footnote disclosures to explain the various relevant accounting methods and policies.
2. **Existence and occurrence:** Requires the client to only list assets that exist and liabilities and revenues and expense accounts that have occurred.
3. **Rights and obligations:** Recognizes the fact that the financial statements should include items only if the client has the right to them and only if the liabilities are the obligation of the entity. For example, a mortgage payable shown on the balance sheet of XYZ Corporation must be a mortgage on a building owned by XYZ, and not owned by XYZ Corporation's mother-in-law for her vacation home. All obligations (liabilities) on the corporation's balance sheet must be for the company.
4. **Completeness:** All transactions must be included and presented.
5. **Valuation and allocation:** All account balances on all of the financial statements should be valued properly, in accordance with generally accepted accounting principles.

Keeping these assertions in mind, you answer the question by reading the answer choices. Answer a. is an activity that an auditor would perform. However, the auditor traces from a ledger back to a source document, such as a shipping document, to satisfy the assertion test for existence, not valuation. Answer b might indicate valuation. Turnover ratios are analytical procedures. Most analytical procedures are performed to satisfy the assertion of completeness. You should consider this answer, just in case you cannot find a better one. Click on the second answer response and continue to read. In answer c., asking about receivables that have been pledged indicates rights and obligations. If the receivables have been pledged, they are not free for use by the client. This fact must be disclosed in the notes to the financial statements. So far in the analysis, answers a. and c. are clearly not valuation. Answer d. is the very best example of valuation since accounts receivable are to be valued in accordance with generally accepted accounting principles (GAAP) at net realizable value. Net realizable value indicates that uncollectible accounts have been estimated and the value is subtracted from the overall receivable balance.

Reading each and every answer response may be exhausting. Reading each answer response takes time and energy, but it is the only way you can say for sure that you have carefully considered all answer possibilities and that you have made every effort to select the best answer for the circumstances described. You will earn many more points by following this process. In other words, it matters enormously that you read all four answer explanations, looking for the best answer, as often there is more than one correct answer. The AICPA examiners want you to choose the best, correct answer. It's one of the major keys to being successful on the AUDIT exam. The next key to success is to deal with the AUDIT simulations.

AUDIT SIMULATIONS

The overall simulation question format is discussed in Chapter 8, The Simulation Component: No Fear, It's Here. Working the AICPA sample exam at www.cpa-exam.org is essential to candidate success. A single simulation sample provides a rich experience for candidates to see that it is easy to search the table of contents. Reread Chapter 9, The Research Component: How Many Hits? shortly before taking the AUDIT exam. How should you learn the proper phrases? By learning the concepts that are asked in the multiple-choice questions. The same topics will be search phrases in the research tab of the simulations.

Relax; most of the AUDIT simulation work tabs provide answer choices. You are not asked to create an answer from scratch. Rather, candidates are given answers to choose from. Before selecting a choice, read the company profile information and study the selected financial information. Based on the specific information, your answer will vary. For example, if the client is a retail establishment, internal controls and valuation of completed inventory would be treated differently than if the client is a service industry where labor costs would be the primary issue. A retail company's inventory is different from a manufacturing company's inventory. A manufacturer must maintain controls over raw materials, work-in-process, and finished goods. A manufacturer also must have controls over the costing system to arrive at the proper inventory costs. Take your time to think about the environment in which the company operates.

As mentioned in Chapter 8, begin by opening each work tab to note what it is the examiners want you to do. Then read the content of the information tabs. This technique will save you time. Now you know what to look for when you read about the company. Don't forget that the Resources tab may contain information that will help you solve the work tab questions.

AUDIT—THE COMMUNICATIONS TAB

Chapter 7, The Communications Component—Formerly Called Essays, makes it clear that most of the grading points in the communications tab are awarded for writing well, rather than content. Avoid the use of bullet points, abbreviations, and lists. Use full sentences. Most AUDIT communication questions require candidates to explain a general issue to a client or to a colleague. Recognize the audience. Avoid the use of jargon by clearly explaining any phrases, such as "substantive tests" or "attribute sampling." Define the terms in the beginning of the memo. Don't lose sleep worrying about what the examiners will ask you to write about. Content is not the important factor here—writing well is. Most of the ten points are awarded for writing well. Keep your response relevant by addressing the question requirements. Candidates can earn as many as 10% of their total examination points in the communication area by staying on topic and by writing well.

Should you use mnemonics to remember key AUDIT concepts? As discussed in Chapter 12, Study Strategies to Improve Your Memory, this is a dangerous exam strategy. Most often mnemonics are used to generate lists, and lists are a very small part of the AUDIT exam.

AUDIT—THE RESEARCH TAB

Save the research section of the simulation testlet for last. Using the time management tools suggested in Chapter 22, Time Management, pace yourself. Search no longer than the time allotted. If you run out of time on testlet 4 (the first simulation testlet), paste the most relevant paragraphs that you have found so far and move to the next testlet. Overall, Research tabs are worth only three to four points each. Don't risk missing double-digit points by working overtime to solve a research question. Move on to testlet 5, and forget what you did or did not do in testlet 4. There are many more points in the next testlet that will be easier to earn. You have three choices.

1. Continue to spend time researching for the correct answer.
2. Exit testlet 4 leaving the research section blank and move on.
3. Paste a semirelevant paragraph and move on.

The results are very different. If you choose 1, you risk giving up as many as fifteen exam points. Testlet 5 contains some easy selection-type answers. Choice 1 will cost you greatly. Get over the perfection mentality of the typical accountant and move on. You can't risk fifteen points!

Choice 2 is a better choice than 1. At least you have moved on to attempt the last exam testlet (the second simulation) and, it is hoped, to earn the remaining fifteen points. Why would you leave anything on the CPA exam blank? At least paste something there that is semirelevant. This will demonstrate to the graders that you know how to use the research function. Leave nothing blank!

If you choose choice 3, at least you have completed the simulation. You know that your answer may not be the best, but you have given it a try. You simply cannot afford to expend one more minute on the first simulation. Move on and try to earn as many points as possible. Move on to earn as many as fifteen more points. Move on to pass AUDIT!

The AICPA offers a free software tool for candidates with NTS to practice the AUDIT research. See www.cpa-exam.org for ordering information

PERSONALLY SPEAKING

I love auditing! As director of the Northern Illinois University CPA Review, I have the pleasure of saying that no other university in the nation has performed as well on the AUDIT section of the CPA exam as the Northern students. In our CPA review courses, I teach most of the AUDIT area (over 80% of the content), and I have come to understand what makes this section so difficult. Candidates must think—not just compute using established formulas, but take concepts that they have learned and then apply them to real-life situations. Before candidates can apply concepts or begin auditing, they must possess a basic foundation of terms. As demonstrated, having a clear picture how a test of control differs from a substantive test is very important. Be wary of CPA review materials that simply list audit procedures or audit definitions. This basic knowledge might help you earn 20 to 30% of the points. This is not enough to pass the exam.

As of the publication date of this book, there are over 100 auditing standards, 12 attestation standards, and 11 statements on standards for accounting and review services. Don't ignore any of these areas. The standards are fair game. Order the free AICPA software and search the AICPA Professional Standards. Skim all of the various standards. Yes, I know the professional standards are difficult to read and interpret. Don't spend time trying to memorize them. Just skim them. After you have given all of the hundreds of pages a quick once-over, you are ready to examine review manuals and software to determine how comprehensive the coverage is. For example, if your review materials omit the areas of compilations and reviews of nonpublic entity financial statements, they are of low quality. You could easily miss 10 to 12% of the total examination points. Ouch, that would hurt.

Whatever you do, do not skip any topical area that is listed on the AICPA content specification outlines (CSOs). For a complete listing of the AUDIT topics, refer to Exhibit 1 in Chapter 2. Audit sampling, for example, is not an easy area. Try to learn some of the concepts. Even some knowledge will carry you a long way. If you skip the area entirely, it could be just your luck that several of the questions require sampling knowledge. Consider purchasing an audio CD. Auditing is tested with words. Hearing these words and learning the definitions, along with hints about how to apply the definitions, is a very effective and efficient method. Repetition, repetition, and more repetition is a wonderful way to learn. The more times you listen to the audio, the longer you remember the concepts.

Fight the urge to hurry to complete this exam. I always tell my candidates to read each multiple-choice response as if their life depends on it. See answering these questions as serious business. Select your answer, but continue on—read the rest of the answers to validate your first choice. If you misread a question by missing a "not" or a "least likely," you will discover this after you read **all** of the answer choices. You will catch your mistake.

Visualize the situation—audit planning usually indicates that the auditor is in the office preparing to audit the client. Could the auditors examine records, systems, and journal entries if they are sitting in their office? Certainly not! During the planning stage, auditors are thinking about what they plan to do. They have not yet begun the fieldwork where they visit the client's premises to obtain detailed documents. During planning the auditor has the client's most recent interim financial statements. If they are a continuing auditor they also may have last year's audit documentation. Let the picture help you. During the planning phase, auditors are simply preparing a plan to audit—they are not yet auditing.

Prepare emotionally as well as technically for this exam section. If you have done your work, you will find AUDIT to be very draining. Expect to be tired during the last hour of the exam. Working three testlets of thirty multiple-choice questions each is an exhausting process. Your eyes will hurt from straining to read the screen. Your scratch paper is your friend. To remain engaged, write down key words for each question. The act of writing will help you formulate the correct answer. From time to time, close your eyes and think. Don't always be in a hurry to select an answer. A slow, well-paced approach is better than hastily selecting an answer just because it sounds good.

Over the years, the areas that give candidates the most trouble in AUDIT are internal control processes and auditor communications. By "auditor communications," I mean the various types of written communication that an auditor uses, such as communications to the audit committee and several types of audit reports. These areas are not fun to study. There is much to retain. Candidates have trouble earning these points because they don't try hard enough. Several candidates have reported that they failed AUDIT because they did not follow my request to read the audit communication materials twice. Notice I said **read** instead of **memorize**. Don't get bogged down by trying to memorize all of the various audit reports. You will go crazy and never be successful. Simply read these reports for a basic understanding of the presentation. You will not be called on to prepare an audit report from scratch. You will be given answer choices. Keep it simple—don't add to the challenge. Read for a basic understanding. Then practice the multiple-choice questions to test whether you can apply what you have learned.

What's the recipe to Northern Illinois University's high degree of success? The recipe contains equal parts of hardworking candidates, quality instruction, quality materials, and a savvy exam approach. You, too, can be successful. Establish a disciplined study plan, have some fun creating memory devices, and work as many questions as you can. As you work questions, learn from the answers to the question. Getting a question wrong during practice is no crime. It's only practice. By practicing, you will remember. By practicing, you will pass AUDIT!

CPA EXAM TIP:
Allow more time to prepare for AUDIT than to prepare for REG or BEC. It's the longest CPA exam section.

17 FINANCIAL ACCOUNTING AND REPORTING: TOUGH IT OUT

Financial Accounting and Reporting (FAR) is a four-hour section of the CPA exam. The overall format is 80% financial accounting topics, 10% governmental accounting, and 10% accounting for not-for-profit entities. Candidates believe it is the most difficult of the four sections, and the pass rate usually supports that belief. The topics tested cover four semester-long accounting courses.

1. **Intermediate accounting**—the **first semester.** Typical topics include the balance sheet, income statement, monetary current assets and current liabilities, fixed assets, inventory, and the introduction of basic time value of money issues. If you were studying from the world-famous *Intermediate Accounting,* 11th edition by Kieso, Weygandt, and Warfield, you would review chapters one through thirteen.

2. **Intermediate accounting**—the **second semester:** Topics such as accounting for bonds, pension, leases, deferred income taxes, investments, and stockholders' equity are heavily tested. The statement of other comprehensive income and the statement of cash flows are key. Special areas, such as recognizing accounting errors, accounting changes, and revenue, are always important topics.

3. **Advanced accounting**—a one-semester course: This course leads to an understanding of how to combine financial statement information to produce consolidated financial statements.

4. **Governmental and not-for-profit accounting course:** Usually this is a one-semester course or is taught as part of an advanced accounting course.

Just reading the list of testable topics is enough to make most candidates cringe. This is tough stuff. It's no wonder that FAR is known as the most difficult area to pass. Candidates must have a knowledgeable command over 150 financial accounting standards as issued by the Financial Accounting Standards Board (FASB), 40-plus governmental accounting standards as issued by the Governmental Accounting Standards Board (GASB), and special accounting issues encountered in not-for-profit entities. What a huge list! How do candidates manage the vast technical breadth of topics? That is the topic of this chapter.

MANAGING THE VAST TECHNICAL BREADTH

FAR is the most diverse exam section. One minute you're answering a question about a capital lease, and the next minute the subject is pension accounting. The amount of detail tested on this section is overwhelming. Preparing and following a study plan to guide you through the maze of numerous topics is almost a requirement for passing FAR. Candidates must know something about everything.

A common mistake is to study some topics very well and to overlook other subjects entirely. Do this and you are asking for failure. You must be well versed in numerous areas. The top-ten list of all-important subject areas for the FAR exam is

1.   Bonds
2.   Pensions
3.   Leases
4.   Investment and financial instruments
5.   Multiple-step income statement
6.   Classified balance sheet
7.   Converting information from cash to accrual and vice versa
8.   Statement of cash flows
9.   Other comprehensive income
10.   Deferred income taxes

Any of these topics can be tested. Yes, there are other areas such as inventory, accounts receivable, cash, and the financial accounting concepts, that also must be studied. You will be asked questions about these topics, too, but this list identifies the key areas that remain the heart of the FAR exam. Think of the list as the classics of the CPA exam. Don't leave home without your top-ten list of FAR knowledge.

It is dangerous to ignore governmental accounting and accounting for not-for-profit entities. For now, let's focus on the topics covered in the two semesters of a college intermediate accounting class.

FAR COMMUNICATIONS

Here's where you can shine. It is not difficult to write about financial accounting topics. That's right—the governmental accounting and accounting for not-for-profit entities issues are tested using only the multiple-choice question format. All of the simulations cover financial accounting issues. This may change in 2005. Review the concepts covered in Chapter 7, The Communications Component—Formerly Called Essays. Recall that the exam is positively graded. You are awarded points for correct statements. Points are not deducted from your grade. Don't be overly self-conscious. Write well. Begin with a paragraph that clearly identifies a thesis statement. Use additional paragraphs to develop main ideas and to support what you say. Watch for fragments and run-on sentences. Watch for missing or incorrect punctuation, especially your comma usage. Don't forget to run spell-check after each time you make a change in your answer. Proofread your memo after each change.

Let the words in the communications tab speak to you. For example, let's say the requirement was to discuss with a client the topic of off-balance-sheet risk of accounting. What does "to discuss" mean? You must complete two major tasks—define what off-balance-sheet risk is and give examples—and then you must make any statements that you feel will support your thoughts in the area. Don't know anything about the topic of off-balance-sheet risk? Don't worry—begin by rephrasing the question in a statement. Then, looking at the words "off-balance-sheet," develop a definition that discusses the fact that some accounting transactions that are important to financial statement users could be omitted from the basic financial statement presentation. What effect would this have on the financial statement presentation? Certainly it would result in some activities that should be disclosed in the notes to the financial statements. The users must be made aware of all possible liabilities, even if the liabilities are not yet recorded. Try to list some examples.

Be careful when writing communication essays. Do **not** insert journal entries, and avoid referring to DR for debit and CR for credit. Speak in terms of an asset increasing or a liability decreasing rather than a debit and a credit. If you must discuss a formula to help the reader compute an amount, do not use numbers. The communication essays are answered with words. Make statements such as: Add the amount of the actual interest paid for the period to the amount of accrued interest. Use common language. Accounting jargon will not help you earn points. Write in everyday terms.

Watch for a question that asks candidates how to "report" for a transaction. You must answer with a discussion of the financial statement, the exact section of the financial statement, and any information that should be disclosed in the statement notes. Always get readers to the correct financial statement, then lead them to the correct section of the statement, for example, current liabilities, and then discuss where (first, last etc.). Pretend you are preparing a map to guide readers to the exact place where that account would be shown. Reporting questions are easy and fun. Just use your financial statement knowledge.

FAR RESEARCH

Review the concepts discussed in Chapter 9, The Research Component: How Many Hits? Save the Research tab for last. Don't spin your wheels. Think about the key search term, put quote marks around the phrase, type it in, and hit ENTER. Spelling counts—you must spell all words in the phrases correctly. If you need assistance, open the Communications tab, type the phrase, hit SPELL-CHECK, and see how the words are spelled. Usually you can use the words and phrases that are used in the question requirement.

Shame on you if you do not take advantage of the free AICPA offer. Order the Financial Accounting Research System (FARS) software. It's free—all you need do is to register at the CPA exam Web site, www.cpa-exam.org, and enter your notice to schedule (NTS) number. You are allowed to practice with this software for six months. One or two hours of practice with the software and you can be a pro. There is no excuse for not practicing now that the FARS is free.

FAR: LEARN STEP-BY-STEP

How can you possibly learn all of the concepts tested in this area? Use review materials that summarize the key concepts, present the important formulas and algorithms, and discuss the disclosures according to generally accepted accounting principles. Don't be tempted to study your financial accounting texts. They contain too much information. This area is already overwhelming—avoid trying to study everything. Study **only** what's on the exam.

When you work multiple-choice questions, whether they test financial, governmental, or not-for-profit accounting, study by covering up the answer choices. Teach yourself to work with the question data and to ignore the answer choices. Work the formulas and then uncover the answers to see the amount you just calculated. The idea here is to first visualize the formula, write it down on your scratch paper, and then plug in the numbers. Errors occur because candidates use the incorrect formula, make math mistakes, or miss the real issue. Perhaps you plugged the numbers into the formula incorrectly. If your answer is not there, slowly work it again. Continue to believe in your abilities. If on the second time through, your answer is still not there, sit back and ask yourself if you have the correct formula or if you could be falling into a trap, such as using numeric data that is irrelevant to the issue. Practice computing the answer using formulas. If you are well studied, you do **know** how to compute the answer—it's just a matter of methodically applying your knowledge. Don't forget about the ten points of governmental accounting and not-for-profit accounting.

GOVERNMENTAL AND NOT-FOR-PROFIT ACCOUNTING

Use the same multiple-choice technique as just discussed. Governmental accounting represents 10% of the total FAR points, as does not-for-profit accounting. You have some tough choices of what to do with your time. If you choose to ignore governmental accounting because you are uncomfortable in this area, you will make a huge mistake. You must at least learn the basics.

Not-for-profit accounting is very similar to accounting for other financial statement issues. The focus is on accounting for donor contributions. Candidates must know how to prepare a statement of activities and a statement of cash flows for a not-for-profit entity. Buy a good review manual, and use it as a guide to learn the basics. A 70 to 75% understanding of the overall material is enough to carry you to a passing score.

PERSONALLY SPEAKING

Many candidates report to me that they simply hate the FAR exam. Avoid a negative outlook. Financial accounting is the heart of what we learned in college. It is only natural to feel overwhelmed here. The material is tough, diverse, and quantitative. Yes, FAR is difficult. If you are having trouble answering the questions, remember that so is everyone else. You studied, you practiced, and you reviewed. Yet the material seems foreign as you take the exam. What happened to all of your knowledge? Stop! Take a reality check. You can pass the FAR section with some help. Remain hopeful. The AICPA will help you by equating your score. Points are added to your raw score to improve your performance. In the past, as many as 10 to 15 points may have been added to candidates' raw scores. If this is true, you only had to earn a raw score of 60% to pass the FAR section. Although the AICPA no longer uses curve points, points still are added to your score. Believe in yourself—you **can** pass the FAR section. Relax, take a deep breath, and keep on fighting to answer each and every question. Remain confident. Don't let self-doubt creep in. Hang tough and don't give up too early!

Don't leave home for the FAR exam until you have studied these governmental accounting topics.

- Governmental funds
- How to prepare the government-wide financial statements
- How to reconcile the governmental and proprietary funds to arrive at the numbers on the government-wide financial statements
- How to record a general fund budget
- How to close the budgetary entries
- Other financing sources and uses
- Nonexchange revenues
- Encumbrance accounting
- Capital assets and infrastructure

To learn these topics, purchase review materials. By using them, you can quickly bring yourself up to speed.

As you work through the questions on the exam, do not grade yourself. See each question as a separate challenge. If you must guess, go ahead and do so. Tell yourself that Debra says it is OK. Everyone, even those who have earned a grade of a 99, had to guess on some questions. Your job is to answer the questions. Expect to guess. Leave the grading to the AICPA. Forget about what you don't know. It's too late to improve your knowledge when you are sitting in the Prometric test center. Move on with confidence.

I have the privilege of working directly with many CPA candidates each year. I find that candidates who fail the FAR exam do so not because they are not smart enough to learn the concepts, but because they just give up too early. Plan to spend at least four weeks of solid study learning and practicing the FAR topics after you have taken a review course. Sound like a lot of work? It is! It is what it takes to review the FAR area. It is what it takes to pass this area. You must hang tough! There is no simple solution—learn the concepts, practice the concepts, and you will prevail!

CPA EXAM TIP:
Take the financial accounting and reporting section as soon as you can after your college graduation. If you don't use the material every day, you may lose it. Use it or risk losing it!

18 REGULATION: THE RULE-ORIENTED SECTION

The Regulation (REG) section of the CPA exam is just that—all about regulations. Two primary regulations are tested in REG—the Internal Revenue Service (IRS) Code and various business law regulations, such as the Securities and Exchange Commission (SEC) regulations and AICPA *Professional Code of Conduct*. Overall, the section tests 60% income taxation–related topics and 40% business law topics. For a complete listing of the REG content areas, go to Chapter 2, Content and Overall Exam Format and study Exhibit 2.4, the AICPA Content Specification Outlines for Regulation (REG). Many candidates believe REG is the most rule–oriented section. For some candidates, this translates into an easier section to complete—either you know the material and the rules or you do not. There is very little subjective evaluation. This chapter informs candidates about the REG section and provides ideas of how to study effectively to recall the specific rules. Let's begin by discussing the taxation area.

SCRATCH PAPER USAGE

Expect to use the on-screen calculator. About half of the income taxation multiple-choice questions require numerical computations. Calculator usage tips are provided in Chapter 6, The Multiple-Choice Component. You can make many of the computations in your head or on the scratch paper that is provided. Don't forget to use your scratch paper wisely by sectioning off each page (drawing lines down the page to form columns). At the beginning of the REG exam, just after you have opened the exam and you see that the exam clock is counting down, sit back in your chair, close your eyes, and recall any taxation and business law items you might forget. Write them down now, before you get started on the exam. Jot down key concepts. Chances are you will use at least half of the information while completing the exam. Obviously you cannot do a "mind-dump" of your entire note card file or exam review manual, but you can write down the formulas and items that give you trouble. Remember to write the information on your scratch paper only **after** the exam has begun and only write down key items. Avoid creating a reference booklet.

FEDERAL TAXATION: MULTIPLE-CHOICE QUESTIONS

Before you begin your studies, check to be sure that your income taxation materials are up-to-date. Tax laws are tested within six months of issuance. Pay attention to major tax law changes. Check the IRS Web site (www.irs.gov) for announcements of new laws. Then verify that your study materials address the newly passed regulations. In general, the best way to study income taxation topics is to skim the current year's income tax forms and directions and work questions either in a review textbook or by using CPA examination review software. CPA Review manuals contain questions asked on previous CPA exams. You can learn by working these questions. There are only so many ways to test a topic such as gross income—inclusions and exclusions. To demonstrate the idea of learning by doing, examine this multiple-choice question.

> With regard to the inclusion of social security benefits in gross income for the 2004 tax year, which of the following statements is correct?
> a.   The social security benefits in excess of modified adjusted gross income are included in gross income.
> b.   The social security benefits in excess of one-half the modified adjusted gross income are included in gross income.
> c.   The maximum amount of benefits to be included in gross income is 85% of the social security benefits.
> d.   The social security benefits in excess of the modified gross income over $32,000 are included in gross income.

At first glance, this question appears difficult. It really is not. Candidates must know the amount of social security income that is included in gross income. Read the question, identify the requirement—the amount of social security income to be included in gross income—and then read the answer. Yes, you read that correctly: Read the answer to learn the point. The answer is c. Now you know—a maximum of 85% of the social security benefits are included in gross income. You have just learned the point. To help you to remember the concept, relate it to something that you are familiar with. The idea is to keep your brain free to remember all kinds of data. This piece is simple—SS 85. I have likened the concept to the christening of a cruise ship—the SS 85. You are cruising free of tax after you have paid tax on 85% of your social security (SS) income.

Directly referring to the questions and then studying the answers not only helps candidates to learn the material more effectively but also helps to increase learning efficiency. Candidates must learn hundreds of taxation details. If you purchase a study source that you know is both comprehensive and up-to-date, such as the *Wiley CPA Examination Review* materials, you are set to begin your study process. Let's try the approach using a computational multiple-choice question.

Perle, a dentist, billed Wood $600 for dental services. Wood paid Perle $200 cash and built a bookcase for Perle's office in full settlement of the bill. Wood sells comparable bookcases for $350. What amount should Perle include in taxable income as a result of this transaction?

a. $0
b. $200
c. $550
d. $600

Begin by taking your best guess. Let's say you believe the answer should be $600. You believe that Perle should include in his taxable income the amount of income that represents the going rate for this service—$600. Now check the answer provided in your software or review manual. Upon looking, you see the answer is c., $550. What have you learned? You will have learned nothing, unless you refer to an answer that includes detailed answer explanations. Quality review materials should inform you that an exchange of services for property or services is called bartering. A taxpayer must include in income the amount of cash and fair value of the property or services received in exchange for the performance of services. Now you have learned the concept. Let's try to answer the question again. Using this rule, we must include cash and the fair value of the property (the bookcase's fair value). The answer is computed at $200 plus $350, or $550. We did it! What's the concept to be learned? Exhibit 18.1 shows an example of a note card that a candidate would prepare to remember the preceding concept (rule).

Exhibit 18.1: Income tax rules for exchange (bartering) of services/goods

Cash
Plus: Fair Value of
Property/Services Received
Amount to Include in Taxable Income

For most candidates, reading is a very ineffective method to learn income taxation topics. Rules are much easier to learn by working actual questions rather than merely by reading the rules.

Are you wondering how you will remember several concepts? Studies prove that when students work a question and get the question wrong, they remember the concept longer than if they worked the question and answered it correctly. The problem with this approach is that most candidates detest getting a question wrong. They prefer to answer everything correctly the first time. That's the accountant coming out in you. Get over it. Get to work and learn by doing.

The approach just described works very well to learn multiple-choice concepts. However, income taxation topics are also tested using simulations. What do candidates need to know to earn points on the simulations?

FEDERAL TAXATION: SIMULATIONS

The overall simulation question format is discussed in Chapter 8, The Simulation Component: No Fear, It's Here. Before you begin your studies of the income taxation area, take the AICPA sample REG exam as presented at www.cpa-exam.org. Take your time to understand the REG simulations. First, you will see that some of the tabs are similar to multiple-choice type questions. They ask questions using a pop-up box showing various answer selection choices. This question type is nothing more than a glorified multiple-choice question with more than four answer choices. The learning methods discussed earlier in regard to the multiple-choice format apply here, too. By learning the multiple-choice concepts, you also will be learning the concepts tested in many of the simulation tabs. Three unique work tabs require special skills.

1. Tax schedule preparation tab
2. Communications tab
3. Research tab that asks candidates to identify the IRS code section and code subsection

FEDERAL TAXATION: THE COMMUNICATIONS TAB

Chapter 7, The Communications Component—Formerly Called Essays, makes it clear that most of the grading points in the Communications tab are awarded for writing well, rather than for content. Avoid the use of bullet points, abbreviations, and lists. Use full sentences. Most tax communication questions require candidates to explain a general tax issue to a client or to a colleague. Recognize the audience. Avoid the use of tax jargon by clearly explaining any tax phrases, such as alternative minimum tax or the dividends received deduction. Define the tax terms in the beginning of the memo. Don't lose sleep worrying about what the examiners will ask you to write about. Content is not the important factor here—writing well is. Most of the ten points allocated to the communication area are awarded for writing well. Keep your response relevant by addressing the question requirements. Candidates can earn as many as 10% of their total examination points in the communication area by staying on topic and by writing well.

FEDERAL TAXATION: TAX SCHEDULE PREPARATION TAB

Testlets 4 and 5, the two simulation testlets, often require candidates to prepare tax schedules. Not an entire tax return, but a portion of the tax return, called a schedule, such as a Form 1040, Schedule A. Candidates often try to guess which tax schedule will be tested. Rather than guessing, you should have knowledge of the key schedules, such as the Form 1040 Schedules A, B, C, and D. What if they ask about a relatively obscure schedule, such as schedule F, profit or loss from farming? No one can be expected to know each and every tax form. Take a deep breath, read the form, read the data given in the question, and do your best. Recall, the examiners will adjust the exam score using a process called equating, by adding points to help candidates pass. If the schedule or form was difficult for you, most likely it was difficult for other candidates, as well.

Spend some time on the IRS Web site, (www.irs.gov.) Pay special attention to Circular 230, which is listed as a key study source in the content specifications outlines (CSOs) that describe the topics tested.

Take a look at your own personal tax return. Ask to see the corporate tax return for the business where you work. Purchase review materials that contain samples of IRS tax forms. It is much easier to learn something when you can see it. Don't forget to study corporate taxation topics as well as estate and gift taxation issues. Comprehensive review materials should include these areas.

FEDERAL TAXATION: THE RESEARCH TAB

Chapter 9, The Research Component: How Many Hits? provides information on how to handle the research section of the simulation. As of the publication date of this book, the AICPA does not offer a free software tool to practice tax research. Most universities are now requiring students to utilize tax database search tools. Candidates who have no practice in such tools should purchase CPA review tax simulation software.

Working the AICPA sample exam at www.cpa-exam.org is essential to candidate success. The single simulation sample provides a rich enough experience for you to see that it is easy to search the table of contents for code section numbers as long as you can identify the proper phrase. How will you learn the proper phrases? By learning the concepts that are asked in the multiple-choice questions. The test will ask candidates to search for the same topics using the search tool.

Should you memorize code section and subsection numbers? No, do not memorize code sections. No one has enough brainpower to do that. Trust your ability to read the question requirement to identify the proper search phrase.

Save the research section of the simulation testlet for last. Using the time management tools suggested in Chapter 22, pace your progress. Search no longer than the time allotted. If you run out of time on testlet 4 (the first simulation testlet), paste the most relevant code section and subsection that you have found so far and move to the next testlet. Overall, Research tabs are only worth three to four points each. Don't risk missing double-digit points by working overtime to solve a research question. Move on to testlet 5, and forget what you did or did not do in testlet 4. There are many more points that are easier to earn. Because the simulations test only income taxation topics, the exam will end on the income taxation topics. However, don't forget that the exam begins with three testlets of multiple-choice questions that not only test taxation topics but also business law topics.

BUSINESS LAW TOPICS

To learn law topics, use the same approach as demonstrated for the income tax area. Learn by doing the questions. The advantage here is that the simulations test only tax topics, not law topics. You are now preparing for any area that currently is 100% multiple-choice. Law topics do not change as frequently as the income tax area. If you took two business law classes in college, you should have covered most of the topics, with one exception—ethics and professional and legal responsibilities.

Don't underestimate the area of ethics and professional and legal responsibilities. This area represents 15-20% of the total exam points. College business law courses do not cover this area. The topic is presented in auditing textbooks. Review your audit textbook, making sure it is not more than two years old. Another useful reference source is the AICPA Web site. Go to the ethics section of the www.aicpa.org Web site and click on ethics. Read the AICPA *Code of Professional Conduct* and the ethics quizzes. You just might see some of the same questions on your CPA exam.

Avoid overpreparing for the contract area. Business law professors spend entire courses on contract issues. Remember, the CPA exam tests candidates' knowledge as it relates to the skills needed by accountants and auditors, not lawyers. Contracts issues are tested, but they comprise only a small portion of the law points.

Don't leave home without your SEC knowledge. The 1933 and 1934 securities acts are extensively tested. Go to the SEC Web site (www.sec.gov) and skim, do not read, the Securities Acts. Note that as of the publication date of this book, the Sarbanes-Oxley Act of 2002 has not yet been tested. This act will most likely be added to the AUDIT section of the exam in 2005.

Commercial paper and bankruptcy are tested. Learn when an instrument is negotiable. Learn the bankruptcy preferences.

Some of the law topics appear to be more accounting than legal applications. Questions regarding title transfer concepts, such as FOB shipping point (title transfers when the goods are picked up and loaded on the common carrier's truck) and FOB destination (title transfers when the goods arrive and are accepted by the purchaser), are asked frequently.

For the most part, you won't need your calculator to answer business law questions. However, look for the classic question that requires you to compute the amount of an insurance loss. Use the coinsurance formula to arrive at the proper number. You will find this formula in almost all review course manuals. If review course materials do not mention this concept, don't use them. They are not quality reference materials.

Traditionally, under the pencil-based CPA exam, the areas of forming, operating, and dissolving a business were tested along with the above topics. These areas have been moved to the Business Environment and Concepts (BEC) section. The only partnership and corporate type questions that you will see here deal with income tax issues.

Don't forget—testlets 1 to 3 test both income tax and law issues. The testlets will not be partitioned off between the two areas. Also, remember that pretest questions—up to 20% of the total multiple-choice questions—are not counted in your total exam score. They are trial questions that the AICPA is using to preview candidate preparedness and to test new types of questions. As of this book's publication date, the AICPA has stated that only tax issues are tested in simulations, and that there will be twenty-four multiple-choice questions in each testlet of the REG exam; the other three CPA exam sections could contain twenty-four to thirty multiple-choice questions.

Yes, the REG exam is rule-oriented. Practice the rules, and you will pass.

PERSONALLY SPEAKING

Income taxation has always been my worst area. I would dream of opening my CPA exam to find an entire exam testing taxation topics. Although my dream did not come true, I did pass the exam because it was curved. I know that my performance was poor in the taxation area. However, I prevailed and you will, too. I passed because I knew the basics.

For some candidates, income taxation is relatively easy. They work in the field every day. The amount of study time for this area varies depending on candidate experience. No matter how much experience you have, take the time to reread the REG section of Chapter 7 before you arrive at the Prometric test center. Even very experienced candidates can encounter tax forms and schedules that they are unfamiliar with. Whatever you do, remain in control. Move slowly, read all information at least once, and experiment by searching through the table of contents. Scrolling takes time, but eventually it will get you to where you need to be.

The key to passing REG is simple! Work the questions to learn the concepts, practice the AICPA sample exam, and review key tax forms. While taking the exam, watch the time clock. Avoid spending too much time on one testlet. Three hours can fly by.

I believe the REG exam is the second easiest section to pass, a close second to the BEC section. The simulation research component has not proven to be very difficult. Remember, it is not the computer that helps you pass this exam. It is your content knowledge that gives you the power to pass. If candidates fail REG, it is because they did not carefully manage their time or they did not study the content. Areas where candidates tend to receive low scores are

- Law—property issues
- Law—understanding the uniform commercial code (UCC)
- Law—the *Professional Code of Conduct*, especially independence issues and auditor retention and use of workpaper documentation
- Tax—the alternative minimum tax
- Tax—taxpayer preparer's responsibilities
- Tax—estate and gift taxation

This list is not all-inclusive. Don't take a chance. Study all areas listed on the CSOs. View the current CSOs on the CPA exam Web site at www.cpa-exam.org. Study only when you are able to concentrate. A rule-oriented section such as REG requires great focus and concentration. If you are tired, take a nap and resume your studies later. If you study when you are tired, you won't retain much later.

Get plenty of sleep the night before you test. Move through the test in a very methodical way. Select your answer and change it only when you are 110% sure that your first answer is incorrect. There are only so many variations the examiners can use to test tax and law knowledge. If you study, you will see many repeat questions. What are you waiting for? Begin your studies now!

CPA EXAM TIP:
Understand the AICPA *Professional Code of Conduct*. View the Code and take an AICPA ethics quiz at www.aicpa.org.

19 BUSINESS ENVIRONMENT AND CONCEPTS: IT'S NEW, IT'S DIFFERENT

The Business Environment and Concepts (BEC) section of the CPA exam is the shortest section, requiring only two and one-half hours to complete. As of the publication date of this book, the questions were 100% multiple-choice format. Wow, what a break! Do you think that passing the BEC section will be a breeze? Watch it; it's dangerous to think that way for two reasons.

1. The content tested is widely dispersed, cutting across five areas of discipline—economics, information technology, finance, managerial accounting, and business law.
2. Of the content tested, much of it is new to the CPA exam, with 70% of the material being tested for the first time on the computer-based test (CBT) that launched on April 5, 2004.

Of the four examination sections, the BEC section presents the greatest challenge to educators, CPA candidates, and CPA exam review providers; the challenge is to determine the type of questions asked. To date, very few sample questions have been released—five on the sample exam and ten in a white paper issued by the AICPA in October of 2003. With so few examples and so much new material tested, candidates must give this area due respect. Don't attempt to wing it. Read this chapter to learn more about the BEC section.

BEWARE OF FORMAT AND CONTENT CHANGES

The BEC section is slated for changes, such as the addition of simulations, that may begin as early as 2005. For now, this book concentrates on the multiple-choice question format. Before candidates begin their preparation process, they should visit the www.wiley.com/cpa Web site for the latest updates in the BEC area as well as all other areas of the CBT. The AICPA announces content and format changes on the CPA exam Web site at www.cpa-exam.org. Candidates, don't get too comfortable; the computer-based CPA exam is a work in progress subject to format and content changes.

BEC FORMAT AND CONTENT

When the exam launched in 2004, the BEC question format was 100% multiple-choice. Candidates must complete three testlets ranging from twenty-four to thirty multiple-choice questions per testlet. The format is the standard, four-option, radio-bullet choice selection as described and demonstrated in Chapter 6, The Multiple-Choice Component. The 100% multiple-choice format is temporary. As soon as the AICPA gathers enough information about candidate awareness and preparedness in this area, it plans to add simulation testlets. Currently, no information is available about the subject matter or format of the simulations.

The content of the current BEC exam is general and diverse. Exhibit 2.5 in Chapter 2, Business Environment and Concepts, presented the examination content specification outline (CSO) showing this breakdown per section.

1. Business structure: 17–23%
2. Economic concepts: 8–12%
3. Financial management: 17–23%
4. Information technology: 22–28%
5. Planning and measurement: 22–28%

Your first step in the preparation process for this area should be to visit the www.cpa-exam.org Web site to obtain the current, detailed BEC content specification outline. The AICPA, in recognition of the fact that this area is not only new but also very diverse, has posted additional content detail in a publication printed October 10, 2003. This nineteen-page document provides the best available information about the BEC test, including ten sample questions. Don't let the breadth of the material scare you. Only entry level knowledge is required. Think basic; this area is primarily definitions with fewer calculations than you might think. Most candidates however, won't remember all of the listed content items. Be careful here—don't risk making more out of this area than it is. Get focused on the material by at least purchasing a CPA review manual to guide you in your preparation process. If you attempt to study this area by referring to old textbooks, you will spend far more time than is necessary. Study the five content areas enough to know the basics. Divide your study process up among the five areas. Tackle one area at a time, reviewing the overall basics as explained in the next sections.

AREA I: BUSINESS STRUCTURES, 17–23%

Roughly twenty points of the BEC exam is a topic formerly tested in the business law area of the pencil-based exam. The testable concepts focus on the three forms of business organizations: sole proprietorships, partnerships, and corporations. Candidates must know how to form, operate, and terminate each of these business forms. Questions will focus on the general characteristics of each business type and the advantages and disadvantages of each form of business. Begin your BEC studies with business structures. Review materials provide many good examples of earlier questions, as this area has been tested as part of the law section of the CPA exam for over fifty years. You will get an idea of the question depth. With so many earlier questions available, you will see firsthand that the tested concepts are simple and discrete. For example, you should be able to determine the recommended business form based on certain stated facts and circumstances. You also must be able to list the factors to support the use of a calendar year-end or a fiscal year-end for both financial reporting and federal taxation purposes. Once you learn the factors, you have this area mastered. You are ready to move on. Based on the business form, you should be able to differentiate between the rights, duties, legal obligations, and authority of owners, partners, stockholders, and management. Be able to discuss more than one corporate form of business, such as subchapter C and subchapter S corporations. Study general, limited, and limited liability partnerships. This area is tested mostly using words, but always be prepared to compute the allocation of partnership profits and losses. Don't be overly concerned—you are not expected to know the issues based on a legal viewpoint. You are a potential CPA—you need the accountant's perspective. CPAs don't prepare the legal documents to form the business. CPAs simply counsel clients as to the nature and form of business that is best for them. Keep the picture of a trusted business advisor in mind. Help your clients to form, operate, and terminate the business types discussed.

AREA II: ECONOMIC CONCEPTS, 8–12%

Economics professors would tell you the CPA exam tests primarily microeconomic concepts. It is not necessary, however, to prepare by reading an entire microeconomic textbook. That would be overkill. Stick with the basics. Knowledge of key economic measures, such as the Consumer Price Index (CPI), gross domestic product (GDP), and the gross national product (GNP) are essential. Candidates should understand the effects of inflation, deflation, expansion, and recession on the economy. How do Federal Reserve actions affect the economy? What is the difference among real, nominal, and effective interest rates? Note the use of basic economic concepts. The questions do not reach beyond the entry-level sophomore college courses. Note how general the topics are. International issues are tested, as candidates must be able to analyze foreign currency hedge transactions as well as the effect of exchange rate fluctuations on financial position and operations. Market influences, such as the characteristics of supply chain management, are also testable topics.

Don't make the mistake of omitting this section from your study plan just because the area frightens you; the concepts are basic. Therefore, it takes less time to prepare for economics than it does for other areas. For example, the content specifications state that candidates should understand the purpose of transfer pricing. If you know that a transfer price is the price charged when one segment of a company provides goods or services to another segment of the company, you are off to a great beginning. An accounting issue arises when goods and services are transferred across international borders. Multinational corporations operating in several countries can save taxes, duties, and tariffs by transferring goods from one of their own segments to another segment. Less foreign exchange rate risk occurs. Do you see that the CPA exam knowledge is at an entry-level, introductory, sophomore-level course? The economic concepts tested on the exam are basic. Keep your CPA exam knowledge at the **general, fundamental level**. Purchase up-to-date review materials, and you will find the area of economics to be quite easy.

AREA III: FINANCIAL MANAGEMENT, 17–23%

Here's where your junior-level finance class knowledge comes in handy. The topics tested in Area III, Financial Management, are those learned for the first time in the fundamentals of finance course. Capital budgeting tools, such as present value, internal rate of return, payback method, discounted payback, and discounted annual cash flows, are must-know concepts. Candidate knowledge includes definitions, examples, and calculations of the aforementioned items. Just like the economic concepts area, finance topics are tested using simple examples. Specific ratio calculations, such as inventory turnover, debt to equity, and working capital, are key. Your understanding of cash discounts used in credit terms for accounts receivable is also tested. Most candidates won't require much time to refresh their basic knowledge. If you use good-quality review materials, you can budget three evening study sessions three hours in length and, after a total of nine hours, almost have this area mastered.

You are **not** required to reread an entire fundamentals of finance textbook. Just refresh your knowledge in the areas tested on the CPA exam. You don't have the luxury of taking time to review all of the hundreds of finance calculations available. Cut to the heart of the matter—learn the items listed in the content specifications.

AREA IV: INFORMATION TECHNOLOGY, 22–28%

Good grief! you say. The area of information technology (IT) comprises almost one-third of the BEC exam. Stop fretting—again, it's the basic, fundamental knowledge that will carry you. For example, the content specification outlines state that candidates should have the knowledge to define basic IT concepts such as batch, real-time, and distributed processing. Most accounting systems classes cover this material early in the junior year. Don't think that you must possess an in-depth understanding of electronic commerce. It's the big picture that counts. There are no calculations and formulas to learn here. Take it easy, keep calm, utilize a review manual, and you should be able to complete your studies here in about eight to ten hours. Not a bad return for as many as 28 points out of 100.

AREA V: PLANNING AND MEASUREMENT, 22–28%

The term "planning and measurement" stumps many candidates. Spend some time acquainting yourself with the content specifications. This area tests roughly ten points of managerial accounting concepts; the remainder tests planning, budgeting concepts, and performance measures. The cost/managerial concepts, such as defining, identifying, and calculating fixed costs, variable costs, standard cost variances, and regression analysis, will most likely be familiar to candidates. Performance measures, such as total quality management and the balanced scorecard technique, might be new concepts to some. At a bare minimum, know the definitions of all items tested. The content specifications indicate definitions and/or calculations that will be required. The AICPA has not shared with candidates the ratio of definitions to calculations. Don't worry about trying to figure it out. Get busy learning and the percentage breakdown will be of little value to you. You won't care, as you will be prepared for whatever the AICPA Board of Examiners decides to test.

PREPARE TO LEARN

Your best preparation method may be learning by working questions. In other words, go to the questions to learn the concepts. For example, work through an IT question like this one.

Which of the following statements is correct concerning internal control in an electronic data interchange (EDI) system?

a. Preventive controls generally are more important than detective controls in EDI systems.
b. Control objectives for EDI systems generally are different from the objectives for other information systems.
c. Internal controls in EDI systems rarely permit control risk to be assessed at below the maximum.
d. Internal controls related to the segregation of duties generally are the most important controls in EDI systems.

Use this question to learn at least one concept. Let's assume that you read the question in your review manual or on screen, and you do not know the answer. You guess answer b. Upon checking your response, you find that answer a. is correct. What have you learned? First, since your answer selection b. was incorrect, you learned that the control objectives for EDI systems must be similar to the objectives for other information systems. Next, you learned that in EDI systems, preventive controls are more important than detective controls. Upon reading the answer explanation, you learn that the auditor would rather prevent problems than detect problems after it is too late to correct them and data could have been stolen, lost, or manipulated. You also should see that answer c. was there to pull candidates into thinking that internal control risk cannot be assessed below maximum in an EDI system. Yes, internal controls can be assessed below maximum.

This approach is called learning from the question. Go ahead, dive in, work the questions, and learn. It's a very efficient as well as effective learning method. Candidates have found that they can cut their study time in half learning from the questions.

PERSONALLY SPEAKING

I believe this area is the easiest of the four exam sections. Is that because it is the shortest section? It's not the amount of testing time that makes me think BEC is the easiest section, but rather the nature of the content. It's five distinct areas that are very well defined in the AICPA content specification outlines. The areas are also more definitional, requiring a few calculations and little or no interpretation of data. Candidates could spend two weeks of total study time and be very well prepared for BEC.

Are you beginning to think you should take the BEC section first in your CPA exam journey? I wouldn't. Remember the eighteen-month rolling window rule. Once you complete the first CPA exam section successfully, you have a total of eighteen months to pass the remaining sections. The eighteen-month time period begins from the date you took the first section that you passed, not the date you received your score. By the time you learn your score, three to four months could have gone by, leaving fourteen months in which to pass the other sections. I suggest taking and passing a more difficult area first. It's less stressful to prepare for an easier section than a more difficult section as the time clock is running down.

Many candidates prefer to take two exam sections each testing window. If this describes you, combine the BEC testing experience with a more difficult section, such as the Financial Accounting and Reporting (FAR) exam. Prepare for the longer section first. Save BEC for later in the testing window after you have taken a short rest in between exam sections. If you are reading this textbook in late 2004 or early 2005, however, consider taking BEC soon, before the simulations are added.

Candidates report that they expected the BEC section to be much more comprehensive than it really is. It's more of a survey of the topics listed. This reaction indicates that a general, fundamental knowledge is required. CPAs are business advisors who should be knowledgeable about a great many topics that affect the business environment. A good reference source for economics, IT concepts, and basic finance issues are short, condensed paperback study booklets that cover the basic definitions and are sold in college bookstores. Then answer questions using a CPA review software product. Learn by doing the questions. Think overview, think basic, study the fundamentals, and believe that you can pass this section. I know you can!

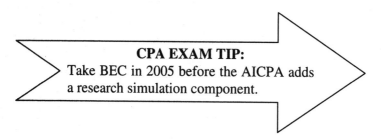

CPA EXAM TIP:
Take BEC in 2005 before the AICPA adds a research simulation component.

20 SURVIVING THE PROMETRIC EXPERIENCE

Informal studies show that fewer than one-third of today's college graduates have taken a computer-based examination. People are often fearful of situations in which they have no experience. This chapter explains what to expect from the Prometric experience and how to react should an issue arise. Read this chapter to learn from others' experiences. Follow the established rules, and you will see that taking the exam is much easier than preparing for the exam.

WHERE IS THE CPA EXAM GIVEN?

The computer-based CPA exam sections are given at secure test administration sites known as Prometric test centers. Prometric is a well-established exam vendor that delivers millions of computer-based examinations annually. The most current list of test centers can be found at www.prometric.com/cpa. Be careful to check for CPA exam locations: not all Prometric test centers are secure enough to offer the high-stakes CPA professional examination. Currently over 300 centers in the United States and its four jurisdictions offer the CPA exam. No international sites have been approved. The AICPA indicates that it is unlikely to offer the CPA exam outside of the United States in the near future. Candidates do, however, have some increased flexibility as they are permitted to sit for the exam at centers outside of the state in which they apply to sit. For example, a candidate could sit for the Auditing and Attestation (AUDIT) section in Denver, Colorado, and sit for the Financial Accounting and Reporting (FAR) exam in Los Angeles, California. Candidates have a great deal of flexibility in scheduling their test center location, exam dates, and exam times.

FLEXIBLE SCHEDULING

Flexibility is the name of the game. It's up to each candidate to select the day, time, and test center location. Be careful to plan ahead. Due to eligibility and security concerns, no candidate will be permitted to schedule an examination appointment at Prometric fewer than five days prior to the appointment date. Test center hours vary, with most centers offering the CPA exam Monday through Friday, from 9 a.m. to 6 p.m. Many centers also offer evening and Saturday hours. Before your plan is set in stone, verify your selected test center hours of operation. Don't make assumptions—if your planned date is a holiday, double-check that the center will remain open that day. Add at least an extra one-half hour to the examination time. For example, if you were scheduling an appointment to take the Business Environment and Concepts section (BEC), you would allow for at least three hours of time at the center; two and one-half hours of actual examination time and one-half hour to check in. To get your first choice of dates and locations, candidates are advised to schedule an examination appointment at Prometric at least forty-five days in advance. Before scheduling can occur, candidates must file for an authorization to test (ATT). Refer to Chapter 3, Scheduling and Applying for the Exam, for a description of how to apply. Allow at least four to six weeks for the approval process and payment of the applicable examination fees (also discussed in Chapter 3). Upon payment of the fees, candidates receive a notice to schedule (NTS). You must receive a valid NTS before you can schedule your examination.

As you will read in Chapter 21, Nerves of Steel, it is recommended that you visit the Prometric test center prior to the test to verify location and travel time. Why increase exam anxiety by selecting a distant test center? As of the date of this publication, there are at least two scheduling methods: Candidates can make examination appointments online via the Prometric Web site, www.prometric.com/cpa, or by calling Prometric's candidate services call center at 1-800-580-9648. (Hearing-impaired candidates using a teletypewriter [TTY] may call 1-800-529-3590 to schedule appointments.) In the early months after the launch of the computer-based exam, candidates reported that the third scheduling option, calling the local test center directly, did not always work. Some test centers indicated that they could not complete the request directly at the site.

Before you call, have your NTS in front of you. You are required to provide certain information listed on your NTS when making your examination appointment. Leaving a voice mail message does not constitute a valid appointment. Candidates using the online registration method receive instant confirmation of examination appointments. Those candidates who register via telephone receive verbal confirmation from the Prometric call center representative. Candidates do not receive written confirmation. Candidates intending to take the exam in Guam should visit www.2testGuam.com or telephone 1-671-475-5000. Guam registration procedures are slightly different.

Prometric sites are prepared to accommodate special testing requests. Each state and jurisdiction regulates the granting of special test accommodations. Should you require assistance, begin by contacting the applicable state board of accountancy. All parties—Prometric, the AICPA, and the state boards—follow the guidelines of the Americans with Disabilities Act. The type of accommodation will be shown on your NTS. Notification of the accommodation also is sent to Prometric. Neither you nor your Prometric exam proctor can make any changes to the accommodations that have been approved. If you believe your accommodations are incorrect, contact your board of accountancy before proceeding.

Double booking of examination appointments is not allowed. Candidates will be approved to take an individual exam section only once during any one testing window. This is to prevent candidates from previewing an exam section one week and then taking that same exam section the next week at another test center. The rules are clear; candidates will be approved to sit for an exam section only once in each testing window.

Candidates may reschedule an existing examination appointment. The easiest method is to use the scheduling tool at www.prometric.com/cpa, since the system is available twenty-four hours a day, seven days a week. Appointments changed thirty days or more before the scheduled time usually are processed at no additional cost. Changes made within five business days to thirty days before the exam date require payment of an additional fee. Consult the Prometric Web site for exact details. Saturday is considered a business day. No refunds are given for cancellations or no-shows. The entire exam fee is forfeited.

FOLLOW THE RULES

Follow the rules and you will survive. Candidates report that the Prometric test center personnel are very polite and efficient. To date, no major problems have been reported. The centers are quiet and the computers work as promised. Don't expect the exam proctors to make exceptions for you. If you forget your NTS or the two required forms of identification, you will be barred from sitting for that exam section. Leave prohibited items, such as watches, food, beverages, plastic bags, and writing instruments, at home. You will be given everything you need to complete the exam. The center provides you with a pencil and scratch paper. If noise is a problem, you can obtain a special set of earplugs at the test center. You will not be permitted to bring your own earplugs.

Examples of behavior that will not be tolerated during the exam are

- Repeating acts of misconduct after receiving prior warning(s)
- Tampering with computer software or hardware
- Attempting to remove items from the testing room
- Copying, writing, or summarizing exam questions on any material other than the scratch paper issued to you

If you suspect center staff of misconduct, such as looking over your shoulder to obtain confidential exam material, you should contact the security division of Prometric at 1-800-347-3781. You can use the same number to report suspected cheating. Report content issues to the AICPA Examinations team via fax at 1-201-938-3443 within four days from the date of completing the referenced examination section. Your fax should include the precise nature of your concern, the rationale, and, if possible, references. It also should include your candidate identification number. The AICPA will not respond directly.

PRACTICE BEFORE YOU GO

The AICPA reports that the cutting and pasting functions performed during the simulations have caused candidates some concern. Confusion can occur in three primary areas.

- Cutting and pasting to fulfill the research requirement. Understand that the entire paragraph, not just a word or phrase, is to be pasted into the research answer box. Review the discussion in Chapter 9, The Research Component: How Many Hits?
- Some candidates attempt to copy and paste information out of the research software into their communication response. Then, when they enable spell-check, the alignment, font, and wording adjust to a rather strange format. Do not copy and paste out of the research software into a Communication tab.
- In the REG section, when completing the Research tab, candidates are required to type the IRS Code section number rather than copy and paste an entire paragraph as in the FAR and AUDIT sections.

All of these concerns could be alleviated if candidates completed the AICPA sample exam at least three times before arriving at the Prometric test center. The AICPA reports that candidates who avail themselves of the tutorial and the sample exams do not experience such problems. Practice is key. Avoid confusion; use the AICPA practice tools that are available to you.

COMPUTER GLITCHES

Are you worried you will experience computer problems? Stop worrying now. The procedures have been in place long enough to prove that the system works. Chances are highly unlikely that the computer will give you problems. You could, however, provoke problems if you are not well versed in the exam navigational processes. It is essential that you practice the sample exams. You must work with the system. The platforms are in place, the center's staff is well trained, and you are not the first person to take this high-stakes professional exam. All of the computer features should work well. In the very unlikely situation that they do not, the test center staff will give you guidance about how and where you report the problems. Some of the very best technology personnel in the world have prepared this exam. The entire process was tested extensively before implementation. Remain focused on your job: to prepare by reviewing the technical content. The computer format is the least of your worries. You know enough about the exam and the Prometric center to feel comfortable. Get back to the business of studying. You must be prepared to answer the technical questions. You are not required to fix computer glitches.

Do you worry about power surges? Don't worry. The technical computer people are a step ahead of you. The exam is saved every sixty seconds. In the event of a power outage, you would lose less than one minute of your work. Don't worry about the computer performing well—that's a given. Be concerned about your performance.

TIME MANAGEMENT

Time management is essential to your survival. Please read, study, and apply the time management techniques discussed in Chapter 22, Time Management. Your whole test experience could be greatly affected by poor time management. You will not be allowed to wear or bring a watch into the testing room. You must control your time using the clock on the top bar of the exam window. Prometric staff cannot assist you in monitoring exam time.

PERSONALLY SPEAKING

Candidates report that Prometric test center personnel operate very professionally. To date, no major problems have been reported. Most centers are quiet, and very few computer glitches have been noted. Here are a few comments that veteran test takers want to share with you.

- Leave your study materials at home. The lockers at the center are very small. Large binders do not fit.
- Wear comfortable clothes but be prepared to wear your sweatshirt or sweater the entire time. Proctors do not allow you to remove clothing during the exam.
- At small test centers (sixteen seats), the proctors are very accommodating. If you arrive early and ask to begin the exam early, your request might be granted.
- Travel to the center alone. Family and friends must cheer you on from home. The center does not allow people to wait in the reception area.
- If you require food during the exam, you must exit the testing room, go to your locker, and retrieve your food. You must consume all food and beverage items outside of the testing room. Try to get by without comfort food. There is little or no time to eat and drink during the exam.
- The actual CPA exam looks and feels just like the AICPA sample exam shown at www.cpa-exam.org. Become very familiar with the sample exams before you take the actual exam. If you don't, you could become flustered very quickly.
- The testing room is quiet.
- The chairs are comfortable.

- The computer screens are seventeen inches wide, and the screen clarity is much better than most computers at my workplace.
- Candidates are videotaped as they take the exam. Don't allow the taping to increase your anxiety level. Five minutes into the exam, you will be too busy to think about the cameras.
- If you encounter problems using the scroll bar within the research requirement, alert the proctor, also report the problem to the AICPA within four business days from the time you completed the exam. Exam content concerns are to be sent via fax to the AICPA at 1-201-938-3443. Include your candidate identification number, the precise nature of your concern, the rationale, and an exact reference to the testlet number and the tab description. Memorize this information before you leave the exam room, as you are not allowed to take information out of the test area.
- Sometimes people need additional scratch paper. The proctors respond quickly to requests for additional scratch paper.
- Leave your personal writing instruments at home. You are given a Prometric pencil to use. You must put all personal items in your locker.

The exam has begun on a positive note. I have received no negative feedback about the testing process. What a momentous change. You will participate in one of the most professional examination processes in the world. This won't be like the typical reality television show. There is no requirement to eat live worms or to walk on hot coals. The experience will be real, and you will survive when you plan ahead, practice the AICPA sample exams, and follow the rules listed in the candidate bulletin (found on the www.cpa-exam.org Web site and the on the www.prometric.com/cpa Web site). You will become a CPA exam survivor!

CPA EXAM TIP:
Take your appointment seriously. Failure to show up for a test appointment will cause you to lose money and possibly the testing opportunity.

21 NERVES OF STEEL

What are nerves of steel? How do you maintain nerves of steel throughout the CPA examination process? This chapter discusses methods to control CPA exam nerves and overcome exam intimidation. Exam anxiety can quickly send you into a tailspin, causing you to second-guess yourself, make simple mistakes, and forget your technical knowledge. Exam jitters don't help. If you are stressed, chances are the stress will cause you to earn a lower exam score. Passing the exam requires a unique mix of knowledge, exam strategy, confidence, and stamina. Don't risk losing control. Be aware of how your nerves can work against you.

YOUR NERVES

The power to pass the CPA exam resides in you. Only you can walk into the Prometric test center and answer the questions. No candidate earns points by being nervous. Points are earned by applying knowledge. Adjectives that describe the nervous feeling you have include jumpy, jittery, fidgety, uneasy, tense, fearful, and agitated. None of these characteristics will help you pass an exam section. It is very difficult to apply knowledge when you are nervous. You must remain calm to pass. Adjectives that describe the calm attitude you need to pass are peaceful, composed, cool, collected, undisturbed, serene, tranquil, and unruffled. Work to remain calm, rather than nervous.

GET THOSE NERVES OF STEEL

Nerves of steel are not available for purchase. No store sells them. Just like the much-desired abs of steel, you must work to develop nerves of steel. No one can expect to have a flat, strong stomach without hard work and exercise. Simply buying the exercise equipment and leaving it in the box is not going to help you. The same situation applies to maintaining nerves of steel during the CPA exam process. Purchasing review materials is not the answer. You must **use** those materials to learn. Knowledge reduces fear. The more you learn, the less fearful you will be. Open the materials and study. Work those questions. View the AICPA exam tutorial and take the sample exams at www.cpa-exam.org. Experiment with the navigational tabs. Use the research database examples to practice. Help yourself by learning the material until you reach a comfort level that allows you to feel confident. Feed your mind with knowledge.

VISIT THE EXAM SITE BEFORE EXAM DAY

Six to eight weeks before you take the first exam section, visit a Prometric test site. Keep in mind that the CPA examination is a high-stakes professional examination that is administered using a high level of security. Don't expect the Prometric center staff to allow you to preview the CPA exam. Don't even ask. Tell them that you just want to look at the reception area to familiarize yourself with the check-in procedures. Locate the restrooms. Drive around the building and note various parking lots, should your preferred lot be full. Note the nearest bus or train connection. Try to travel to the site about the same time of the day you plan to sit for your exam section. Document your travel times. Note whether rush-hour traffic might create a problem.

Just seeing the actual examination location will help keep you calm. Later, when you visualize yourself at the exam, you will have an accurate picture of your surroundings. Trace your route to the exam. If you are taking the exam in a town other than where you live, travel the route to and from your hotel. Be sure the hotel is quiet. Avoid staying at hotels near busy roads and/or railroad tracks. Note the location of restaurants where you might sit and review your notes before you arrive at the test center. Obtain information about the cost of breakfast and/or lunch in nearby restaurants where you can complete a last-minute review of key concepts. If you are staying in a hotel, inquire about checkout time and the availability of coffee, ice, and other items that you consider a necessity. Ask if your hotel room will include a refrigerator, coffeepot, and other essentials such as a hairdryer. Know what to expect.

VISUALIZE YOURSELF IN CONTROL

When you reflect on what it will be like at the exam, always visualize yourself as a person who is in control of the situation. See yourself as calm, collected, and knowledgeable rather than as jumpy, fidgety, and stressed. Picture yourself so attuned to the exam material that you couldn't possibly have time to be nervous. See yourself methodically moving through the questions, working one exam testlet at a time, staying within the time limits, and completing all of the questions. See yourself as successfully searching for answers to the research components. Visualize yourself writing the communication answers in complete sentences with correct spelling. Picture yourself showcasing your knowledge on the communications component. See yourself earning points.

BRACE YOURSELF FOR THE UNEXPECTED

Realize that you won't know everything. Understand that the examiners will ask you some unexpected questions. No matter how much you studied and practiced using previous exam questions, plenty of new questions will stump you. There is no need to get agitated. After reading a question that you can't answer, take a deep breath and say, "Oh, here is a question that I don't know, and now I must guess the correct answer." Go ahead and be brave. Use your practiced exam technique of narrowing down the answer choices. Eliminating one or two of the answers will increase your chances of guessing the correct answer. If you are unable to eliminate any of the four answer options, make an outright guess. Select your predetermined outright guess answer (e.g., when you don't know the answer, select the second of the four choices). Don't waste time thinking about which answer option to select as an outright guess. Use the same answer choice each time as your guess response. Guess consistently and you will be correct some of the time.

Don't panic when you open a simulation work tab and see a question that you know nothing about. Stay in control by first reflecting on your overall knowledge. Skim the question; look for cues and clues that will jog your memory. Release tension by smiling and laughing quietly. Take a deep breath and say to yourself: "Oh, here is a great question." Know that you should not be stumped because you used current study materials and spent time reviewing the material. If you are stumped, it could indicate that the AICPA is pretesting a topical area in which you are unfamiliar. Remember that 20% of the multiple-choice questions represent pretest items that are not counted in your final score. If you studied and don't have the answers, then those who did not devote time to studying are really clueless. Build yourself up. Suppress those negative feelings that focus on how tough the exam is. Feel good about the fact that you are here, taking the exam. You are doing your best.

Use that scratch paper. List some of the elements of the question. Jot down key concepts and formulas. Stare at the points you listed, allowing a mental image to form in your brain. If you studied, you should know some-thing about the topic. Let the words speak to you. For example, a concept such as "accounting for uncompensated employee absences" provides you with clues. An employee has been absent from the job and has not yet been compensated for the absences. What is the accounting issue? If the em-ployee has been promised compensation, the business must accrue for the absence. Form the journal entry: Debit an expense account and credit a li-ability account. The compensation has been earned but not yet paid. Take some time to reflect. Remain calm, and the knowledge will come to the fore-front of your mind. Allow yourself to become agitated, and panic will take over. Expect some questions to throw you. Work to control the situation and to keep calm.

TAKE SOME RISKS

Even the best athletes aren't going to keep winning without taking some risks. Don't be afraid to take some risk. Every now and then, decide that you must go for it. Taking risks means that you answer each and every question to the best of your ability. If that means guessing on a question, then so be it. It is what you must do to earn points. You have no chance of earning points if you leave a question blank. By answering each and every question, you have a chance to improve your score. Leave nothing blank. The CPA exam is positively graded—you earn points by doing. Points are not deducted for incorrect answers. Points are awarded for correct answers. For example, on a communication question, when in doubt, write it down. If the graders don't want the concept, they will ignore it. Stay on topic and write it!

USE YOUR FAVORITE RELAXATION TECHNIQUES

Performers and athletes often go to a corner and meditate or pray before an important event. Others listen to their favorite music. Some might call friends or family to talk about something other than the event coming up. Before exam day, think about your personal relaxation techniques. What works for you?

Maybe your favorite relaxation technique is to sit in a bubble bath and read. Obviously you can't take the exam while bathing. Take a bubble bath the night before. Close your eyes and think about the task at hand. Reflect on what you know. Ignore what you don't know. It's too late to learn new material at this point. You have reached the final stretch. Don't schedule an outing for the night before the exam. To calm your nerves, you must remain focused on the next day's task. Don't schedule a massage for the morning before the exam. You might become so relaxed that you fall asleep during the exam. Schedule a massage the night before the exam to help you sleep. Get a manicure or a pedicure. Do simple activities by yourself. Give your-self time to visualize what you must do. Friends, family, and coworkers might irritate you by their lack of understanding about what it is that you must do. Others tend to oversimplify the process because they don't under-stand the difficulty of this exam. You will remain calmer if you are by your-self.

Keep your relaxation techniques simple on the day of the exam. Some suggestions are

- Chew gum.
- Play your favorite music on the way to the Prometric center.
- Close your eyes and picture a tranquil scene, such as a waterfall with gentle rolling water.
- Do some jumping jacks.
- Go outside and breathe in the fresh air; listen to the birds singing.
- Give yourself a pat on the back; you have done your best.
- Smile at your reflection in the mirror.
- Take deep breaths.

- Complement the test center proctors on their clothing or hairstyle; make others smile.
- Sing or hum to yourself.
- Smile, smile, and smile some more.

Notice that most of these activities are easy to do and are very low-key. Why? You don't want to get yourself stirred up before the exam. Avoid creating a situation that increases your stress level.

DON'T CRAM

Don't study up until the last minute before the exam. Clear your mind. Leave your exam materials at home or in the car. The lockers at the Prometric site are small, and they will not accommodate large binders of review materials. Last-minute study points probably will not remain in your mind throughout the exam. Hastily learned concepts could confuse you more and cause you to forget key concepts that you previously mastered.

STAY CALM, NOT ACTIVE

Pacing around the house or your hotel room will only add to your tension. Your heart will beat faster, and you might become more nervous. Keep your preexam activities to a minimum. Engage in peaceful activities to foster a peaceful state of mind.

FORGET THE OFFICE

Your colleagues know it's exam day. Don't call them; they will just remind you of the many looming issues and deadlines. You can't do anything now about a troubled client or project. Save those concerns for your return the next day.

WATCH WHAT YOU EAT AND DRINK

Eat foods that won't upset your stomach. Having greasy sausage and bacon for a preexam breakfast may lead to trouble later on. Stuffing yourself at a breakfast or luncheon buffet leads to a drop in blood-sugar levels a few hours later. Drinking too much coffee or caffeine beverages not only leads to many restroom breaks, but also can bring on a decrease in energy level as the caffeine wears off. On the other hand, if you are used to morning caffeine, don't try to go without your morning fix. Stick to your normal routine as much as possible. Now is not the time to experiment, diet, or overeat. Do what you normally do.

Try to eat at least ninety minutes before taking the exam. Give your digestive system a chance to work before you enter the test center. Avoid alcoholic beverages—save them for after the exam. Give yourself the best possible chance to think clearly. Stress levels decrease when you take a rational approach to the situation. This is just one exam section. It is not a matter of life or death.

DON'T TRY TO SHOW OFF

If you plan to take an exam section with another person, don't try to impress other candidates by reciting concepts out loud. You just might make a mistake and become really flustered. Keep your technical thoughts to yourself. Clear your mind. Engage in light conversation about the weather, a person's outfit, or the color of the walls. If a candidate asks you about a technical concept, say you don't remember. You could become more confused. Once you have arrived at the center and are sitting in the reception area, there is no time to go back and check your notes. Now is not the time to be helpful. Now is the time to concentrate and focus on the exam.

FORGET ABOUT WHAT YOU DON'T KNOW

So what if you see others at the Prometric test center who appear to know more than you? So what if there are areas that you did not study? You can't do anything about that today. You are at the exam site and must perform with the knowledge that you have today. The exam will begin in a few minutes. There is no time to improve the situation. Nerves of steel require you to keep that positive attitude out in front of you at all times. Go ahead and admit that you don't know everything. Yes, there are content areas where you still feel your knowledge is weak. That's to be expected with an exam of such technical breadth. You are ready to face the exam. Predict that you will respond to each and every question to the best of your ability. Trust that the knowledge you have will be enough to get you a 75 on each section, one exam section at a time. Remain positive and in control.

YOU DON'T NEED TO BE PERFECT TO PASS

Tolerate an average to below-average performance because an average to below-average performance on the CPA exam will get you a score of 75 or greater. Each exam section score is equated, meaning that there could be times where a raw score of 50 to 60% could result in an earned score of 75. Allow yourself some slack and be forgiving if you don't know something. Think about all that you do know. Nerves of steel require you to be positive. Nerves of steel will help you perform at a higher level.

PERSONALLY SPEAKING

All this talk about nerves of steel may make you think you have to be superhuman to pass the exam. What if you lose it right before the exam begins? What if you are calm until you encounter a test question that rattles you? How will you respond with nerves of steel? Think of the exam process as a performance. When dancers make a mistake, they keep dancing until the dance is over. When Olympic skaters fall during a jump, they get up off the ice and keep on performing. This is what you must do. You must keep on trying to complete the exam. You are completing one question at a time. You have no time to deal with frustration now. You must focus all of your energy on moving forward to complete the exam. You must look ahead to each question rather than looking back and worrying about the topics you do not know.

Release the tension before you enter the exam room. I know candidates who must cry before each exam. Okay, break down and cry. Others like to fidget, wiggle their legs, and blink their eyes frequently. I don't care what your technique is, but use it **before** you enter the testing room. Once you enter the room and sit down in front of the computer terminal, you must stay calm. See the computer screen as your friend. Silently say: "Hello, computer. Today we are going to kick some butt." This may not sound professional, but it will help you release some of the anxiety.

More than one candidate has reported that he was so nervous that he could not even press the right keys. When he started the exam, his hands were shaking so much he hit the wrong keys. Stop it! You can't let this happen. You must take a deliberate approach, consciously making the right moves. Begin slowly. The extra time you take in the beginning will pay off down the home stretch. If you hit the wrong keys, you could find yourself staring at some weird screen shots. Proceed slowly at first. Look at the overall navigational system. The system is just like the tutorial and the sample exam located at the www.cpa-exam.org site. Be confident—you know how this works. You have practiced.

Maintaining nerves of steel requires you to forget about what others think. Let's say that the whole world knows you are taking a section of the CPA exam today. Your boss, your clients, your college professors, your friends, and your family all think that you will pass. After all, they say, you have always performed well. Why shouldn't you perform well today? Their belief in your abilities is flattering, but don't let it scare you. Let's say the first six multiple-choice questions are very difficult for you. How will you react? If you think about all of those people who are relying on you to pass this exam, you could overreact and lose your composure. Wait a minute. Are they really relying on you? No, they just believe in you. Get back to the basics—you must continue to believe in yourself even when the going gets tough. Talk to yourself. Maybe those first six questions were pretest questions with which the AICPA is experimenting. So you don't know everything. I told you that you would encounter concepts that you did not know. Just pick up your spirits and move on. You have a performance to complete. This exam is your event and no one else's. It is up to you to do your best. A calm, cool, and collected candidate has a much better chance of performing well than a flustered, shaky, and nervous person. Sit up tall in your chair, read the exam questions carefully, and press those computer keys with confidence. You've got nerves of steel.

CPA EXAM TIP:
Remain calm, no matter what happens. Anger, frustration, and disgust only lead to despair. Smile, work hard, and give each question the old college try. Continue to believe in your abilities.

22 TIME MANAGEMENT

This chapter deals with time management while taking the actual CPA exam sections at the Prometric test center. See Chapter 11, Developing Your Personal Study Plan, for tips on how to manage your time while studying.

Time management during the exam is crucial because the AICPA does not provide any time allotments. During the exam, the only time device is the box in the middle of the top title bar that lists the time remaining for the entire exam. Candidates cannot wear watches into the test center. Clocks are not available. Candidates must be prepared to allocate their time. Take control of the exam by apportioning the total exam time among the testlets at the beginning of each exam section. You will be pushed for time. Spend time practicing with software that counts the time frame down. You will see how this works when you work the AICPA sample exam as presented on the www.cpa-exam.org Web site. You are asking for trouble if you report to take an exam section before you have worked the sample exam. You must see firsthand how each exam function works. Don't take time for granted—time can be your greatest enemy. Plan and apportion your time and apply the appropriate techniques to ensure that you complete the entire exam. Proper time management is essential. Each exam section must be addressed separately. Let's begin with the shortest exam section, Business Environment and Concepts (BEC).

BEC TIME MANAGEMENT

The total time allotment for the BEC section is two and one-half hours. As of the publication date of this book, the BEC section consists of three testlets of multiple-choice questions only. Each multiple-choice testlet contains twenty-four to thirty separate questions spanning the entire AICPA content specification outline (CSO). All three testlets will have the same number of questions. For example, if the first testlet has twenty-eight questions, the other two testlets also will have twenty-eight questions. Could a candidate taking the BEC section on the same day have, say, twenty-six questions in each testlet while another candidate has thirty questions? Yes, two candidates testing the same day could receive a different number of questions. You won't know how many questions per testlet you will have until you open the first testlet. The candidate receiving thirty questions per testlet is not granted additional time. All candidates have a total of 150 minutes to complete the BEC section. Does this seem fair? Fair or not, this is how the CPA exam works. You must deal with it.

There is one simple solution: Allocate equal time to each testlet. You must complete each testlet within fifty minutes. It is very important to realize that the fifty-minute time allotment includes any break time you may choose to take. The clock continues to count down during any breaks. Remember that breaks are allowed only after a testlet has been completed. If you find you are running behind time after testlet number one, skip a break. Exhibit 22.1 shows the suggested time allotment for the BEC section.

Exhibit 22.1: Business Environment and Concepts Time Management

Testlet 1	Testlet 2	Testlet 3
MC 24-30 About 50 minutes	MC 24-30 About 50 minutes	MC 24-30 About 50 minutes
• Includes 20% pretest • See content below	• Includes 20% pretest • See content below	• Includes 20% pretest • See content below
Time remaining at end of testlet: **1 hour 40 minutes**	Time remaining at end of testlet: **50 minutes**	Time remaining at end of testlet: **None**

- Two and one-half hour exam (clock continues during breaks).
- Testlets must be worked consecutively.
- You may move back and forth **within** a testlet.
- All content specification topics are testable within each testlet.
- No simulations for testing windows in 2004; Could be added in 2005.
- Content summary is
    - 30% finance
    - 20% business structure (formerly tested on Law)
    - 20% managerial (formerly tested on ARE)
    - 20% information technology
    - 10% economics

Keep in mind that there is no penalty for guessing on an answer. Therefore, you should answer **all** questions. Before you enter the exam room, select a response that you will use for each guess. Guessing consistently gives you a chance of earning some points. For example, some candidates always select the second response for their outright guess response. Admittedly, this is not the ideal method to use to achieve a passing score. However, it will save you time for those few questions where you are totally clueless. No matter how much you prepare, there is always a chance that a question or two in each testlet will stump you. Once you admit to yourself that this will happen and that this situation is very normal, you won't fret about it. Make your guess and move on. There is no time to waste.

Another complicating factor is that some questions will require computations and the use of the on-screen calculator and other questions will not. It is wise to establish some time checks within each testlet.

Exhibit 22.1 shows the time allocation for each BEC testlet. Spend fifty minutes on each testlet. This assumes no breaks of any kind. Within each testlet, check your time at twenty-five-minute intervals. What should you do if you are running behind time? You have no choice but to pick up your pace. You cannot return to a testlet once you have closed it. You do have the option of marking questions for review as you work each testlet. Be sure to select an answer even if you plan to review the question later. Doing so will ensure that you have a chance of earning points. Leaving questions blank is a losing proposition. You have shut off any chance of earning points. Use of the guessing technique is better than leaving any question blank.

Time is your enemy only when it is uncontrollable. You have the power to control the time by allocating and managing the total exam experience. Refer to Chapter 21, Nerves of Steel, for ideas on how to control the entire experience. Sometimes it requires you to talk to yourself. Sometimes you must be brave and give it your best attempt. Whatever you do, you cannot look back. This advice applies to all four exam sections. You have no time to waste. Therefore, you always must move forward both physically and mentally. You can't be thinking about a question that was asked in the first testlet when you are working questions in the second testlet. You can't change your answer now. Your focus must remain on the task at hand—the current testlet.

Candidates report that time is tight for all sections. However, because at this time, the BEC section is only multiple-choice format, time pressure will not be as much of a concern as it is for the other three exam sections. Your next challenge is to control the time on the Regulation (REG) exam.

REG TIME MANAGEMENT

Your total time for the Regulation (REG) section is three hours, or 180 minutes. The REG exam contains a total of five testlets. The first three contain twenty-four multiple-choice questions. Yes, the AICPA has designated the number of questions to always be twenty-four. Before you relax, re-member that there are two more testlets in the REG section that utilize the simulation format. For details of how the simulations work, refer to the AICPA sample exams at www.cpa-exam.org and review Chapters 7 and 8 of this book. The time clock reports time in hours and minutes. For example, forty-five minutes into the REG exam, the clock will show time remaining of two hours and fifteen minutes. Always think in terms of hours and min-utes rather than total minutes. Exhibit 22.2 shows the suggested time allot-ments for each of the five testlets. Again, the time allotments include break time. Because the test is only three hours, it's best if you don't take a break. Candidates report that time does not usually permit a break during the REG section. You must tough it out. Be sure to visit the facilities before the exam begins. Limit your beverage intake before the exam. If you are a smoker, chew nicotine gum. Take your prescription medicines before you enter the test center. The test takes only a short time. You can make it.

Exhibit 22.2: Regulation Time Management

Testlet 1	*Testlet 2*	*Testlet 3*
MC 24 About 30 minutes	MC 24 About 30 minutes	MC 24 About 30 minutes
• Includes 20% pretest • 60% taxation topics • 40% ethics, business law, and legal and professional responsibilities	• Includes 20% pretest • 60% taxation topics • 40% ethics, business law, and legal and professional responsibilities	• Includes 20% pretest • 60% taxation topics • 40% ethics, business law, and legal and professional responsibilities
Time remaining at end of testlet: **2 hours 30 minutes**	Time remaining at end of testlet: **2 hours**	Time remaining at end of testlet: **1 hour 30 minutes**

Testlet 4	*Testlet 5*
Simulation About 45 minutes	Simulation About 45 minutes
• Communication— includes writing skills • Research (generic) • Other (see www.cpa-exam.org tutorial)	• Communication— includes writing skills • Research (generic) • Other (see www.cpa-exam.org tutorial)
Time remaining at end of testlet: **45 minutes**	Time remaining at end of testlet: **None**

- Three hour exam (clock continues during breaks).
- Testlets must be worked consecutively.
- You may move back and forth **within** a testlet.
- All content specification topics are testable within each testlet.
- Simulations—spell-check can be enabled; grammar check is not available.

Note that the time allotment for each simulation is equal. What if you encounter trouble on the first simulation? Should you take extra time to complete it, in the hopes that the next testlet will be easier and quicker to complete? Don't risk it. Robbing time to complete any of the testlets is very dangerous. You could risk having to leave an entire testlet blank, costing you as much as fifteen total points. Remember, the multiple-choice sections are worth 70% of the total exam points, while the simulations are worth 30%. Leave a simulation blank and it will cost you dearly. Use a special approach to time management for the simulations.

SIMULATION TIME MANAGEMENT

The clock is running. You open testlet 4 and there it is—a simulation. At first it may appear overwhelming. Then you realize it is just like the sample exams that you worked on the AICPA Web site. Candidates report that the sample exam is nearly identical to the actual exam. By spending time at home, slowly reviewing each work and informational tab, you can move more quickly than someone who is seeing the format for the very first time. Your first strategy should be to open each work tab to see what it is that you must do. Jot down a few key items on your scrap paper. Now return to the directions, company profile, and resource information tabs. By reading the question requirements first, you have determined what information is important to complete the work tabs. This method helps to decrease that overwhelmed feeling. You can ignore some items of information until you need them. Your first priority is completion of the total exam. Complete it piece by piece. Save the research component for last. Work the drop-down box and more structured questions first. Complete the communication section after you have answered the structured work tabs. Don't forget to review the resource tab for helpful information that might provide clues to your answer selection. Yes, you are controlling this exam, and you are very aware of the time limitations.

What should you do if you are having trouble locating the relevant research paragraph(s)? Enter what you can. Completing the rest of the exam is far more important than eating up time struggling to find the exact wording. Remember that you are not permitted to edit the research component. Simply enter entire paragraphs or code sections by using the appropriate copy and paste routines. Note that the copy and paste routine for the REG section is different from the copy and paste routine for the Auditing and Attestation (AUDIT) and the Financial Accounting and Reporting (FAR) sections. Practice all of the sample exams until you become very comfortable with all of the functions. Practicing only one exam section is like reading one chapter of a book—a chapter in the middle. You have missed the details. Give yourself every chance to be successful—practice until you know it! Practice will give you the confidence to move through the exam at a quicker pace. Time management is a critical process!

FAR TIME MANAGEMENT

Good morning! Most likely the FAR exam is scheduled to begin in the morning. Since this exam section is 240 minutes long, candidates spend the better part of a day at the test center. Check-in time is thirty minutes before the exam start time. The FAR and AUDIT time allotment should allow you to take at least one break during the testing process. Exhibit 22.3 presents the time allotments for the FAR section. Stick to the time suggestions.

Exhibit 22.3: Financial Accounting and Reporting Time Management

Testlet 1	Testlet 2	Testlet 3
MC 24-30 About 50 minutes	MC 24-30 About 50 minutes	MC 24-30 About 50 minutes
• Includes 20% pretest • 80% financial topics • 20% government and not-for-profit	• Includes 20% pretest • 80% financial topics • 20% government and not-for-profit	• Includes 20% pretest • 80% financial topics • 20% government and not-for-profit
Time remaining at end of testlet: **3 hours 10 minutes**	Time remaining at end of testlet: **2 hours 20 minutes**	Time remaining at end of testlet: **1 hour 30 minutes**

Testlet 4	Testlet 5
Simulation About 45 minutes	Simulation About 45 minutes
• Communication— includes writing skills • Research FARS • Other (see www.cpa-exam.org tutorial)	•• Communication— includes writing skills • Research FARS • Other (see www.cpa-exam.org tutorial)
Time remaining at end of testlet: **45 minutes**	Time remaining at end of testlet: **None**

- Four-hour exam (clock continues during breaks).
- Testlets must be worked consecutively.
- You may move back and forth **within** a testlet.
- All content specification topics are testable within each testlet.
- Simulations—spell-check can be enabled; grammar check is not available.

Although the REG exam specifies twenty-four multiple-choice questions, the BEC, FAR, and AUDIT sections can have anywhere from twenty-four to thirty multiple-choice questions. The first testlet will serve as your clue. Each testlet has the same number of questions.

One technique that works to save time and to maintain exam focus is to read the question portion of the multiple-choice question first, before answering it. Look at this question.

On December 1, 2004, Leslie Corporation declared a property dividend of marketable securities to be distributed on December 31, 2004, to stockholders of record on December 15, 2004. On December 31, the marketable securities had a carrying amount of $60,000 and a fair value of $78,000. What is the effect of this property dividend on Leslie's 2004 retained earnings after all nominal accounts have been closed?
a. $0
b. $18,000 increase
c. $60,000 decrease
d. $78,000 decrease

Savvy candidates will read the last sentence first. **"What is the effect of this property dividend on Leslie's 2004 retained earnings after all nominal accounts have been closed?"** The question is asking about the retained earnings effect of a property dividend. Save time and skip all date references except for the date of declaration. You don't need to use all information to answer the question. Remember, all dividends decrease retained earnings. Since this is a property dividend, the gain on the securities would increase retained earnings by $18,000. The answer is quick and it is simple—retained earnings will decrease by $78,000 for the dividend less the $18,000 increase to retained earnings for the increase in the market value of the securities. The answer is $60,000. The other dates were extraneous information. Save yourself time. Read the question first. This technique works very well for FAR and REG income tax questions.

What happens if the computer screen freezes or there is a power outage? As discussed in Chapter 20, Surviving the Prometric Experience, provisions have been made to assist you. Your work is saved every sixty seconds. You do not need to hit a save function during the exam. Your work is automatically saved. The exam proctors are trained in methods to adjust your time if the screen freezes. The CPA exam is a high-stakes professional exam with a great deal of visibility. Procedures are in place to deal with every possible problem. Trust the system. Today you will complete a section of the CPA exam. That is your mission. You don't have time to think about problems occurring with the system. Your time must be spent focusing on the questions and providing answers to those questions.

The FAR, AUDIT, and REG sections contain a work tab within the simulations called "communications." Chapter 7, The Communications Component—Formerly Called Essays, deals with the specifics on how to prepare an appropriate response to such a question. You must complete the entire simulation, which includes the communication component, within the time specified for testlets 4 and 5. This includes taking the time to hit the spell-check function. Remember, spell-check is not automatic. You must tell the computer to check your spelling. Many of us rely on computers to automatically adjust our spelling. Take the time to check spelling after you have written your communication response and proofread. Why proofread before hitting the spell-check function? Candidates often make adjustments and additions to their work. You will want to spell-check the final product.

AUDIT TIME MANAGEMENT

Here's the long haul! The AUDIT exam is scheduled for four and one-half hours or a total of 270 minutes. Most college students have never taken an exam this long before. Use a software review product and create practice exams of this length. See the practice as part of your dress rehearsal.

AUDIT is the longest section and as such will require you to work at remaining focused. Concentration is key. If you must, write information down on your scrap paper. Write yourself notes such as "NOT." What does this note mean? It is telling you to select the response that indicates what an auditor would be "least likely" to do. A "YES" on your scratch paper tells the candidate to look for the answer response that is "most likely."

Your eyes will feel the strain. Rest your eyes by occasionally closing them. Blink more often, and look up at the ceiling. Remember that you are not permitted to bring eye drops into the testing area. You must store such items in your locker, which you can access during breaks.

Exhibit 22.4 presents the time allotments for the AUDIT section.

Exhibit 22.4: Auditing and Attestation Time Management

Testlet 1	*Testlet 2*	*Testlet 3*
MC 24-30 About 55 minutes • Includes 20% pretest Time remaining at end of testlet: **3 hours 35 minutes**	MC 24-30 About 55 minutes • Includes 20% pretest Time remaining at end of testlet: **2 hours 40 minutes**	MC 24-30 About 55 minutes • Includes 20% pretest Time remaining at end of testlet: **1 hour 45 minutes**

Testlet 4	*Testlet 5*
Simulation About 55 minutes • Communication—includes writing skills • Research—AICPA Professional Standards • Other (see www.cpa-exam.org tutorial) Time remaining at end of testlet: **50 minutes**	Simulation About 45 minutes • Communication—includes writing skills • Research—AICPA Professional Standards • Other (see www.cpa-exam.org tutorial) Time remaining at end of testlet: **None**

- Four and one-half hour exam (clock continues during breaks).
- Testlets must be worked consecutively.
- You may move back and forth **within** a testlet.
- All content specification topics are testable within each testlet.
- Simulations—spell-check can be enabled; grammar check is not available.

PERSONALLY SPEAKING

How do I know the suggested time allotments work? Several hundred candidates taking the Northern Illinois University CPA Review course have tested my suggestions and reported that they were appropriate. I am not looking for a pat on the back. I am just providing you with a reason to trust the suggestions. Over my many years of working with CPA candidates, I am saddened to hear reports of candidates who did not finish the exam. What a waste of effort and money. Answer the questions to earn points. It's that simple.

Accountants are usually poor time managers, especially when they are taking exams. As a group, accountants tend to be perfectionists. We want everything to be correct. We will spend extra time just to make things balance. Don't keep searching for a better research answer unless you have time to spare. It is not about perfection—it is about completing the entire exam.

Continue on and don't look back. One 62-year-old taking the REG exam told me he was so plugged in to the exam experience that he lost track of time. He was enjoying the process so much he forgot about the little time box ticking away at the top of the computer screen. He ran out of time. The proctors are trained to end the exam. They will accept no excuses from you as to why you require additional time. Yes, the proctors are nice people, but they have a job to do.

Candidates and educators always ask me why you cannot preview each testlet before you begin the exam. The answer is exam security. Candidates could collaborate in the restrooms and use the research function to check multiple-choice answers. Each testlet must be worked in consecutive order. Breaks are allowed only after a testlet is completed and before you begin the next testlet.

For those candidates who are concerned about medical problems that require periodic food and drink, be aware that exceptions are made only in rare cases. If you believe your problem requires special exam accommodations, contact your state board of accountancy. Special accommodations can be made for well-documented medical reasons.

I always seem to be the one who breaks the computer or experiences trouble with the software. Why does this happen? I react too quickly. I am a driven person who types quickly and is very impatient when it comes to computer response time. Don't act like that during the exam. Work deliberately, moving through the exam at a medium speed. Working too slowly or too quickly can be equally dangerous. Give the computer time to register your request. Have I stressed the importance of taking the AICPA sample exam located at www.cpa-exam.org? I believe I have. Again, I urge you to complete all four sample exams so you can proceed with confidence.

See the ticking time box as your friend rather than your enemy. The time box gives you an excuse to guess and move on. The time box tells you when you have done what you can. Complete the entire exam and exit the test center knowing that you did your best. You answered all of the questions; you have a fighting chance.

CPA EXAM TIP:
Use only the agreed-on allocated time. Spending additional time on a testlet could result in a greater loss of points—you can't leave a testlet blank and still pass any section of the CPA exam.

23 IT'S SHOW TIME

Are you beginning to think the CPA exam is similar to a survival outing where you must learn how to exist in a vast wilderness without food, water, and the comforts of home? Just like a wilderness adventure, you will survive better if you are properly prepared and trained for the outing. Throughout the study process you are building stamina every day. You have spent a great deal of time preparing for the event. Your knowledge base of concepts is growing stronger. You can almost feel your brain growing with all that newly acquired knowledge. Still, you could commit a treacherous mistake by arriving at the exam without the proper materials, attitude, and commitment.

Yes, the time has finally arrived to perform at the exam. The final dress rehearsal is here. This chapter explains what to do in the final hours before the exam. Simple things like knowing what to wear, what to bring, and how to act at the exam can make a big difference in your performance.

WHAT TO WEAR

Wear comfortable, loose clothes. So what if you gained weight during the study process? Break down and buy yourself some new jeans or sweatpants that feel comfortable. You could be hot during the exam, or you could be cold, depending on the time of the year, the time of the day, and the conditions at the Prometric test center. A special word about temperatures: If you are seated under an air-conditioning or heating duct that bothers you, report it immediately to your proctor. The blowing air will only bother you more as each hour ticks on. The best time to switch computer stations is before you sit down and log on. Check your chair out, and make the proper height and back adjustments before you begin, while the proctor still can assist you and make any necessary switches.

What you wear into the testing room is what you must wear for the entire exam. Candidates are not allowed to remove **any** clothing during the exam process—not even simple things, such as glasses, hair ribbons, and hair clips. Be sure you can tolerate your attire for the entire testing process. You may prop your glasses up on the top of your head, but you are not permitted to set them down on the desk.

Speaking of glasses, leave your contact lenses at home. Who needs to be beautiful at the CPA exam? Wear glasses that have been prescribed within the last year and that you know help you to clearly read a computer screen. Under the stress and pressure to read so much information, your eyes could dry out. Purchase some lubricating drops and store them in your locker. You may access your storage locker, located in the center's reception area, during your breaks.

All coats and headwear (unless required for religious reasons) must be stored in your locker. Candidates who wear blazers that look like jackets or coats may be asked to store them.

Wear shoes that can accommodate swollen feet. Sitting in one position for long periods of time can cause swelling. Anything that is tight may distract you. Think about what you plan to wear and be sure it is right for you.

Wear barrettes, clips, headbands, or whatever it takes to tie or clip hair back out of your eyes; constantly fixing your hair takes time and may cause loss of concentration. Keep it out of your way.

Should men shave? If you are used to a clean-shaven face, a growing, stubbly beard could cause you to itch and/or fiddle with your face. If you normally shave, then shave for the exam. If you are used to an unshaven face over weekends, go ahead and be grubby.

Ladies, what about your purses? The Prometric storage lockers are narrow, and will not accommodate a large bag. Candidates report that a three- to four-inch binder is too large to fit in the locker. Keep your handbag small for this event. Leave backpacks, tote bags, large binders, or briefcases in your car, at home, or in your hotel room. You will enter the exam with the clothes you are wearing and with your notice to schedule (NTS) paperwork. That's it. The rules are strict.

PROHIBITED ITEMS

Watches or time devices are strictly prohibited. You will use the clock on the computer, at the top of your task bar, to control the exam time. The clock will count the minutes down for you. You are also not allowed to bring scratch paper, writing instruments, rulers, cell phones, Palm Pilots, and other such devices into the examination room. Security is tight around this exam. Candidates receive a complete listing of prohibited items along with their appointment summary that outlines their testing time. The list of items is also printed on the www.cpa-exam.org Web site under "Uniform CPA Examination Candidate Bulletin." The basic rule, however, is simple: Candidates are not allowed to bring any items into the test center room. All personal items must be stored in the Prometric reception area in a small locker. This could create problems. What about your medications? What about smoking? After all, candidates are nervous and may desire food and/or a puff on a cigar or cigarette. Are candidates who take medications given a special exemption? I think you know the answer—no medications, smoking materials, food, or beverages in the testing area. It's a sterile environment. Eat before you go. Bring nicotine gum along and pop a piece in your mouth before you enter the testing area. Think about your medication requirements when you schedule your testing time. If you absolutely cannot work out a solution, check with your state board of accountancy about taking the exam under special accommodations. Don't take this step lightly, though. Doctor verification must be well documented.

You are permitted to eat and drink and perhaps even smoke while on breaks—if you have the time.

BREAK POLICY

Your first priority is completion of the exam. Breaks, however, are permitted only after you have completed a testlet. What's a testlet? If you don't know by now, you are in trouble. But just in case you started reading this chapter first, testlets are a group of questions either in multiple-choice format or case study format. Read Chapters 16 through 19 for a detailed discussion of what each exam section's group of testlets looks like. Understand that your only option for a break will be in between each testlet. The test center staff will confirm that you have completed a testlet prior to your break.

You are **not** required to take a break. The clock keeps running during the break. The restrooms are outside of the test area. As suggested in Chapter 22, Time Management, you should allow a minimum of five minutes for a break. Think about the exam time section limit. For example, Auditing and Attestation is four and one-half hours long. Most people will want to take at least one break. Locate the restroom as you enter the center. This will help you to gauge your time. Are you allowed to visit your locker during a break? Yes, you may go to your locker to retrieve your purse, medication, or food. Most Prometric reception areas contain water coolers. Remember, though, the clock is ticking. Your time is precious. After a break, the proctors will go through a series of procedures to check you back in. Allow time for this! Now that you have an overall picture of the process, it's time to discuss what happens on exam day.

EXAM DAY

Today you will complete a section of the CPA exam. Taking your first exam section will be the roughest. After you have taken a section, you will know firsthand how the procedures work. Remember, though, the procedures apply each and every time you sit. Jump out of bed ready to go. Begin the day with a positive outlook. Leave any bad attitude at home. You can make or break your entire exam experience just by the way you act. Refer to Chapter 21, Nerves of Steel, for some last-minute advice about controlling the exam. Review Chapter 22 as well. Accept well-wishers' statements of "good luck." Maintain a positive attitude—just your outlook alone will help to keep you calm and in control. You are alive today. You are here, ready to go—it's show time!

PREPARE FOR THE SHOW

Check to be sure you have the necessary paperwork. You must bring your Notice to Schedule (NTS) to the exam along with two other forms of identification. Be careful here. Several widely acceptable forms of identification, such as a green card or a social security card, are **not** acceptable. Be sure your selected identification agrees exactly to the name as shown on your NTS. You will receive a list of acceptable forms of identification along with your NTS. Follow this procedure to the letter. Exceptions are not tolerated. What a shame it would be if you arrived, ready to show the AICPA examiners what you know, only to be sent home for lack of appropriate identification. Be ready for the show.

Don't call home or the office shortly before the exam. Talking to friends is always wonderful, but this is not the time. It's time to put your game face on. In other words, it's time to focus on the exam and only on the exam. Don't let a problem at the office or at home be your center of attention. Whatever is wrong right now, you can ignore for now and deal with it later in the day. For now, smile at the people in the hallways, smile at the Prometric receptionist, and smile at your friendly Prometric proctor.

Arrive early—at least thirty minutes before your scheduled exam time. Keep any conversation light—the weather, a person's nice shoes, and the color of the carpet. Don't talk about anything that requires you to expend brainpower. Save it for the exam. Smile pretty when the proctor takes your digital photo. Don't think about exam content now. Allow the staff to check you in. Keep it light and happy.

TIME TO BEGIN

It's time to start your engines. Well, maybe not quite, but it is time to log on to the computer. After checking your identification and taking a digital photo of you, your proctor will usher you into the testing area. Sit down, check your surroundings, and make yourself comfortable. Yes, get comfortable. You will be asked if you wish to use earplugs. If you do, the center will provide them for you. Be careful when making this decision. Earplugs filter out the outside sounds, but they also magnify your internal body sounds. Are you prepared for that? Earlier chapters advised you to practice doing software questions in a less than totally quiet environment. You will be surprised—once you begin you should be so engaged in the process, that you won't even notice who or what is going on around you.

Once the proctor says that you may begin, take a deep breath and think. Write down some last-minute lists in the booklet containing four sheets of scratch paper that the center has provided. You will also be given a pencil. Once the proctor says "Begin," your time is your own. Make that list now before you forget. Be careful not to write anything down until you are given the go-ahead. We don't want your exam attempt to be invalidated.

Don't think about what is happening around you. Yes, you are being watched. In fact, you are being videotaped the whole time you take the exam. Who cares? You are rather cute in your calm, cool, and collected state of mind right now. The camera crew that gets to videotape you is lucky. Being filmed is definitely not a worry of yours. You are now focused on the content. You worked the sample exam at www.cpa-exam.org and you are very familiar with the format. You have studied the content. Now it's all about you showing them what you know.

USE YOUR SCRATCH PAPER WISELY

Is there a shortage of scratch paper? Not really, but the proctors will give you more only when you can show them that you have totally exhausted all sides of the paper. Using your scratch paper wisely relates more to what to write down rather than how much to write down. Staring at a computer screen for more than two hours is tough. Not only do your eyes become dry and strained, but your brain tends to become disengaged. You must fight the urge to disconnect from this exam. Here you are at the real event! This is not a trial run. This is the real thing. Each and every question counts, so you must read each and every question carefully. Write key words down on your scratch paper. What good is this? Jotting down key words helps people focus. If the question says which of the following is "not" the item, write down "NOT." Blink often to allow your eyes some rest. If you hit a tough patch of questions, remember that some of these questions (as many as 20%) could be pretest questions that do not count toward your final score. Keep the general scoring process in your mind—there is no need to be perfect. You have some margin for error. Don't exceed your time parameters. No one will tap you on the shoulder and warn you about your time usage. It's all up to you.

DON'T BE DISTRACTED

Don't be distracted by any issue. For example, if you are having problems entering a response in the research question area, you may not be using the expected response format. If your responses do not generate the expected color changes in the pencil icons, continue testing. Don't waste time worrying about what you can't control. Move on to complete all questions. You have four days to fax the AICPA to alert them to your issues. The most important issue now is to complete the entire exam section within the allotted time frame.

Attempt to answer all questions. There is no penalty for guessing. Don't waste time deciding which answer to choose for an outright guess. When you don't have any idea what the question is asking, select the second response and move on. By consistently selecting a guess response, you save time and you also are sure to make a few correct guesses. Since you must work all testlets in consecutive order (beginning with number one and moving forward), it is imperative that you follow the suggested time guidelines presented in Chapter 22.

Don't think back over previous questions. You did what you could do at the time. If later you think about an additional point, it's too late. You can't go back to a closed testlet. You are allowed to move back and forth only within a testlet. Once you close a testlet, it's done. I am sure everyone looks back to some extent, but realize it's dangerous. You can't undo what you have completed. Shrug it off—you must concentrate on the next play. This is game day and the real event. Move on until you finish.

THE END

No, it's not the end of you—it is the end of this exam section. You followed the tips presented in this book, you studied diligently, and now you have done your best. There is nothing more to do for this exam section. It's time to prepare for the next show and to wait for your results. Each exam section gets easier as you become more familiar with the format. By the time you finish all four sections, the proctors will know you by name.

PERSONALLY SPEAKING

Yes, it is nice when people recognize you, but don't think you can leave your identification at home. You must follow all test center procedures for each and every test session. The Prometric staff can't relax, and neither can you. Unless you have just completed your last exam section, you have work to do. You must move on to take another exam. You are in the control mode—why not continue?

What do I mean by the control mode? I mean that you have controlled this exam section. You did not let the exam take control of your emotions. Show time is all about keeping the show going. If you stumble, you must pick yourself up and keep on going. Expect rough patches with groups of questions that you are unfamiliar with. If you used reputable review materials and you don't recall studying these topics, then probably no one else is prepared for such material either. Maybe the examiners are pretesting candidate knowledge on a new area. Being in control means being thick-skinned. Nothing can upset you.

Can things go wrong at the exam? Sure, the lights could go off, the computer screen could freeze, there could be typos on the exam itself. All of these things have happened, but guess what—the candidates survived. Those candidates who not only survived but remained calm to deal with the glitch passed the exam. Things can go wrong, and things will go wrong. In most cases, the AICPA is one step ahead of you. There are built-in mechanisms to deal with most problems. For example, the computer automatically saves your work every sixty seconds. At most, you will only lose one minute of your work. There is no need to worry about what to do in these situations because the staff has been well trained to handle problems. It is not your worry.

I always ask nervous candidates if they feel better when they are nervous. They stare at me incredulously as if to say: How can nerves make you feel better? That's the point—worry won't help you pass the exam. As I told you in Chapter 21, it is the calm candidate who passes. Look at the exam as an opportunity to bring that exam section to closure, to show the examiners what you know, and to show them how calm you really are. You deserve to be a CPA. I know you can do it. I believe in you!

CPA EXAM TIP:
Pay attention to the list of prohibited items. Do not break the rules. Doing so, could result in a loss of a testing opportunity.

24 THE WAITING GAME

A CPA exam section is over! You survived the testing experience, and now you must play the waiting game. During the first year of the computer-based exam, scores and diagnostic information will be sent from the American Institute of Certified Public Accountants to the National Association of State Boards of Accountancy (NASBA) at the **end** of each testing window. Why the long wait? The AICPA Board of Examiners evaluates exam results and determines a passing score using a "candidate-centered" method. In candidate-centered methods, the focus is on looking at actual candidate answers and making judgments about which sets of answers represent the answers of qualified CPAs. This means that the passing scores cannot be finalized until a group of candidates has completed the exam. In the early stages of the computer-based test (CBT), a panel of experts must analyze the data and apply professional judgment to determine the appropriate response levels. A cut score, defined as an initial benchmark used to determine the passing level, must be compared to each candidate's actual performance. While the overall grading process has become more technologically driven, the score evaluation process continues to require human judgment. The AICPA hopes to shorten the score release time as more candidate performance data becomes available. Check the CPA exam Web site, www.cpa-exam.org, for expected score release dates. For now, anticipate scores to be sent at the end of each testing window. What should you do while you wait? Should you begin studying other sections?

WHILE YOU WAIT—WHAT'S NEXT?

Your first priority should be to catch up on home and work activities. Take a few weeks to do just that. Spend time with your family. Reward them for the sacrifices made while you were preoccupied studying. Then begin your studies for the next section. Put the previous section behind you. You did your best and there is no looking back now. Prepare for the next section. If you don't, you could run out of time.

While flexibility is one of the greatest benefits to the new CBT, it also can be one of the greatest problems. Don't let scheduling an exam become a problem for you. Establish a plan to complete all four sections and stick to the plan. Don't procrastinate. You must allow for the possibility that you might fail a section or two upon the first attempt. The eighteen-month time period will go by quickly. Begin the next section soon. Waiting is never easy. Candidates usually feel uncertain about whether they passed a section or not. You must wait for your score. Remember, you are not alone. The same rules apply to all candidates. Some candidates must wait longer than others. A candidate taking an exam earlier in a testing window will wait longer to receive scores. But that same candidate also will have longer to prepare for the next section if he or she begins soon after completing a section.

Is it wise to wait for feedback before beginning a new section? No, the type of information that is released about candidate feedback is not worth waiting for.

WAITING FOR FEEDBACK

What type of feedback do candidates receive about their exam performance? The exact format is discussed in Chapter 25. However, don't expect to receive a detailed listing of how many questions you answered correctly and incorrectly. The feedback will be very general, related to the AICPA content specification outlines. See Exhibit 24.1 for an example of the general categories for the Auditing and Attestation (AUDIT) section.

Exhibit 24-1:   Category Sections of the AICPA Content Specification Outlines for AUDIT

I.	Plan the engagement, evaluate the prospective client and engagement, decide whether to accept or continue the client and the engagement, and enter into an agreement with the client.
II.	Consider internal control in both manual and computerized environments.
III.	Obtain and document information to form a basis for conclusions.
IV.	Review the engagement to provide reasonable assurance that objectives are achieved and evaluate information obtained to reach and to document engagement conclusions.
V.	Prepare communications to satisfy engagement objectives.

Note that the feedback categories are very general. Candidates must move on. It is foolish to wait for feedback that is this general in nature. It is also just as foolish to hurry to complete all four sections just to say that you completed all four sections of the CPA exam in one testing window. There is a big difference between the word "completed" and the word "passed." You are going for the passing score. You must develop a plan and execute the plan with determination.

The type of feedback shown in the exhibit is of some value and might help you regroup should you find out that you failed a section. However, it is not of value to you when trying to decide whether you should move on to the next section or not. You must move on. You don't have time to waste. Think about how quickly those months will fly by. For example, let's say Candidate A took the AUDIT exam on April 5, 2004, the launch day for the CBT. That candidate won't receive the AUDIT results until July 15, 2004. If he waits until then to find out whether he passed, almost three and one-half months of the total eighteen months will have gone by. By that time the candidate is well into the next testing window and has only six weeks to schedule, study, and sit for another exam section. You can't afford to waste time like this. Altogether, Candidate A has until October 4, 2005, to complete the remaining three exam sections. The following testing windows would remain:

July 16– August 31, 2004	October 1– November 30, 2004	January 1– February 28, 2005	April 1– May 31, 2005	July 1– August 31, 2005	October 1–4, 2005

Notice only four full test windows remain. The first and last time periods are less than full windows. Because candidates are not allowed to sit for a section more than once in a test window, time is already rapidly passing by. The eighteen-month clock does not begin ticking until you pass a section. If Candidate A had failed the AUDIT section, the eighteen-month time limitation would not yet apply. Use the maximum number of days that are available. Plan your exam experience around your life. But don't let your life take over. If you do, time could become your enemy.

PERSONALLY SPEAKING

Before the CBT launched, CPA candidates told me that they would take all four sections within one testing window. When I asked them why, they would simply reply: "To get it over with." This statement amazes me. Completion of the exam is the final goal, but there really is a big difference between getting it over with and passing the exam. What's the hurry? Never hurry just to say it's over. If you did not take the time to plan, study, and practice exam questions, you may find yourself sitting for the same exam section a second or third time. A wiser strategy is to proceed along the CPA journey at a pace that gives you enough time to study and pass each section upon the first attempt. In the long run, this is a far more effective and efficient plan. The cost of testing alone should serve as a reminder that it is wiser to move forward with a well-designed plan. After each exam section, take stock of what you have completed, how you feel, and what you think you are capable of doing next.

If you have just completed one section, are you ready and able to move on to the next section? Perhaps a work commitment (e.g., busy season) is keeping you from taking the next section. Maybe you feel too burned out to continue. There are valid reasons for skipping a testing window. Go ahead, take a breather, and wait to see how well you score before you tackle another new subject. It is smart to admit that you require more time to prepare than what you initially thought. You aren't alone. What looks good on paper may not execute well in real life. You might decide to postpone the next section. It's mature of you to admit that your first plan was overly ambitious. Move on and revise your plan, keeping in mind that testing occurs only in the first two months of each calendar quarter. The third month is closed, which means no tests are administered during that month. Postpone your schedule only when you are almost 100% sure that you have failed that section and that you will be required to repeat that same section.

Maybe you feel so invigorated that you are eager to move on to the next section. You believe you performed well and you want to keep that momentum going. The CPA exam journey is **your** journey. Design a plan that works for you. Be considerate of your employer and your family. Be realistic; what can you complete within each testing window? Also, don't forget the eighteen-month deadline that states you must complete all sections within eighteen months of the date you sat for the first successfully-completed section. Don't risk running out of time. It's a personal decision; you are the one in the test center taking the exam. You are responsible for fulfilling your plan. Do it your way but remember the parameters. The eighteen-month rule is applied with little or no exceptions. Prepare your exam plan to include enough time to complete all four sections within eighteen months. Don't wait too long; there isn't time to delay. I strongly suggest that unless you have a valid reason for postponing a section, you should begin preparing for the next section within a few weeks of taking a test. Stretch the exam-taking process over twelve months. Then you will have two extra testing windows to use if needed. There really isn't time to wait for scores from one section before you begin the next section. As my father would say: "Get a get along!" There's no time to waste. Begin your journey now!

CPA EXAM TIP:
Don't wait for your exam score. Move on to take the next exam section. There is no time to waste.

25 REGROUPING AFTER AN UNSUCCESSFUL ATTEMPT

It happens—you failed an examination section. Does this mean that you are a failure? No, you are **not** a failure. Reregister to sit for that same exam section in the next testing window. A failed attempt is only a temporary setback. Continue to believe you can pass the CPA exam. Turn the failed attempt into success. You tried the CPA journey and your road map took you on a few detours. Look at the exam attempt as a learning experience. When you try the journey again, you will know where the roadblocks are. You will improve your route and steer clear of problems. Does this sound ridiculous? It shouldn't because you do know more now about the CPA exam than you did before you took it. You can use your knowledge to assess what you did right and what you did wrong. Correct the errors and make the right moves the next time. Determine how close you are to achieving your goal.

EVALUATING YOUR RESULTS

Candidates who score less than a 75 in an exam section receive a report referred to as "Uniform CPA Examination Performance Information." See Exhibit 25.1 for an example of this report. The sample shows the results for a candidate who was unsuccessful in passing the Regulation (REG) section. This particular candidate earned a score of 65. Look at the overall score as well as the detailed performance information. Note that the height of each bar represents the relative strength of the candidate's performance by exam area. The approximate percentage of the topical coverage is shown below each bar. The example shows six exam areas, plus an additional bar showing a candidate's overall performance on the simulations.

Exhibit 25.1: Uniform CPA Examination Performance Information

Candidate Name:	Generic Candidate	Examination Section:	REG— Regulation
Examination Section ID	1234567891011121	Score:	65
Date Examination Section Taken:	May 25, 2004	Result:	FAIL

Content Area Performance

A profile of your performance for each content area and—if this report is for AUDIT, FAR, or REG—your performance on the objective portion of the simulations are shown below. Because the content area evaluations are based on your answers to relatively few questions, they will tend to fluctuate more than your score each time you repeat an examination section. Therefore, in preparing to retake this examination section, the best preparation is to carefully study all content areas. However, in allocating your preparation time, you may wish to spend additional time on content areas where your performance was low, particularly if that content area makes up a large percentage of the test content. For a general explanation of your content area go to the Uniform CPA Examination Web site at www.cpa-exam.org.

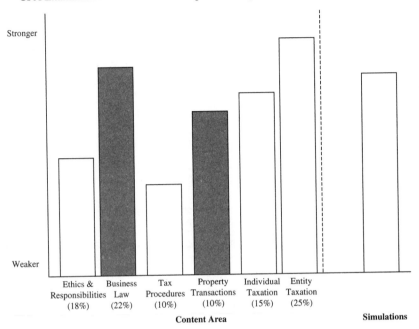

When you receive this form, use it to analyze your strengths and weaknesses. This candidate scored below the halfway mark on two areas: ethics and tax procedures. The lowest bars represent the overall weakest areas. Analyze the extent of your own weakness. Was your performance really weak? This candidate's performance bar is midway between the weaker and the stronger areas. Apparently he scored slightly below average on the tax procedures area and lower yet on the ethics area.

Begin your studies with the area(s) in which the bar is less than halfway high. Put the weak areas in perspective. This candidate's weakest performance was in two areas—procedures, which represented 10% of the total exam points, and ethics, which represented 18% of the total exam points. Ethics is almost twice as important as tax procedures. Test takers should plan to spend more time preparing for ethics than for any other area of the REG exam.

What do the highest bars represent? When the bar is up to the top, it indicates that the candidate's performance for that area was strong. Because your performance was strong in some areas, you can make a strong showing in the next testing window. Register to retake the exam section as soon as possible. There's no time to waste. Begin preparing by working to correct your weaknesses.

Performance results will show you which areas deserve special attention. Plan to spend a great deal of time with those areas. If your overall performance indicates that type of performance, consider taking a review course and spending more time learning the concepts. You have some work to do. It may not be a good idea to retake the section so soon. By the time you receive your results, you may have only a month to prepare for the next testing window. If you are not working and can find quite a bit of study time between now and the next testing window, go ahead and register, but realize that you need to improve. Improvement takes time and considerable effort. You would most likely benefit from a structured review course.

See how the subdivision of topics for each exam section matches the uniform content specification outlines (CSOs) as given by the AICPA. Chapter 2, Content and Overall Exam Format, Exhibit 2.6 shows six areas for the REG exam. Refer to the CSOs for the concepts tested. For example, the tax procedures area tests the topics of federal tax procedures, accounting periods, accounting methods (e.g., cash, accrual, percentage of completion, installment sales), and inventory methods, including uniform capitalization rules. Does this information help? In some cases you may recall some of the details tested. If you do, go to your study materials and be sure to master these topics. If you cannot recall specific questions, be sure that you study all areas. Keep in mind that the computer-based test (CBT) changes each test window. You will not receive the same exam with the same topic allocation. Therefore, the best preparation is to study all content areas one more time. There is no shortcut—refresh your memory for **all** content areas. Now is not the time to pretend that you have no weak areas. When you fail, you are obviously weak in one or more areas; figure out which areas and work to improve them.

REPORTED CONTENT AREAS

The list of topical coverage reported for the Auditing and Attestation (AUDIT) and Financial Accounting and Reporting (FAR) sections remain sketchy. The Regulation (REG) and Business Environment and Concepts (BEC) sections provide more detail to give you a good idea of the areas in which **you are weak**. For example, the performance chart for AUDIT will show overall results for the simulations as well as five content areas.

- Planning—25%
- Internal control—15%
- Obtain and document information to form a basis for conclusions—35%
- Review the engagement—15%
- Communications—15%

Candidates must refer to the detailed content specification outlines to see a list of specific topics. The performance charts are very general. The exam content is not. Don't get a false sense of security—prepare for all content specification areas. You won't get the same exam questions the next time around. Be prepared for everything. Each exam is different.

OVERALL RESULTS

Don't forget that your overall score also provides some clues to your performance. A score of 60 or less indicates that some major weaknesses must be corrected. Consider taking a review course rather than self-studying. Give yourself plenty of time to study and review. Be honest—did you receive this score because you did not study? Did you earn this score because you were tested on material that you have never learned before? New learning takes time. Take a candid look at your time commitment: Can you give it the time it deserves? If not, then don't rush to reschedule. Take the time to learn the concepts. Get some outside assistance to help you.

Lack of knowledge is not the only reason for a low score. Perhaps you were overly nervous or forgot to carefully manage your time. More than 50% of the candidates fail each section. You aren't the only candidate to have earned a low score. Being unsuccessful does not mean that you are a failure. It is a failure, however, to give up or to blame others for your poor performance. Face up to the facts: you must do better the next time. You can do better the next time, especially if you see your performance for what it is: a score on an exam. It is not an indicator of your self-worth as a person or as a business professional. A low score is just another hurdle to jump. Get hopping!

Earning a score of 60 and above shows that you are on your way to becoming a CPA. You are closer than you think. Scores of 61 to 70 mean that some work must be done. Spend more time working actual questions rather than reading about these areas. Learn by doing. If you performed poorly on one or two categories, spend considerable time by correcting the weaknesses for these areas first. If you remember struggling with a particular simulation work tab, such as a communication tab or research tab, then the format of the question may have hurt the score as much as the lack of technical knowledge. If this is the case, spend extra time working the sample exam and practicing with the free AICPA research software. However, keep in mind that simulation questions are seldom repeated in the next testing window. Prepare for the entire content outline. All items are testable.

Oh-so-close with a 70 to 74. Yes, a score of 74 is a valid score. It's not only valid; it's the saddest situation possible. Ouch! If you received a score of 70 or above, chances are that no one particular area was weak. Most of the bars will be closer to the "stronger" category. Use a software product. Work all of the questions and track your results. Review by working questions. Learn from the questions that you answer incorrectly. Let the results guide your work. All candidates who earn scores of 65 and higher should sign up for the next testing window. It won't take you that long to review. You have a solid knowledge base. If you remember the statement of cash flows as being something that gave you trouble, begin your study program with this area. If governmental accounting caused concern, and you still feel lost, sit down and read your review materials page by page. Make note cards as you go. Recite concepts out loud. Use all of the study strategies described in Chapter 12, Study Strategies to Improve Your Memory.

Was corporate taxation a problem? If you remember that the topic was tested and required a Schedule M-1 reconciliation that you were unable to complete, then allocate more practice time to studying the various tax schedules. It is doubtful that you would be required to complete an M-1 reconciliation in the next testing window. Simulations change frequently. If your score in individual taxation was high, just do a quick review. Do an average review of the other areas, where the bar was at midlevel.

USE CURRENT MATERIALS

If your review materials are now older than one year, you should purchase new materials. The CPA exam tests new standards and Internal Revenue Service Code sections within six months of issuance. Do not waste your time studying old material! Study materials must be up-to-date. Don't assume that accounting never changes. In the last three years, as much as 30% of the AUDIT concepts have changed. Major recent FAR changes include a new financial statement entitled "other comprehensive income." FAR is also undergoing numerous changes as the accounting profession decides how to account and report for derivatives and financial instruments. Swaps and hedging are new testable topics within the last few years. Look for some change in governmental accounting. Every year expect several tax law changes. Spend the time and money to obtain information about the latest changes. Don't waste your time studying old material. Study old material and almost always count on failure. Spend the cash to obtain new materials. Make the investment in the future. The return on your investment will be great. Money spent on new materials will seem a small investment to make to help boost your chances of success. Give yourself every possible chance to complete the exam successfully.

SCORE REVIEWS

Whenever you fail an area, you may ask your board of accountancy to submit a request to the AICPA for a review of your papers. Requests for such reviews are accepted for a limited time after candidates receive their scores. Check the Web site at www.cpa-exam.org or refer to the literature mailed along with the examination scores. The service is not free. For example, sample fees charged in the state of Illinois have been as high as $50 per exam section. Chances are that the review will result in a "no change" in the grade status. Do not count on receiving a grade change. Statistics show that grade changes are rare. For a candidate who receives a 74 on one or more exam sections, the reality is tough to face. You came within one point of a passing score. This is especially sad when a candidate receives four scores of 74, resulting in an outright failure by the loss of four total points. Although the statistics are grim, the situation is real. Face the reality and move on. Keep in mind that the AICPA has already applied careful grading techniques throughout the grading process. Take some comfort, however, in the fact that you came close to passing.

When you come close to passing by receiving scores in the 70s and 60s, it is an accomplishment. The results show that you are almost there. Take the time to think about where you felt weak. Use your review manual or software to identify topical areas, and then rank the topics as to how you felt about them when you were taking the test. For example, most review manuals show that there are six important areas in the AUDIT exam.

1. Audit planning
2. Understanding and evaluating internal control
3. Performing substantive tests
4. Communication and audit reporting
5. Statistical sampling
6. Auditing with technology

Do you remember trying to answer questions on these areas and feeling inadequate? Perform a simple ranking of the individual areas using this scale.

1. Very weak and needs considerable improvement
2. Remember having some trouble with the more difficult areas
3. Don't recall having problems; knowledge level seems to be adequate

Where do you go from here? Design a study plan to spend more time studying the areas that you ranked 1. and less time on the areas you ranked 3. Don't plan to begin your studies on your weak areas first. Don't spend much time studying the areas you ranked 3. The best way to study such areas is to skip reading entirely and go directly to the questions. Review the material by working exam questions. You'll be surprised at how quickly the concepts come back to you. That's because you know these areas and have reinforced the concepts earlier by practicing the questions. Once you truly understand a concept, you will never forget it. Spend your time studying areas that you ranked 1.

What if you ranked most of the areas 1? You have considerable work to do. It might be wise to forgo the next testing window and spend additional time preparing. Perhaps you should sign up for a reputable review course. If you know you did poorly because you did not make the commitment to a study plan and you believe you will change that level of commitment this time around, then go for it. The decision to sit or not sit is up to you. Be careful, though; don't set yourself up for failure. For example, if you are entering a busy season at work and won't have time to study, then sitting in the next testing window will just result in another disappointment and much frustration. Postpone taking the test for a few months.

When deciding whether to sit or not, recognize the general tendency to forget. The longer you wait, the more you will forget. If you ranked your exam knowledge level a 2, you are so close. Register to sit in the next window and make every attempt to find time to study. You have already achieved a very high knowledge base and you need so little to perfect what you already know. If you wait, not only could you forget concepts, the material also could change.

TO REVIEW AGAIN OR NOT TO REVIEW

Do you need an organized review? If you have already taken an organized review and have up-to-date materials, it is probably best to stay home and spend your time studying. If you have trouble disciplining yourself to stick to the plan, take a review course. A good review course not only helps increase your knowledge but also should help psych you up.

Look for a review course that helps you identify and understand the reasons for your failure. It should provide you with sound, practical advice about the corrections that you should make to pass the next exam. If you earned a score of 50 or less, you have a lot to learn. Enroll in a review course to accelerate the learning process. If you have one or two attempts left before your early score rolls out of the eighteen-month time period, take a review course. Don't risk losing a pass for any section.

If you decide to repeat a review course, don't forget to make the commitment and keep it. Attend every class and listen to the instructor as if it were brand-new material. You never know when the instructor is going to insert new material or make changes to concepts that you previously learned. Repeat takers tend to zone in and out, believing that they have already heard the story before. Work to concentrate. Hang on every word. Pretend it is all new to you. Focus on the task at hand.

Often a review course is not really a review because candidates have never learned the material. If you found you were learning material for the first time in the review, you have discovered one reason why you did not pass. It is tough to learn and review at the same time. Take the course again. The concepts will be much clearer the second time through. Think about why you might have failed.

REASONS CANDIDATES FAIL THE EXAM

Lack of technical knowledge may not be the only reason why you were not successful in passing the CPA exam. Did you manage your time correctly, or did you find yourself running out of time? Did you panic and let the exam control you, or did you control the exam? Did your nerves of steel turn soft halfway through? Did the little voice of doubt rise up and scare you? Did you find yourself changing answers without knowing why? Did you leave part of a simulation blank? Did you take the time to proofread your work, making sure you addressed the question requirements? Did you leave the exam early because you thought that there was no way you could have passed? Did you grade yourself as you progressed through the exam? Did you forget to fight, scratch, and claw for points?

There are many factors that could have contributed to your failed attempt. Think about them. The little things like time management really do make a big difference. Maintaining your confidence level is crucial. That's right; you must always believe that you can pass the CPA exam. Don't waste time placing blame on yourself or others. Accept the results, take a big gulp, and prepare a study plan for your next and final attempt.

GO BACK TO CHAPTER 11

You know where you might have gone wrong. Now is the time to go back to Chapter 11, Developing Your Personal Study Plan, and develop a new study plan to fit your new situation. Follow the techniques to develop a schedule. A second review of material reduces the amount of time you must spend to master the material. You have more time now, so use it wisely. Discipline and commitment are still important success factors, but procrastination can be your enemy. Don't waste time. Prepare your plan and stick to it. Maybe this time through you will not have to revise or adjust your study plan. Let's hope you can develop it and closely follow it.

FAILURE VERSUS SUCCESS

You are only one more exam attempt away. Failure is temporary. The only way you can truly be a failure is if you give up. Try and you will succeed. Give up and you will never become a CPA. Being a CPA is not a requirement for happiness, but once you have made the attempt, you will realize that although this exam is difficult, it is also passable. Keep on trying and you will make it.

PERSONALLY SPEAKING

People don't ask you how many times you have taken the CPA exam. They only ask: "Are you a CPA?" Cut yourself some slack—the exam is not easy. Going in you knew that on the first attempt, more than 50% of test takers fail. Some say that on the average it takes two attempts to pass. Although I have no statistics to back up that number, I do know that it is not uncommon to sit more than two times. I really believe that the number of failed attempts could be greatly reduced if people would take the time to understand what the exam tests and to realize that these concepts must be practiced. Michael Jordan always practiced his free throws, dribbling, and even his jumps. He was the master of basketball, but he did not stop practicing until the day he retired. Don't stop studying until the day of the exam. You never know when you are studying the very topic that will be tested the next day.

I can't understand why people study old material. In my capacity as director of the Northern Illinois University CPA Review, I receive e-mails and phone calls from candidates who whine about having to spend more money to obtain updated review materials. Some candidates study with textbooks that are four to five years old! Why are they doing this? Think about it— they are basically saying that topics such as income tax and financial accounting have not changed in five years. I want to cry for them, as they are starting out with a great disadvantage. They are not being fair to themselves. Of course, money may be a factor. The average cost of a review manual or software for one exam section is $45 to $50. However, when you make passing the exam a priority, you will forgo a few meals at a fast food restaurant and buy the latest product. I have the candidates' best interest in mind here, not my own. I want them to help themselves by giving themselves every possible chance to pass. It breaks my heart to see people setting themselves up to fail.

It is sad when people are prepared before the exam and then, during the exam, let the form of the question scare them into self-doubt. Attack this exam with gusto. Attack with confidence, even if it is your second or third time. Continue to fight for points no matter what you encounter. Whatever you do, **don't** grade yourself.

When candidates repeat an exam section, they begin to think they can determine their grade before they receive it. Don't even try. The last exam you took may have required a different knowledge level. If you feel this exam is tougher than the last exam, it may be true just because you now know more than you did before. Now you are recognizing the real issues. Don't compare the current exam to other exams. Move forward without looking backward. Each exam is its own unique instrument. Perform your best on this exam. Leave the grading to the AICPA.

Persistence does pay off. One of my favorite candidates took the pencil-based exam eleven times. He took three different review courses and purchased every supplemental CPA review aid he could find. He joined the Northern Illinois University CPA Review on his eighth attempt. The first time through our review, he found that he was still learning new material. So his eighth attempt was more like a first attempt. He did not pass. He passed two sections upon his ninth attempt. He gained one more section in his tenth attempt. Finally, after eleven exams his tenacity paid off. He became a CPA. He brought four family members to the awards banquet, two of whom had flown in from Ireland. I mentioned how wonderful it was that his family members cared so much that they had spent a great deal of money to attend the celebration. He laughed and said it was nothing compared to the $19,683.62 he had spent taking the exam, enrolling in review courses, and purchasing CPA materials. The total astounded me. He was correct; this is not a cheap affair. Unsuccessful attempts can be costly. Still, I admire him greatly as he stuck with the task. (Two weeks after he found out that he passed the CPA exam, his company made major cutbacks. He kept his job because he was a CPA. The money he spent probably was worth his lifelong career investment in time and in the company pension plan!) In my eyes, he will always be a great person. He never gave up and he crossed the finish line to success.

Make some changes to your study routine. Revise your study plan based on your known weaknesses. Utilize current materials. One never knows when little changes will make big gains. Adjust and go for a passing score!

CPA EXAM TIP:
Failure is only a bump in the road—a hurdle that must be cleared. Establish a plan and move on. We have all failed at something in our lives. We will be measured at how we regroup to meet our goal.

26 CONGRATULATIONS—YOU ARE A CPA!

You have patiently waited for your exam results, taking one exam section at a time. Finally, you receive the letter announcing that you are a CPA! You have successfully completed all four exam sections within a time period of eighteen consecutive months. Are you really a CPA? It depends. Each state and territory of the United States of America establishes rules to regulate the use of the CPA title. Although the uniform certified public accountant's exam is a national exam, the licensure requirements are regulated separately. The title "Certified Public Accountant (CPA)" is conferred by a state or governmental jurisdiction that authorizes the holder to practice as a CPA in that jurisdiction. Be sure you understand the requirements of the state in which you practice. Relax—the difficult part is over. Now you simply follow the rules and pay the necessary licensing fees. First, be sure you apply for licensure in the proper state.

LICENSURE REQUIREMENTS

The letter you receive notifying you that you are a CPA outlines the necessary steps to obtain a license. Before you begin completing the paperwork, be sure you have determined the jurisdiction(s) in which you plan to practice. For example, if you took the exam as a University of Wisconsin—Madison graduate at a Prometric test facility in Milwaukee, Wisconsin, but plan to live and practice as a CPA in Chicago, Illinois, you should apply for licensure in the state of Illinois. To do so, you must meet the Illinois requirements. Make no assumptions here. The practice requirements are not always the same, even for bordering states. States do not always recognize reciprocity. Usually the passing of the examination remains intact, but the additional state rules may vary considerably. Some states, such as Illinois, require that you meet their requirements **before** you apply to sit for the exam. As of the writing of this book, Illinois does not allow CPA exam candidates to fulfill requirements after the fact. For example, if you met the requirements of Colorado, sat for the exam, successfully completed all four sections, and then applied to transfer those scores to Illinois, you may be surprised when the Illinois regulators say: "No, we cannot accept your Colorado passing scores. Since you did not meet the exam requirements in Illinois on the day you sat for the exam, we will not recognize your Colorado scores." Ouch!

Consult the state boards directly. As mentioned in Chapter 3, Scheduling and Applying for the Exam, it is wise to research each state's regulations before you apply for the exam. If you even suspect that you might want to transfer your exam scores to another state, contact both the state in which you plan to apply and the state in which you plan to practice. Don't get caught in a bureaucratic nightmare. Understand the requirements before you sit and pass. It is easier to avoid a mistake than to correct one. View the www.cpa-exam.org Web site and click on the "candidate bulletin" reference. The last few pages of this key document list all of the state board addresses and telephone numbers. There is no excuse for not being thorough. Imagine going to all the trouble to pass this difficult, comprehensive exam only to find out that you are prohibited from practicing in a particular state. Check it out—it's important to your career.

LICENSURE REQUIREMENTS

Many states require the completion of an ethics component. The licensure rules may stipulate a course requirement or an examination. The ethics examination is often open book. You will receive the rules, and be asked to read them and respond to a list of questions. The only mistakes you could possibly make are reading something incorrectly, failing to complete a section, or missing the deadline for completion. Don't take this step lightly. If your jurisdiction requires completion of an ethics component, it is serious business. It's a state law. The constituents of that state believe a CPA must be knowledgeable not only about technical matters but also about matters that affect a person's integrity.

Make a copy of the examination before you begin. Write your answers on the copy. Complete all of the paperwork on the copy so that you don't risk ruining the actual exam. Have a CPA friend or coworker review your answers. After you have proofed and reviewed your responses, carefully copy them over to the actual exam form. Check to see that you have completed all sections.

Take the same care with the ethics examination that you did with the examination application. Prepare a folder entitled "Ethics Examination." Keep a copy of the paperwork you submitted to the state board. Go to the post office and send the document registered receipt required. You want the ability to track the receipt of your exam by recipient, if necessary. Put all the information in your "Ethics Examination" folder. Mark the expected response date on your calendar. Call the board if you do not hear from them on a timely basis.

PROOF OF WORK EXPERIENCE

When work experience is a requirement, often your employer is asked to provide the necessary proof of time worked as well as type of work performed. Public accounting firms are very familiar with the paperwork. If you work for a company or firm that is not knowledgeable about the procedures for documenting experience, your first call should be to the state board. Ask them to provide you with sample letters from previous cases. Your company's auditing firm personnel could prepare a letter to attest to the type and quality of work that you perform.

Make copies of all forms before you give them to employers to complete. Allow them plenty of time to meet the deadline. Give polite, gentle reminders a few days before the due date. Usually this is not a high-priority item for your auditor or employer. Don't take it personally; just give them the time and reminders as needed.

Just as you did for your application and all other required paperwork, keep copies of all documents and place them in a special folder. Note the response dates on your calendar. Follow up on the due dates. Be sure you have affixed the proper amount of postage, and request a tracking receipt.

PROUDLY DISPLAY YOUR CERTIFICATE

Take your CPA certificate to a professional framer. After all, it is a professional certification that you earned through your hard work. Proudly display it in your office. Consider framing other announcements. Some new CPAs are so excited that they even frame their letter announcing the completion of all exam sections.

Add your CPA designation to your business cards and letterhead. Update your resume. You never know when a better job might come along. Now that you are a CPA, you will have an advantage over other candidates. List any and all special accomplishments in the education and professional certification section of your resume. Consider listing the review class you took. Note any special achievements, such as the fact that you passed all four sections of the exam upon your first attempt or within one or two testing windows. Add a line to your resume that states: "Successfully completed all four sections of the CPA exam upon first attempt." What a statement you have just made! You accomplished something that very few people in the world can do. Be sure to mention your accomplishments in your job interviews. List any special state award or AICPA medal that you earned. Maybe bragging just isn't your style; remember that the business world is competitive. If you don't make your achievements known, you might lose out to another job applicant who isn't shy about identifying his or her accomplishments.

Go ahead; let your parents, spouse, or employer submit an article to your local paper. After all, it can serve as good advertisement for your employer. Notify your university accountancy department of your achievement. Passing the exam is an achievement of which to be proud. Enjoy the rewards and recognition. Bask in the limelight. You worked hard to get to this point.

Attend any special awards or certificate presentations in your state. Take lots of pictures to save and show to your grandchildren someday. People have been trying to pass the CPA examination since 1917. This exam is going to be around for a long time to come. You have met the challenge and now you should enjoy the rewards.

CONTINUING PROFESSIONAL EDUCATION (CPE)

Some states require continuing professional education (CPE) to ensure professionals keep technical skills current and as a requirement for renewal of the CPA license. Each state jurisdiction specifies the number of hours to be earned over a set time period. The number of credits is usually specified in hours and may vary by your type of employment. For example, educators and those CPAs practicing in government and private industry positions may not need as many CPE hours as those CPAs who practice in public accounting. The responsibility for maintaining a record of CPE hours usually falls on the individual. Some states request proof each year; others may conduct random verification checks, asking CPAs to provide proof of hours earned when requested to do so. The best proof of hours is certificates of attendance that are issued for each course by the sponsor. Familiarize yourself with the particular requirements of your state. Some states require a certain number of CPE hours in various subjects, such as ethics, accounting, and auditing. Some states limit the number of hours that can be earned in soft skill areas such as management and marketing. Other states limit the number of hours that can be earned through self-study versus public forums.

Where should you go to obtain your CPE hours? Begin your search for CPE at the American Institute of Certified Public Accountants. You will find the details on the Web site at www.aicpa.org. Discounted prices are offered to members. This is just one reason for joining this organization. In fact, once you pass all four exam sections, you should join two organizations: the AICPA and your state CPA society.

The AICPA provides quality CPE in a variety of forms, such as live lectures, self-study texts, web-based programs, and interactive online seminars. Your employer may cover some of the CPE costs. State CPA societies offer reasonably priced, quality programs that involve little travel costs. Not all lectures and programs with an accounting topic qualify for CPE credit. State regulators select approved CPE sponsors. Obtain proof of the sponsor's approval prior to registering for a program.

A certain number of CPE hours are required to maintain membership in the AICPA. The number of hours varies by professional classification, such as public accounting, corporate finance, government, and education. Some CPE programs may count as fulfillment of both the state and the AICPA requirements. Spend some time learning about both the AICPA and your particular state regulator's CPE requirements. Keep your payment receipts. The dues and fees you pay for CPE are usually deductible to some extent on your income tax return.

By passing the CPA exam, you have demonstrated that you are technically competent and current. You should continue to do whatever it takes to remain at least at that same level of competency throughout your professional career. Don't let your skills become rusty. The accounting and auditing profession is undergoing frequent changes. Earning CPE hours will not only help you to stay on top of changes and new developments, but by attending courses, you have a wonderful opportunity to network with other professionals.

NETWORKING

Passing the CPA exam is truly an individual experience. Only you could go to the Prometric test center and complete each section. Now that you are a CPA, you will find that remaining current is much more of a group experience rather than an individual experience. Some of your best learning experiences may not occur in a classroom setting but by interacting with other CPAs. Don't be afraid to volunteer to serve on a committee at your state society or one of its local chapters. When you pass the CPA exam, you will be the most current and well studied on all accounting subjects as you ever will be. In the future, you probably will focus on a few select areas, such as tax, consulting, auditing, or fraud, and will no longer be as knowledgeable in all facets of the accounting profession. Volunteer work will help you to meet people, define your preferred area of focus, and reward you with new challenges. Networking with other professionals may alert you to new professional opportunities.

SAYING THANK YOU

So your boss wasn't exactly supportive throughout your CPA journey. Your spouse and/or friends were not behind you 100% of the time. Forgive and forget, as you probably had your bad days, too. Forget about the negative times and move on with your life. Take the time to thank your boss, colleagues, and family. Tell your friends you couldn't have met the challenge without their support. It takes so little to be humble and thankful. The rewards from what you have achieved are many. Share the glory and the recognition. You really could not have done it without the support of outsiders. Be a gracious winner.

WHAT'S NEXT?

Your first priority probably will be to catch up on home and work activities that you have ignored during your exam preparation. After you have taken a few weeks to regroup and catch up, you should begin to consider obtaining at least one more additional certification. Three certifications relate closely to the CPA exam.

1. Certified Internal Auditor (CIA)

2. Certified Management Accountant (CMA)
3. Certified Fraud Examiner (CFE)

All of these certifications are earned by passing a rigorous examination. Much of the CIA certification tests the auditing and general business knowledge that you learned for the CPA exam. There is a great deal of content overlap. If you are a CPA, you will be exempt from taking one or more sections of some professional examinations. Why not continue to use the technical knowledge and examination strategies that you have perfected? The organizations that support and administer the three certifications listed are

- CIA (Institute of Internal Auditors in Altamonte Springs, Florida) (www.theiia.org)
- CMA (Institute of Management Accountants in Montvale, New Jersey) (www.imanet.org)
- CFE (Association of Certified Fraud Examiners in Austin, Texas) (www.cfenet.com/cfe/)

BELIEVE AND ACHIEVE

How does success feel? You have accomplished a very important goal in your life. Use your newly acquired certification as a tool to open doors for yourself. Never lose your desire to achieve. Do you remember how the journey to become a CPA began? You started by believing in yourself. You supported that belief with hard work and dedication to the task at hand. The lessons you have learned will benefit you throughout your life. When the task is difficult, believe first in yourself. Continue in life with hope and determination.

Congratulations—you are a CPA!

PERSONALLY SPEAKING

Passing the CPA exam probably will rank among your greatest life accomplishments. Being a CPA has given me many opportunities. I have traveled worldwide and always have been respected for my integrity and knowledge. I take the title "CPA" seriously. I realize that I am blessed with an ability to understand and analyze technical information. I know I possess a unique skill.

Did you make any promises to yourself when you were studying for the exam? I did. I promised myself that when I passed the exam, I would use my title to gain experience in areas where I could share my knowledge with people who needed my help. Yes, I do work for pay, but I also have used my status and achievements to help others who are less fortunate by donating time to many organizations. I hope you do, too. Here are some suggestions for giving back to the society that has given you so many opportunities.

- Volunteer to prepare tax returns for senior citizens

- Serve on a not-for-profit board, such as a religious or community organization (Hint: You are very qualified to serve in the treasurer's position.)
- Become active in your state society of CPAs. Work your way up to serving on a technical committee where you can influence the standard-setting process of the profession.
- Contact government officials about traveling to developing countries to assist them in updating their banking and accounting models.
- Be a role model for children. Travel to schools and share stories about the commitment that you made. Let them know that the road to success is not an easy one. Remind them that the pleasure that you receive from achieving is far greater than the sacrifice it takes to get there.
- Be a role model for society. Be honest at all times. Maintaining a high degree of integrity is critical for a CPA. The rest of the world counts on you to be honest. Follow through.

Remain proud of your achievement. I am so proud to be a CPA that my license plate reads "BE A CPA." I want the whole world to know that I have achieved success. Congratulations—you too, are successful. Congratulations—you are a CPA!

CPA EXAM TIP:
You are now a CPA. Use your skills to make a difference in the world. Act ethically in all you do. Be a role model for others.